Solving for Democracy

Tony Bracks

CONTENTS

Acknowledgements

Thanks to my wife Angela for designing and creating the book cover and for her generosity of spirit in the years dedicated to writing this book.

Thanks for the writing support of my sister Carolyn Bracks who has transformed the text. As well to my friends Bob Crowley, Thane Cooper and Dr Ron Bewley, for their invaluable feedback.

Thanks also to the many learned authors whose work I have used to both research our current democratic systems and to investigate the possibilities to improve the process. The brilliant work of Fareed Zakaria was invaluable in clearly outlining many of our problems and posing the critical questions. In fact, many of this book's answers are in direct response to the questions he posed. Other works of influence include those of James Surowiecki, Jane Mayer, Bruce Bueno de Mesquita and Alastair Smith. A range of other useful books and papers are listed in an appendix.

Preface

It started with a mistake. In December of 2014 I was travelling with friends to watch a sporting event in Adelaide. Over the course of an evening dinner and quite a few drinks, thoughts turned to deeper discussions. I spoke about my views on the important things to be fixed in the world. Firstly, fix the funding of elections and of politics, to enable democracy to better represent the will of the people rather than the will of those with the money. Secondly, improve the media to enable a more unbiased and effective portrayal of politics, without which the electorate could not have a clear view of the world. And thirdly, improve our education system to ensure that we can make more reasoned and well considered decisions. To me these were the critical things to fix which would allow many other problems to be solved. I had a proposal for changes to each which would significantly improve the process. Much debate ensued, most of which was probably more affected by alcohol than by reason itself. The night ended, and we returned to our lives.

However, over the next few weeks doubts crept in - was I getting to the heart of the problem? My career had largely been spent building computer systems which facilitated trading in equities and derivatives markets. Computer programming is not perfect and inevitably bugs and flaws can work their way into large and complicated trading systems. Solving those problems quickly was critical in the competitive investment banking environment. One of the most important lessons was that of root cause analysis. Unless you find and fix the underlying causes, problems did not go away, and there was an enormous cost. There was often little value in resolving symptoms, rather you must find and fix the root cause of issues.

When I applied this reasoning to my three critical issues, I realised why something did not feel quite right. For two of these issues, I was actually dealing with the symptoms of the problem rather than the underlying cause. Election funding was an imperfection of the election process. The problem was not so much that money *did* affect democracy. Rather, the problem was that money *could* affect democracy. The root cause was that our elections

3

and democratic processes were not impervious to the undue influence of money. Instead, our democratic process needed to be able to make the best decisions without any influence from money. We need to fix this root cause and make democracy simply immune to undue influence.

The exact same logic applied to the media. We need to make our democracies capable of producing the right policies, without being dependent on the balanced and effective coverage of politics by private media organisations. Getting to the right policies should be possible *without any* dependence on the media. It should be possible to make effective democratic decisions without a requirement for the media to keep either the public, or our critical decision makers, informed.

The fact that democracy was adversely influenced by both money and an imperfect media was a problem within the democratic system itself. This was what really needed fixing. Fixing the symptoms would not solve the deeper problems. Democracy should produce the right decisions regardless of undue influence. Ideas needed to change. Our democratic process needed to change.

As well as finding the right causes of our problems, we also need to find the right solutions to our problems. Solutions that not only get the heart of our problems, but that are effective in the real world. My experience had taught me that solutions must be simple and elegant. Overly complex solutions are unlikely to work in the real world, and systems that are too simplified are liable to miss important requirements. What is required is an elegant solution, which models how the real world works in the most natural and simple way. As well as this, if there is a known, working process then it should be reused. There is little point, as well as greater risk, in reinventing the wheel.

When I looked around for what other experts were saying on this issue, I found that many of our brightest minds seemed to be dealing with symptoms. Many experts seemed simply resigned to the status quo, since democracy was both entrenched and was the best option that we had. The solutions which had been proposed were impractical or ineffectual – they would not work in the real world. The causes of our democratic problems were thus not currently being solved.

So, my thinking was that, with my experience in analytical problem solving as well as in science, I could apply a fresh mind to the problem. A mind that was not bogged down in any attachment to the current system. A mind motivated to apply critical thinking and the scientific method to solve the subjective problems within our democratic process.

About three years later, having done quite a bit of research including reading about 30 related books and research papers, this book is my solution. I have identified many more problems than just the two listed above. Each problem has been associated with its underlying causes. Those root causes have then been addressed or removed entirely. Nothing changes in the overall structure or functions of our democracy, just in the processes that deliver those functions. Replacement democratic processes have been chosen from known working solutions. But absent the many root causes of our current problems, the new democratic process could be vastly and measurably better than our existing system and could produce significantly better government and better governance.

Introduction

"Indeed, it has been said that democracy is the worst form of government, except all those other forms that have been tried from time to time"- Winston Churchill

Democracy has been the most successful form of government that the civilised world has seen. Stable and successful democratic societies have become commonplace. And yet Winston Churchill clearly has a point, democracy can seem the worst form of government.

Representative democracies still elect incompetent governments. Conflicts of interest and corruption plague stable democracies. Often the most popular leaders turn out to be the poorest leaders, and our most capable people are unwilling, or unable, to get elected. Self-interested politicians put themselves first and many sensible but "courageous" policies are shelved for decades. Our democracies choose the best of the politically possible policies, rather than the best of all possible policies. Politics invariably trumps policy. Most democratic governments struggle from one election cycle till the next with short term populist solutions, unwilling and unable to plan for the long term benefit of nations. Our democratic system has left many of society's problems unresolved to this day.

This book will demonstrate how our ineffective democratic process has allowed incompetence, partisanship politics, entrenched delays and poor planning to lead to an enormous cost for society. We will see how the flaws in our democracies have led to untold suffering, as well as to tens of millions of unnecessary deaths. Many trillions of dollars are wasted every year which could otherwise have been spent for the benefit of all. We will see this impact in areas including medicine, science, journalism, finance, economics and international relations. While our democratic governments are unable to create sensible long term strategies many opportunities for a better future are lost. Only a small subset of the recent problems with democracy will be presented. There are undoubtedly many, many more. As we will show, the causes of our problems are within the process of democracy itself, the examples merely demonstrate the result of our current implementation choices.

We will also see how, in the future, our flawed and slow political decision making could lead to even greater catastrophes as our governments struggle to deal with a range of new technologies, diseases, drugs and risks.

Accepting that democracy is the best form of government is not sufficient, we cannot continue to ignore the obvious problems within our democratic process. We will present a compelling case for change.

By identifying and removing each underlying cause of problems from within the democratic process, we will be able to deliver a simple, working and effective solution. A solution which preserves the functions of democracy but delivers those functions through a vastly more effective process.

The world still faces many tragic and difficult problems. Deadly regional conflicts, hopeless poverty, devastating diseases, systemic human rights abuses and the risks of man-made climate change – are just a few among many. The most important problem to be fixed however is not any individual issue itself. The most important issue to fix is the democratic process itself, which is tasked with dealing with society's problems. If we can improve our ability to make the right decisions as democracies, then we will have the capability to solve the bigger issues. If we can improve our democratic governments, then we can potentially move forward to deal with all of our issues effectively. By removing the underlying causes of problems from within democracy, then we can create a better future for us all.

We can never be certain that the decisions of our democratic leaders, or our decisions collectively, are perfect. We are human after all. But what we can do is to ensure that the process behind our decision making is set up to give us the greatest chance of getting the best decisions possible. We can get the democratic process right. We can also have an effective governance framework over those decisions, to ensure that the poorer decisions are reviewed and then avoided.

The purpose here is to deliver a democracy without politics, without conflicts of interest, and without the undue influence of special interest groups. One whose leadership is free to plan for the long term. One whose power is contained not within the hands of individual politicians but within its strengthened processes. One in which the underlying causes of our current problems have been entirely eliminated. A democracy which is strengthened and enhanced to protect the stability of democracy itself.

By the end of this book, we will have developed a democracy that is truly representative of the collective will of the people. A democracy which enables the best possible policies to be identified quickly and implemented effectively. A democracy designed from the ground up to be, of the people, by the people and for the people.

Solving for democracy

"Elections, open, free and fair, are the essence of democracy, the inescapable sine qua non. Governments produced by elections may be inefficient, corrupt, short sighted, irresponsible, dominated by special interests, and incapable of adopting policies demanded by the public good. These qualities make such governments undesirable but they do not make them undemocratic" - Professor Samuel P. Huntington, Harvard University

On global conflict

In 1962, the B-59, a submarine from the former Soviet Union, was heading to Cuba in international waters of the Atlantic Ocean. At the time, the Soviet Union and the United States were in a standoff over Soviet nuclear missiles which had recently been placed in Cuba. It was the height of the Cuban missile crisis during the Cold War. Global tensions were extremely high. The missiles in Cuba could potentially initiate a nuclear first strike against continental US and obliterate much of the US before the US military could react. Soviet warships had been sent towards Cuba in response to the US naval blockade. The Soviet submarine was being actively pursued by American destroyers. The Soviet commander had been out of contact with his superiors for a number of days after the sub was submerged, so had no idea whether or not the Cuban Missile Crisis had escalated. As the pursuit continued, the Americans decided to drop depth charges - as warning shots, to force the Soviet submarine to the surface. The submarine having been detected, was in an extremely vulnerable position. The Soviet submarine commander, Valentin Grigorievitch Savitsky, now knew that the Americans were firing at him. He had to decide how to respond to this life threatening issue for himself and for his crew. If he surfaced to communicate with his home base, then he would be an easy target for the US ships. The commander concluded that for the Americans to fire live weapons, the crisis must have escalated while they were out of contact. He made a critical decision, that he should respond with live fire and launch his nuclear torpedoes at the American surface ships (nuclear torpedoes were missiles

9

fired at surface ships from a submarine, that were armed with a nuclear weapon to increase the destruction caused). He consulted with his political officer. His political officer agreed with the decision and gave his approval to fire on the US ships. However, under Soviet rules of combat, he needed further approval from his peer (and technically fleet commander), a man named Vasili Alexandrovich Arkhipov. Commander Arkhipov was not convinced and adamantly refused to sign off on the launch. After a tense and heated discussion, the submarine commanders, running low on power, chose that the best option was to risk surfacing, where contact was then made with the Americans. Had Arkhipov approved the launch, nuclear torpedoes would have been launched at US forces and a global war could have begun. Thus, a single man when faced with an extremely difficult decision, potentially prevented global nuclear war and changed world history.

Critical decision making in leadership can clearly have significant consequences. In a complex world, when faced with identical circumstances, different people can make completely different choices. During the submarine stand-off two out of three leaders decided that the best option was to return fire. If the critical decision had been left up to a single individual or even up to two individuals, then the planet would have faced global warfare between nuclear armed superpowers. At the time the process to support the individuals in their tough decisions happened to have produced the right result. And yet the outcome could have been different. Having an effective process is obviously important in critical decision making.

In government effective decision making is also critical. The decisions made during the Cuban missile crisis to avert global nuclear war included those of the US and USSR governments themselves. The democratic process itself chooses our leaders and parliamentarians, constructs their support and power bases, selects our laws and chooses our executive government. Having an effective process for our democracies has far reaching consequences, from the welfare of the individuals in any given country, right up to the potential for global warfare. It is interesting to note that in our current democratic governments it can be left up to an individual to decide whether or not to go to war and one person can effectively control the nuclear launch codes. Is this our best option, especially when that person is a politician? Do we have enough of a built in failsafe against flawed individual decision making?

Democracy and democratic governments are a critical part of the modern world. Our governments manage our economies, our infrastructure, our education, our welfare systems, our judicial systems and provide a vast array of other services. Modern liberal democracies have the responsibility to protect citizens from risk and harm, including from hunger, from disease and from domestic and foreign enemies. They protect from the imperfections and heartlessness of unfettered capitalism. They protect us from ourselves and ensure our safe futures. They set the boundaries for what is acceptable in society by establishing regulatory frameworks for safety and our well-being. Depending on the country, the OECD estimates that modern government expenditure is around 20-25% of the size of total yearly production (GDP). Since the cost of government is high, even getting decisions around the size of government right is also important. Government decisions are made virtually every day to ensure that society produces the best results for its citizens. Getting our government decision making right allows us to manage the welfare and advancement of billions of people throughout the world.

And yet our democratic governments are far from perfect. There have been many experiences of poor democratic decision making and poor governance over the years globally.

In this book, we will see examples of how poor government decision making has allowed tens of millions of people to lose their homes and their livelihoods. We will see examples of political gridlock, of intentional manipulation and malevolence to adversely influence our democracies and to harm people's very health and wellbeing. We will see many avoidable circumstances where government delays and political obstructions have allowed and even led to the loss of millions of lives in even our most liberal of modern societies. Yet the examples that we will present are a mere subset of the greater whole of problems and concerns. The examples merely demonstrate the many consequences of the existing flaws within our democratic process, as well as serving to encourage us to quickly deal with the problems.

11

Note also that although it may seem that there are many tangents within the book, please be patient, as each issue discussed has a specific purpose in delivering the right democratic solution.

We will present a compelling case for change. The many problems demonstrated demand action for solutions. Without change and improvement soon, there will be more unnecessary cost, more pain, more suffering and potentially many more avoidable deaths. The issues that will be described are both avoidable and fixable. The causes of those problems will be identified, and reasonable and effective resolutions will be proposed.

The first democracies were the Greek city states, then came the democracy of Rome and thirdly our current western democracies. This book develops a structure for the next democracy. This new democracy builds upon and learns from those that came before. The starting point for our discussion is that of representative democracy. Our underlying belief is that any effective democracy must be as Abraham Lincoln described so memorably: "of the people, by the people and for the people". That is, any new democracy must be a fair representation of the collective will of the people, governing for the best interests of all in society. We aim to deliver on this essence with an improved democratic process. The basic structure of democracy will largely remain, only the imperfect processes will be changed. That is, the functions of democracy will not change, instead how we deliver those functions will improve. The intention is to fix each and every identifiable weakness within our democratic processes, and to replace those flawed processes with known working solutions. We will create a democratic process, absent the causes of its current problems, but with a reinforced system to protect the integrity of both decision making within the system, and to protect the democratic system itself.

Throughout the book a range of examples from our recent history will be presented. These are separated from normal text with a title beginning with "On". For example, "On 89 votes", or as above, "On Global Conflict". These real world experiences demonstrate both the issues with our democracy, as well as the consequences of those issues. Although some of the examples may not at first seem directly relevant to a book on democracy, with a better

12

democratic process each issue could have been avoided. It is often the less obvious experiences which best demonstrate the consequences of flaws within our democratic process. All of the examples do demonstrate key flaws within democracy. Each example is followed by a brief analysis which describes both the underlying problems as well as their relevance to the democratic process.

In the final section of the book we will present a view of how our improved democratic process would work. A new democracy that will ensure both effective governance as well as effective collective decision making. A new democracy without the causes of its current problems, but with a reinforced process to reliably produce better outcomes. A democracy which is capable of producing long term decisions based on both our best collective wisdom, as well as on the best available information and analysis. A democracy which can be better for us all.

The problems of our democratic process

"The best argument against democracy is a five-minute conversation with the average voter" - *Winston Churchill*

Our challenge is to evaluate our democratic process and to eliminate the underlying flaws. We have experienced hundreds of years of western democracy, implemented in more than one hundred different nations. This gives us ample scope for consideration. We will mainly focus on the problems from recent times - as an indication that the problems are ongoing. It is believed that this is a reasonably representative and comprehensive sample. The purpose with our list is to assess the scope of the problem so that we can then understand both the need for change as well as the areas for potential reform. The issues are many; the concern here is that people have become so inundated with the problems of our democracy that they have become immune to them and are no longer cognizant of all of the issues. Problems have been broadly grouped together and some overlap is inevitable when attempting to identify subjective and complex issues.

For each issue identified we will also establish the root causes of the problem. When root causes are identified and addressed the potential for recurrence is vastly reduced. By the end of this book, we plan to have addressed (and removed) the overwhelming majority of the root causes of issues and problems raised. The few remaining underlying causes cannot be removed since they are intrinsic to democracy itself, rather than being within the implementation choices of democracy. Those will be dealt with separately through a more robust and effective governance framework within our new democratic process.

Politicians

"But a democratic franchise in a modern state rarely avoids the creation of a political elite of office holders. Elected members are not elected because they are necessarily of the people but more mundanely because they want to be elected and can attend lots of party meetings and social events in the evenings, and even that in some countries is a somewhat ideal picture compared to money and patronage. Perhaps the best that modern democracies can hope for is not the avoidance of political elites but 'the circulation of elites', as Joseph Schumpeter suggested in his Capitalism, Socialism and Democracy (1942)" – Bernard Crick, PhD, from Democracy: A Very Short Introduction

As people

We need politicians in our current democratic process. Politicians run for office within political parties and if elected, propose legislation and then vote in legislative assemblies on our behalf. This system is not without its difficulties, especially for those politicians themselves. An individual trying to enter politics first needs to campaign within a political party for a party nomination. This inevitably involves finding allies to support the campaign. Once nominated, they then need to campaign for the election, which may require them to leave their job and devote themselves full time to the campaign. Leaving their job is a risk since there is no guarantee that they would be elected. This can be extremely difficult for people of limited means. The elected term is only for three or four years in many countries, so they may be looking for work again after a few years and a subsequent election. If they do actually get elected to office the fate of their re-election can be out of their control due to overall party and leadership issues invariably overriding their own electoral performance. Once they enter politics their whole life is open to potentially unfair and harsh public scrutiny and their personal history displayed for all to see. The personal public scrutiny can involve manipulation and misrepresentation and at times even blatant lies. The job can be extremely busy, with time spread between the need to do their job as a member of government, as well as to campaign for electoral success and to sell their success to colleagues in a competitive environment. Greg Combet, an ex-Federal Government Minister in Australia was quoted as saying that he "averaged two days a month at home" and that "…In the lifestyle of a cabinet minister, there is barely time to consider public policy issues properly". For many people the potential risks, costs and the unfair public scrutiny for themselves and for their families deter them from entering politics. Most people in society currently choose not to serve and this is especially true for many of our most qualified and capable candidates.

On the other hand, the financial rewards of political service can be quite generous. In many countries, the pay for politicians can be significantly better than the average wage and after years of service there are many benefits paid. Pensions can be generous for politicians. And that is not to mention many of the other legally grey kickbacks and job offers that may be offered by those companies that are well served by prior policies. There are a large number of politicians who go on to work in senior positions for companies which have been the beneficiaries of their policies. There are also potentially offers from your own political party for further government political service (including ambassadorships).

It does not seem controversial to say that our politicians are not the best and brightest from our society – they are more likely quite far from this ideal. The current democratic process leads to a relatively small number of people from the overall population offering to serve in politics, and those that do choose to serve are potentially doing so for the benefits that they could not achieve elsewhere. There are many disincentives that discourage the election of good quality political candidates, and many incentives that can attract poor quality candidates for the wrong reasons. Throughout this book there are a range of examples and discussions which demonstrate the power of incentives, and the consequences of poor incentives. Misaligned incentives inevitably produce poor quality candidates in our governments. While those poor incentives remain, we will continue to have less than perfect politicians. For us to achieve the best possible decisions from our government which are in the best interests of all, we need to have the best possible representation in our legislative governments. The poor incentives need to be removed. We can then free up our democratic process to deliver better results.

So, we will build a democratic process where both the appointment of our decisions makers and their subsequent decisions cannot be influenced by misaligned incentives.

Corruption

"In framing a government which is to be administered by men over men, the great difficulty lies in this: you must first enable the government to control the governed; and in the next place oblige it to control itself" - James Madison, Founding Father and 4th US President

It has been estimated by Daniel Kaufmann, a senior fellow at the Brookings Institute, that global bribes currently total more than a trillion dollars annually. Corruption in developing nations in particular has had an enormous cost, including the theft of significant state assets. Indonesia's President Suharto as well as Philippines' President Marcos are well known for the accumulation of billions in assets while in democratically elected governments. Many other politicians have accumulated in a similar way, both personally and for their families. Corruption has led to the killing of officials tasked with the investigation of issues and has led to riots, as well as the deaths of voters and election officials.

In India several senior politicians and ministers have been named as suspects in multiple murder investigations. Many successful politicians and legislators have known criminal records. Some elected politicians have acted more like feudal barons than political leaders. As Fareed Zakaria writes, "The political system there can only be described as 'bandit democracy.' Every year elections are rigged; ballot boxes are stuffed". Patrick French, a British historian, noted in 2011 that every member of India's lower house under the age of 30 was a member of a political dynasty, which would hardly be considered a democracy that was a fair representation of the entire populous.

Politicians have repeatedly made themselves rich from the spoils of their power while the poor remain penniless. In Serbia, Slobodan Milosevic reportedly accumulated more than a billion dollars while in power. Be it representative democracy, or even the pseudo, one party state currently in China, where significant power is concentrated in the hands of a relatively

17

small group of publicly known people, the incentive for corruption is strong. In China, albeit admittedly not perceived to be democratic, there are regular corruption scandals, with the government currently in the midst of a national crackdown on the apparently thriving practice. It has been reported in the Economist that "the 50 richest members of the China's National People's Congress are collectively worth $94.7 billion—60 times as much as the 50 richest members of America's Congress".

In Russia, opposition politicians have recently been jailed and publicly murdered. Critics of the government, both in the general public and the media have been poisoned, killed, or have simply disappeared. In the Ukraine, Victor Yushchenko was poisoned with dioxin while opposition leader in 2004. He was nonetheless still elected to be Prime Minister in spite of significant facial scarring. Anwar Ibrahim, opposition leader in the Philippines, was famously and publicly convicted and jailed for sodomy, in what was generally perceived as a politically influenced move by the government. In Venezuela in 2017, opposition leader Henrique Capriles was banned from politics for 15 years by his political rival's government, for alleged "administrative irregularities" in his previous role as governor.

In Britain, there has been widespread misuse by British parliamentarians of their allowances and expenses in the parliamentary expense scandal of 2009 and the cash for influence scandals of 2009 and 2010. In Italy, three-time Prime Minister Carlos Berlusconi has been engulfed in political scandals for his entire career and has been convicted of a criminal offense. Former French president Jacques Chirac was convicted of embezzlement of public funds. Francois Fillon, a previous French prime minister and frontrunner in the Presidential race, lost support when it was publicized that he paid his family members large sums from the public purse, for jobs they never did. In Brazil in 2016, President Dilma Rousseff was impeached after a corruption scandal. Less than a year later, the President that replaced him, Michel Timer was involved in another Presidential corruption scandal involving potential pay-offs to silence corruption witnesses. Former two term Brazilian President Luiz Inacio Lula da Silva was sentenced to 9 ½ years jail on corruption and money-laundering charges. Also, in 2017, President Park Geun-hye of South Korea was impeached from the Presidency and later charged. The scandal was described by Park Tae-woo, a professor at the Institute of Sustainable

Development of Korea University, "Barring the Korean War, it's by far the biggest crisis in South Korea's history". Israeli leader Benjamin Netanyahu was reportedly indicted by police after allegations that he accepted tens of thousands of (US) dollars in gifts from wealthy businessmen. He was also caught on tape allegedly doing deals with the media for better coverage. Pakistan PM Nawaz Sharif resigned in 2017, after his country's Supreme Court disqualified him from holding office due to his family's financial "irregularities". The BBC reported that, "Not a single one of the 17 prime ministers that preceded him (Sharif) have completed their full term in office". South African President Zuma was beset by corruption scandals, including the reported expenditure of $US 16m on "security upgrades", which basically rebuilt his palatial home. Three recent Governors of the state of Illinois in the US (containing the city of Chicago), were later convicted of crimes and spent time in prison. Two Premiers (leaders) of State Governments in NSW, the most populous state in Australia, have resigned in the last 20 years after corruption scandals. Political corruption has been significantly more widespread than just the high profile cases like US President Richard Nixon. These have been just a few examples from recent times. Democratic government is rarely free of corruption at a senior level.

Having corrupt politicians in government may be seen to be a root cause of problems and it clearly does contribute to many issues. Yet corruption itself is not the underlying cause, it is more a symptom of the problem. The true root cause is that of the opportunity for corruption itself. If we take away the possibility of there being any potential benefit from corruption, then politicians will have no capacity for corruption, no matter their personal morals or ethics. If we could remove the possibility of a politician gaining advantage through voting in a certain way, then there is a significantly lower chance of corruption. If we take away the option of politicians who have governed over particular industries, to later secure jobs from those same industries then the incentive for corrupted policies reduces.

The root cause of corruption is that it is possible to gain benefits from voting or leading in a particular way. Any system where an individual or small, known group holds power over decisions that can have significant financial or personal consequence is open to the potential for corruption. If that power can be maintained easily through a distortion of the electoral process, then the likelihood of corruption will increase.

Experience has shown that increasing the detection of and punishments for corruption can ironically increase the level of illegality. This is because the corrupted power holders will then resort to greater extremes to protect themselves from the law. Even so, monitoring and policing should be part of any general democratic governance process.

However, implementing a system to enforce integrity, to monitor for corruption and to police breaches, only deals with the symptoms of the problem. If we can instead largely remove any potential for individuals to gain from corruption, then we can avoid the problem. Any new system of government must ensure that power is contained in the system itself, and not in the hands of a select group of politicians. Bypassing the potential for corruption is by far the best option. This is both possible and practical.

We will later build a democratic process in which legislators and leaders cannot gain advantage through corruption.

Conflicts of interest

".... the self-interested calculations and actions of rulers are the driving force of all politics" - The Dictator's Handbook, Bruce Bueno de Mesquita and Alastair Smith (both professors at New York University)

On Fidel Castro
Up until 1960, the CIA had tried on at least two occasions to depose and/or kill Fidel Castro of Cuba. Castro was considered to be too much of a threat to the US by establishing a communist government so close to home. A task force had been specifically created to depose the Cuban government. However, as the 1960 elections drew near, Nixon instructed his Cuban task force, "Don't do anything now; wait until after the elections". At the time, domestic political concerns reigned supreme in the decision making process. This delay gave Fidel Castro crucial time to build both his defence forces and his intelligence against any upcoming US action. The subsequent US

sponsored invasion of Cuba at the Bay of Pigs was an unmitigated disaster, for a whole range of reasons - which at least in some part included that of the Nixon mandated delay.

Previously, America had been using U-2 flights over the USSR and China to gather intelligence about the capabilities of its rivals for power. However, the flights came at a cost. U-2 planes had been shot down in the USSR and China and had caused President Eisenhower significant domestic embarrassment. Eisenhower was caught spying on the Soviets at the same time as he was meeting with them to improve relations and he clumsily lied about the flights afterwards. It was reported that, "Eisenhower walked into the Oval Office on May 9 and said out loud: 'I would like to resign'" (he did not follow through on this). Suffice to say that U-2 flights had become an extremely sensitive political issue.

After President Kennedy was elected, he appointed John McCone as director of the CIA. Robert Kennedy around that time wrote to his brother John, "The time has come for a showdown, for in a year or two years the situation will be vastly worse," he wrote, "If we don't want Russia to set up missile bases in Cuba, we had better decide now what we are willing to do to stop it". As described by Pulitzer prize winning author Tom Weiner, "The overthrow of Castro was 'the top priority in the United States Government,' Bobby Kennedy told McCone on January 19, 1962. 'No time, money, effort, or manpower is to be spared.'" The new director soon predicted that Cuba would get hold of Soviet nuclear missiles. "If I were Khrushchev," he said, "I'd put offensive missiles in Cuba. Then I'd bang my shoe on the desk and say to the United States, 'How do you like looking down the end of a gun barrel for a change? Now, let's talk about Berlin and any other subject that I choose.'" He warned the President of his views on August 15th, 1962. The President at the time reportedly did not agree with McCone.

On August 29, 1962, a U-2 flight over Cuba detected a Soviet surface to air missile site of the type that could shoot down U-2 planes. Kennedy shortly afterwards suspended all U-2 flights over Cuba - it was election time and he could not afford another U-2 incident. For 45 days, the US did not have any information on what weapons the Soviets were setting up or had already set up in Cuba. Later, while fears of the Cuban missile remained escalated and when war was a realistically looming possibility, the American president left for the election campaign trail. "The president walked out of the meeting, leaving two military options on the table: a sneak attack on Cuba and a full-bore invasion. His parting words were a request to see McCone the next morning before leaving for a campaign trip to Connecticut. General Carter, McNamara, Bundy, and a few others stayed behind." The President had to spend time on an election while dealing with the real potential for global nuclear confrontation. Eventually after the successful election, McCone was finally able to convince Kennedy to permit U-2 flights again and Soviet nuclear missile sites were very soon found. However, for a period of time, domestic political concerns had again contributed to a decision to delay action which could have detected the existential military threat of nuclear weapons on America's doorstep.

In a relatively short period of time, on three separate occasions and for two different US Presidents, domestic political concerns had influenced significant US foreign policy efforts. Two important actions had been delayed and at a critical moment, time had been taken out for elections. Domestic political concerns had potentially affected the risks of global conflict. In our representative democracies, politicians do need to manage their popularity and do need to take time out for election campaigning. This is not just during election cycles as successful politicians will inevitably continue to campaign while in government. The clash between domestic political concerns and what is best for the nation arises in every modern democratic state. At times, when what is best for the country may not be what is in the best interest of a political leader, the decision making process itself may be unable to produce the most secure national outcome.

A better democratic system would enable the tough leadership decisions to be made by considering only the relevant information, without any concern for personal consequences and without having to spend valuable time campaigning for personal success.

The book, *The Logic of Political Survival* was written by four esteemed professors of political science - Bruce Bueno de Mesquita, Alastair Smith, Randolph M. Siverson and James D. Morrow. In it they demonstrate, using a range of experiences from our recent history, how in politics it is the self-interested politician who is likely to succeed. A politician or leader without a view on what is best for themselves and in particular for their own success and survival, will be significantly less likely both to get elected initially and then to continue as a representative of the people. This is a problem with the nature of politics. If politicians do not put their own electability concerns first, then they will likely be unable to work on the concerns of the state since they will not gain or remain in power. This can be especially difficult when the interests of an individual politician conflict with the interests of the state. The state's best interest can simply be secondary. The fundamental concern for a politician must be for their own popularity and ability to gain votes. Having a keen sense of one's own electability is a core criterion to be a successful politician. When political self-interest conflicts with the greater good, poor political decisions follow.

As one example of many, Wisconsin Senator Russ Feingold in the US was a strong campaigner for more strict campaign finance laws. He was also the incumbent Senator up for re-election in 2010. He took a principled stance against campaign finance by special interest groups and took no such donations. His opponents did not take such a stance. Outside special interest groups like SpeechNow.org were keen to protect their interests. The principled Feingold, campaigning for what he thought was right, was not able to match his opponent's campaign. The expensive advertising campaign against him was very effective and he lost the election, as have many other principled politicians like him. Principled politicians, whose focus is on the greater good without an ability to gain votes, struggle to survive.

Most western democracies have laws and guidelines designed to restrict politicians from making decisions that have a direct and personal benefit. For example, there are asset registers for new politicians in some countries to make public any potential conflicts of interest. Yet complex ownership structures can mask the true owners and beneficiaries. Benefits from political decisions can be complex, politicians can benefit in many ways indirectly through subsequent direct favours or future jobs, benefits for friends and relatives, even aside from more typical political donations. Where there are large amounts of money to be made and significant personal benefits to gain, individuals can be extremely creative and resourceful in getting around the rules. No matter how effective society becomes at policing conflicts of interest, smart determined people will still be able to work around our current democratic process as benefits can happen in numerous subtle ways.

In 1995, the then Treasury Secretary Robert E. Rubin recommended and fought for the removal of the Glass Steagal act, which restricted banks from taking risky investments in other asset classes besides basic banking and lending services. This reform was something that Citigroup had been lobbying for to allow it to increase its profits. In 1999, the Gramm-Leach-Bliley Act was approved, and Citigroup was allowed to invest in more risky business areas. Shortly afterwards, Robert E Rubin resigned as Treasury Secretary and joined Citigroup at an annual salary of $US 40 million. Citigroup's profits increased substantially as they invested in newly approved asset classes. Even though the new investments classes eventually almost resulted in Citigroup's own collapse by this time, Robert E. Rubin had already banked quite significant cash payments and bonuses from Citigroup.

There have been similar situations globally where government leaders have approved the allocation of large infrastructure projects to certain companies and those government decision makers have taken high paying roles with the same companies in later years. It is, of course, possible that companies employ the ex-politicians for their knowledge, experience and their potential influence on their ex-colleagues in future deals. It could also be true that the roles given are done as an implicit payback. Either way, the potential for corruption is large. "Jobs for the boys" is not uncommon in politics. Even if there is no direct corruption involved many political decisions for government leaders are extremely complex and any undue influence can make a tough decision even tougher.

In our present system, the key success criteria for a politician is to gain votes; qualification and capability are actually secondary in any political contest. Candidates elected are often not those best able to govern. The new democratic process must then remove the conflicts associated with maintaining popularity, as well as removing the potential personal consequence from any decision making process. We need to be able to both populate our legislative assemblies and make government decisions without conflicts of interest getting in the way. By removing the misaligned incentives and the sources of conflicts, our society will be able to get the best decisions possible.

We will build a democratic process which cannot be influenced by conflicts of interest.

Politics trumps policy

"All of us who are concerned for peace and triumph of reason and justice must be keenly aware how small an influence reason and honest good will exert upon events in the political field" - Albert Einstein

On tax reform

In a 1985 cabinet white paper, then Australian Treasurer Paul Keating argued in favour of a goods and services tax (GST, also called a sales tax or consumption tax). At the time, most western democracies had already implemented some form of this tax. The tax allowed a significant broadening of the tax base for the government. It was the key reform in a tax package that was presented as a way to make the Australian tax system fairer for all Australians. At the time, the option was overruled by the Prime Minister Bob Hawke, amid opposition from the government's key backers. Although the policy may have been in the nation's interest at the time, the Prime Minister did not want to take a risk on delivering a new tax on voters. A few years later Keating himself was promoted to became Prime Minister. His opponent in the subsequent 1993 election was an economist named John Hewson, who quickly outlined his own policy of a GST for Australians. Keating at the time was an unpopular politician and was well behind in the polls. Even though he had previously championed the idea, Keating then used the GST as a point of differentiation and ran in opposition to it. Keating's skills as a politician, as well as some key mistakes from his opponent allowed him to win the election. At the time, the election had been called "the unwinnable election" for Keating because he was so disliked by the electorate. However, the significant public concern about the GST (and the scare campaign associated with a new tax), effectively turned the election.

Politicians often run campaigns for policies that they do not believe in merely to gain power. Politicians also win elections on poor policies even though the weight of evidence may be against them, simply because they are better at politics than their opponents. John Hewson did not succeed politically and soon left politics. The GST had been used as a tool of a politician against his own personal view. Having policies that are against politicians own personal convictions and that are not the best for society is clearly not the best way to run our democracy.

Skilled politicians have more weapons in their arsenals than an opponent with only evidence and reason. Stoking people's unjustifiable fears, misrepresenting policy, manipulating evidence and personal attacks are amongst many other tools available to a skilled political campaigner. Savvy media skills can add to a lopsided debate. A skilled politician can defeat an opponent whose policies would otherwise stand the test of time. While the democratic system remains grounded in public arguments, presented though media outlets, to generally busy and largely disinterested voters, the winning policy will invariably be the better sales pitch, over the better policy. Politics inevitably trumps policy.

Western democratic societies generally support freedom of speech. Yet freedom of speech comes with a cost. Politicians are free to say whatever they want whether true or untrue, whether manipulative or fair, whether sensible or irrational. These claims and arguments by politicians do influence voters, who have little time to investigate and who can be confronted with conflicting claims by the opposing sides of politics. It can be difficult for voters to know where the truth lies. It is ironic that in our courts of law, where we decide issues affecting people's lives, basic rights and property, there are rules of evidence. There are procedures to be followed in our courts. And yet in our public debate on policy - which potentially affects the livelihoods of millions of people - we have no similar system of rules. There is no real mechanism to control political lies, or distortions, or misleading arguments. It is merely up to political opponents or the privately run media to refute. In our courts we can force false statements to be retracted, evidence to be removed, arguments to be nullified. But no such controls are available in our public political discourse over our nation's future.

26

In an ideal world we would ensure that democratic decisions are dependant less on sales and political skills and more on the validity of the policies themselves. We would remove the cause of problems, which is the capability to manipulate the underlying legislative and policy discussions, as well as remove the impact of any unavoidable public manipulation. A better democratic process would ensure that manipulation of the public process is simply ineffectual. The new democratic process will then be designed in this way, to ensure that politics and manipulation play no part in critical decision making.

Accumulated wisdom lost

"The financial crises of the past two decades, and our failure to predict them, have wreaked havoc on more than just the global economy.... But these crises and scandals do not mean that the science of economics is inherently unreliable. Most of them occurred because we ignored what we knew" – Professor John P. A. Ioannidis, Stanford University

On lessons lost

At the height of the Depression in the 1930s nearly half of the 10,000 US banks had failed. Billions of dollars were lost. Countless people were left penniless. There were a range of causes of the Depression, but the banking collapse contributed to the severity of the problem. In the ensuing years legislators in the US looked for ways to ensure that the banking system could remain solid in the future, since the stability of savings held in retail and commercial banking system was essential to the economy. Many actions were taken to protect the country from a potential repeat of the Depression. From the carnage, the Glass-Steagall act arose (it was actually contained in the Banking act of 1933). The act was designed to ensure that the commercial banks could withstand any future possibilities. Essentially, the act restricted commercial banks from engaging in investment banking since investment banking has much greater risk. In this way, the commercial banks would be significantly less likely to fail. Many nations followed with their own similar banking regulations to safeguard their nations financial well-being.

27

For around 75 years the banking system globally remained solid. Throughout the 1990s however, the finance industries' powerful lobbyists complained that costly regulation reduced investment opportunities and flexibility in the economy. Over a period of time, a range of protections and restrictions on the banking sector were stripped back. The finance sector wanted to be able to both invest in and to sell a greater range of products. The profits of the banking sector could then increase, which meant that individual bonuses would soar. This culminated in 1999, when President Clinton repealed the final remnants of the Glass-Steagall act through the signing into law of the Gramm-Leachy-Bliley Act. US banks were again free to invest in other forms of banking, including investment banking and insurance. Over the next few years, the US investment banks expanded their businesses significantly, investing in a whole new range of products, including a number of newly created, complex and unregulated derivative products. These products were bought and sold by the banks and were structured around a range of product areas, including mortgages. The products earned huge profits, as well as substantial bonuses for those employees and managers involved in the business. But the products contained significant long term risk.

Eventually the derivatives products imploded as the vastly overvalued mortgage market in the US collapsed. The financial debt contagion spread throughout the world. Companies, charities and governments alike, who had invested in theoretically safe "AAA" rated products, were devastated. Many of the world's largest banks were left with toxic products on their books, whose value had either plummeted, or worse, whose value had become an enormous and unknown liability. Significant banking and finance institutions like Citigroup, Bank of America, Bear Stearns, Fannie May, Freddie Mac and many more, either did collapse, or risked collapse. The collapse thus brought on the US Great Recession. At around the same time, real estate markets collapsed in the Netherlands, the UK, Spain and Ireland, undermining their banking systems. As some banks began to fail, the global interconnectedness of the banking system, which cross funded itself through the short-term money market, meant that a critical source of funding for banks globally disappeared overnight. Many global banks suddenly found themselves with significant funding difficulties and systemic global financial devastation followed. Even the more protected and solvent of the banks also faced difficulties, since they did not know which other global banks - which owed them significant cash, may default. Globally, many banks were bailed out (or were backed and guaranteed) by governments and reserve banks. After the collapse in the US more than 300 major lending institutions failed, and more than 2 million homes were repossessed. The US government, concerned over a further collapse of the banking system and a repeat of the Great Depression, eventually spent more than $14 trillion dollars (near to the entire GDP of the US in 2007) on a range of banking and industry bailout packages.

After the Depression, when the Glass Steagal act was first implemented, it was probably inconceivable to consider that at some point the act would be repealed by government, and banks would again be allowed to participate in high risk investments. It was probably assumed that the leaders of our democratic system would not be so foolish to again risk the foundations of the economic system. However, special interest groups were able to convince the government of the day to effectively roll the dice. Afterwards, subsequent governments had no option but to commit trillions of dollars to ensure the stability of the financial system. In the modern global financial system this was not just a problem for the US. The interconnectedness of the globalized banking system means that banking collapses in one locale can affect banks globally. After the banking crisis in the US that contributed to the Great Recession, financial institutions, companies, charities and governments globally lost billions of dollars in investments that they believed had been placed in secure products. Many of the risks that led to the crisis remain. Importantly, the democratic decision making process itself, that led to an avoidable recurrence of a banking crisis, remains exactly as it was before the crisis.

Many of us probably assume that politicians have learnt from the mistakes of the past. There is, however, no way to ensure that they have actually done so. With the ongoing and regular changeovers of democratically elected governments there is a continual stream of new politicians and policies. It is also difficult for any leadership to learn lessons from its predecessors, especially when the previous leadership was generally from another political party. Although there may in theory be a sensible handover of power from one to the other, there is very little trust. Any advice comes with significant

29

risk. Politicians are not really in the game of helping their replacements do well, especially when they and their party will still be in direct competition for the next election. The process discourages trust and makes ongoing co-operation difficult.

As we have seen, this has cost society repeatedly. It is also not just a problem with the transition of government. The lessons of the Great Depression were lost at great cost globally. Extraordinarily, the lessons then learnt again, from the Great Recession of 2007/8, have once again been rewritten and unwound in legislation in 2017 at the behest of US special interest groups. Examples elsewhere in this text show that the lessons of the dangers of government interference in intelligence agencies' conclusions was lost (from both the Cold War and the Vietnam war) and repeated by the US government in the second Gulf War. In his farewell address, Dwight Eisenhower warned of the dangers of influence of the military industries on politics. We see elsewhere in this book how these lessons were largely lost, with the enormous US government expenditure on defence which has been justified through manipulated analysis of external threats. Recent democratic history is riddled with the repeated policy failures of democratic governments more concerned with politics than with sensibly heeding the past lessons. These lost lessons can have severe consequences for society.

In an ideal system, government policies would improve over time based upon the lessons from the past. There would be a mechanism to ensure this. In our existing system this can only happen through the individual capability of our politicians; it is up to them to study and learn lessons from the past. In modern society, the accumulated wisdom is effectively maintained in some ways through the public service departments. Yet in our adversarial political system new governments can have pre-conceived notions of distrust for these public servants and can often ignore their advice.

A better option is to change the political and party process itself, to avoid the policy swings, conflicts of interest and distrust. This would seem essential in order to enable effective ongoing leadership. Removing an adversarial political system would allow the potential for leadership co-operation. In an ideal world, with each new policy proposal there would be a documented case describing the justification for that policy. When new policy is then

30

proposed similar older policies and experiences could be assessed and subsequent results considered. As well, the results of any change should be measured and documented.

We will build a democratic process which can preserve and benefit from the lessons of the past.

A degradation to despotism

*"As only a politician can, Putin ended this academic debate. Within months of his inauguration, he successfully reasserted the Kremlin's power against every competing authority and demonstrated that the old Soviet institutions have life in them yet. When formal measures were not enough, he used his powers of 'persuasion'. Legislators and judges who refuse to vote with the Kremlin are denied their salaries and perks (the Russian parliament does not have control over its own salaries, let alone over other governmental funds). This explains why the upper house of parliament was willing to vote for the reduction of its own power and size, not an everyday occurrence in politics."
- The Future of Freedom: Illiberal Democracy at Home and Abroad, Fareed Zakaria, PhD, Harvard*

On "nearly perfected" government

When a professor at Princeton in the early 20th century, future US President Woodrow Wilson praised Prussia (now Germany) for an "admirable system...the most studied and most nearly perfected...[It] transformed arrogant and perfunctory [bureaucracies] into public-spirited instruments of just government". Germany was then considered a model of democracy. Germany at the time had many of the hallmarks of modern liberal democracies - a formal constitution, freedom of expression, a public service to support the people, the rule of law and a freely elected democratic government. However, following the harsh reparations expenses imposed after the first world war, combined with the ravages of the Great Depression, many people wanted change. In the 1932 national elections the recently formed Nazi Party - which promised change and work for all, gained the most votes. And in the follow up election of 1933 the Nazis received 44 percent of the vote and were asked to form a government. Adolf Hitler had

31

been democratically elected. After Hitler assumed the reins of government, he gradually and skilfully removed the democratic controls on power. Hitler then imposed his own autocratic rule. What was once an open and free society began to degrade into a tightly managed, state controlled totalitarian regime. Democracy was turned into totalitarianism from within. Hitler's regime went on to start a war that cost the lives of tens of millions of people and destroyed the German state.

A black swan event is described as an event that deviates from the normal experience and is extremely difficult to predict. Few in Germany in the early 20th century could have predicted the depression and then the destruction of their mature and seemingly enlightened democratic system. A democratic degradation into despotism probably seems extremely unlikely to most of us now, who live in seemingly stable western democratic states. This collapse into despotism, however, has happened repeatedly in quite a few democratic nations in the past century. The structure of our democracy is largely the same as it was under Germany in the 1930s, nothing substantial has changed in our democratic process since then.

The independence of the three arms of government is considered critical to the stability of the democratic system. No individual or group should control more than one of these pillars of democracy. Yet popular democratic leaders in the past have manufactured reasons to incrementally reduce the power of parliament, the constitution, the judiciary. Iraq was essentially a democracy until an elected Saddam Hussein turned the nation into a dictatorship. In Venezuela, Hugo Chavez was elected under a democratic system before he gradually removed the fundamental controls that limited government power and brought the government under his control. A similar devolution of democratic controls has happened in many democracies in the 20th century, including in Italy, Russia, Kyrgyzstan, Peru, the Ukraine, the Philippines and Argentina.

It is absolutely a risk, albeit small, that any democratically elected leader could chip away at democratic freedoms and protections. Over a period of time, using some perceived crises as a trigger, the leader can assume greater and greater control until it is too late to arrest the slide. In 2017, the Turkish population voted to give greater power to their President Recep Tayyip Erdogan and increase his control over the judicial arm of government. In the same year, the Polish parliament passed legislation which removed the Supreme Court and allowed the legislature to appoint a new judiciary directly. Voters can be concerned at the threat of violence and conflict or can be frustrated at the impotence and obstructionism of a democratic parliament. The political gridlock that is common in many democracies can lead to frustrations within the electorate about a government's inability to resolve problems. People may then increase the power of popular politicians to enable them to fix the problems. Minor changes to a political power structure may seem harmless to busy and frustrated voters, but those changes can lead to the destruction of essential controls on power. Individual voters, when faced with very real threats of violence and turmoil, are less concerned with democratic theory and the importance of the separation of powers. This risk increases when an external or existential concern is present or is manufactured by the democratic leadership. History is ignored at our peril.

As democracies were constructed, the fathers of democracy spoke of a requirement to separate the powers of the three arms of government to ensure that any power allocated was not abused by individuals. As democracies stand however, elected governments and their underlying political parties effectively control two key arms of government. A newly elected government leader directly appoints the executive arm of government. The problem exists in (Westminster style) governments where a cabinet of elected members of parliament are selected to run the executive arm of government. In this case, executive leadership is from within the legislative government (and its political party) itself. These ministers are all from the one side of the political spectrum. A similar concern exists within a Presidential style of democracy, where the President directly appoints the executive arm of government. The President himself is usually appointed from within a political party. In both forms of government then, the political party itself can potentially control both the legislative and the executive arms of government. The potential to be irresponsible rises. When a single side of politics controls two arms of government there is the potential that this group can gradually decrease the controls on power and hence degrade a democratic state towards authoritarianism.

33

In the US, with the legislative arm of government also appointing Supreme Court justices, the potential exists (and is often realized), for one side of politics to effectively control all three arms of government. The separation of powers – a cornerstone of western democracy, can then break down. As we have seen in the many countries mentioned above, the degradation to despotism is not merely a theoretical possibility, but a realistic potential.

It always seemed a reasonable argument, that society had learnt the lessons of the second world war and its dictators. The human race would not again risk such carnage and destruction. We would not allow a modern, educated democracy to again follow the path into authoritarianism as happened so tragically in Germany. It always seemed that the lessons were so powerful that this was an impossibility. Yet nothing has changed in the structure or processes of our democracies since. Our democracies have consistently repeated their mistakes from the past.

The risks of a degradation to despotism can be difficult to specify. The process can happen gradually and in small increments. By the time a problem is noticed it can be too late. The basic protection against unchecked power is to ensure true independence of the arms of government. Each arm acts as a counter-balance to the power of the other arms. And yet political parties can control two or even three arms of government.

We will build a democratic process with true independence of each of the arms of government. A process where power is contained in the process itself, and not in the hands of individual politicians or political parties.

The problems of leadership

"War is a mere continuation of politics by other means" - Carl von Clausewitz, Prussian soldier and preeminent military thinker

It has been often claimed that wars are started by leaders, not by the people. One of the responsibilities of a democratically elected leader is the protection of its people from external threats. Just because a leader is democratically elected however, does not mean that he or she is more or less likely to lead a country into war. The pressure of being democratically elected and remaining in power can have strange and unexpected influences when it comes to conflict. Unfortunately, the decision to fight a war can sometimes be a grey area. On the one side, a desire for peace, stability and the safety of innocents inevitably hurt in the fog of war. On the other side, a potentially noble fight against a known tyranny, or a fight against significant human rights abuses and countless deaths. A continuation of peace can involve the tolerance of genocide and large scale human rights abuses in our neighbours' tyrannical societies. When facing these complex decisions even a good leader can be influenced by other factors, including what is best for themselves politically. Standing up to confront enemies with whom a nation may have long standing enmity can lead to improved popularity.

In recent times we have seen examples of these difficult decisions which inevitably become the responsibility of a single leader. The Vietnam war, the two gulf wars, the Falkland Islands war for Britain, the Russian war in Chechnya as well as in the Ukraine, all had significant consequences for the leaders involved. For some, their popularity increased, for others their leadership faltered, and they lost power. Even getting out of wars can have far reaching consequences. After the Gulf War of 2003 and the occupation of Iraq, Barack Obama promised to withdraw US troops from Iraq - as per the existing plan. After his election however, the new Iraq government was not delivering as hoped and ethnic violence was increasing. Circumstances had potentially changed, and the risk and consequences of withdrawing had increased. But Barack Obama honoured his promise and US troops were withdrawn. The subsequent ongoing ethnic divisions and power vacuum arguably contributed to the rise of ISIS. The country then imploded into civil war which engulfed its neighbours. Complex policy decisions can be more difficult for a politician to face when an electorate has no time for the subtleties of policy or for changing circumstances and is unforgiving on broken promises.

In our condition as imperfect human beings it can be extremely difficult for leaders to separate out the conflicting consequences of war for the nation and for themselves. It is difficult for leaders not to be in some way influenced, even if unconsciously, by the consequences for themselves personally.

35

As with the potential degradation to despotism, the problems of leadership can stem from unchecked power in the hands of an individual, as well as from the many conflicts of interest in politics. Our challenge then is to remove or to govern and control the power of individuals in our governments. As well, we must reduce the many conflicts of interest associated with difficult decisions. The new democracy will need to both remove these conflicts as well as to mitigate the risks. Changes will be required to simplify and improve our collective decision making as well to implement a better governance framework for our leaders.

To summarise our requirements related to politicians:

We will build a democratic process which cannot be influenced by misaligned incentives, or by conflicts of interest. One in which you cannot gain advantage through corruption or through political manipulation. A process which can both preserve and benefit from the lessons of the past. One with true independence of each of the arms of government. One where power is contained in the process itself and not in the hands of individual politicians or political parties. *And one which is protected by a sensible governance framework.*

Policies

"When I see a congressman giving his opinion on something, I always wonder if it represents his real opinion or if it represents an opinion that he's designed in order to be elected. It seems to be a central problem for politicians " - Richard Feynman, PhD, Nobel laureate

Our democratic system is expected to produce a list of policies for our future. We start with policy ideas being proposed, then prioritized, evaluated and decided upon. The complexities of the prioritization and evaluation of various competing policies raise significant difficulties. When it comes to the process of democratic policy making there is quite a bit of devil in the detail.

Short-term policies

"Democrats deliver what the people want. Because they have to stand for election and reelection, democrats are impatient. They have a short time horizon. For them, the long run is the next election, not their country's performance over the next twenty years." - The Dictator's Handbook, Bruce Bueno de Mesquita and Alastair Smith (both professors at New York University)

On units of measurement

In September 1999, the Mars Climate Orbiter begun its insertion into orbit around the red planet. NASA had spent $193m dollars on a plan to study the Martian climate, atmosphere and surface changes as NASA continued its research into the planets around our solar system. At a critical juncture in the Lander's motion into the planet's orbit an engine terminated earlier than had been planned. Travelling too fast, the Lander crashed and was destroyed. Subsequently, the Mars Climate Orbiter Mishap Investigation Board was launched to find the cause of the failure. The enquiry into the failure determined that there was likely a mix up, with one team using metric units (SI), and the other team using US customary units (Imperial units). The discrepancy meant that the rockets had fired too briefly to slow the landing craft and it was lost. At the time, the US and its corporations used the imperial system, while most of the rest of the world used the metric system.

Although the metric system had been in place for many decades in many other countries and offered significant advantages, politicians in the US had been unable to legislate for the changeover. The upfront costs and risk of change had been too difficult for politicians to handle, even if the long term benefits were overwhelming. The standardization of metric measurement between countries has produced clear and significant benefits globally. And yet certain countries are yet to approve the conversion and are encumbered with an obsolete and overly complex system. The requirement to handle multiple systems of measurements causes ongoing additional costs and risks.

The errors that led to the loss of the Orbiter were clearly human errors. After the incident, there were a series of changes put in place to ensure that this would be significantly less likely to recur in the future. In fact, NASA already does all of its internal calculations in the metric system, in spite of the fact that the US itself and NASA's US contractors do not. And yet, if the United States and Europe did not still have fundamentally different systems of units of measurement the error would not have been possible. The root cause - of having two different systems, remains. The process of moving to metric contains short-term risks and pain that creates difficulties for politicians. Great Britain has spent more than 45 years converting from their existing system to metric. The US has been unable to get effective legislation passed.

In democratic societies the political focus invariably works within election cycles. Policies focus on the next election term. It is difficult for a politician to gain support for long-term policies when in comparison, his opponent may well offer constituents more popular short-term benefits. Voters have shown repeatedly that they prefer the short-term benefit over the long-term best policies. Those politicians who focus on the short-term survive and the long-term policies are invariably not implemented. There are times when long-term policies have been successfully rolled out by various governments, but these are more often the exception than the rule.

It is also difficult for democratic governments to have a long-term strategy when they are unlikely to remain in power long enough to follow through on that strategy. More likely than not they will have been voted out and the new government may reverse course after being elected. There is also little incentive for a long-term strategy when an individual politician is unlikely to stay around long enough to reap the rewards of that strategy. It is then not sensible for politicians to take much risk with long-term policies.

Ironically one of the few governments to publicly espouse multi decade plans is the Chinese government. Not having to worry about another party stealing their elections, the single party state allows for long-term plans. No multi-party democratic state government has been able to compete with China's long-term nation building plans and the Chinese have had the most sustained period of high growth of any developing nation.

The root causes of our political preference for short-termism relate to the misalignment of incentives and the challenges in managing election cycles. Without the removal of these underlying causes it is difficult for our democratic process to deliver a long-term strategy.

We will build a democratic process which cannot be influenced by short term political concerns.

Broken promises

In many ways, there is not much value in listing examples of the history of broken promises since they are so pervasive. Few people should need to be convinced. Some examples have gone down in infamy, for example, "Read my lips: no new taxes" from George W. Bush. Politicians get away with the non-delivery of promises for a whole range of reasons. This includes the apathy of busy voters who have short memories and much cynicism. It is too easy to promise all sorts of impressive new policies to influence voters during election campaigns and have little intention of delivery. Since the strategy works, the broken policy promises continue. Many promises are also potentially made in good faith but then become difficult to deliver. This can be due to the complexities of governing with multiple minor parties, the lack of a democratic majority in various houses, or "surprise" finance difficulties that only become apparent once in power. Many promises are potentially made cynically to gain power, in the full knowledge that they have little chance of ever seeing the light of day. Essentially, voters often do not get the policies for which they voted.

There is also a consequence on the other side of promises. Once a promise has been made if a politician breaks it there is a potential political cost. For example, a politician may make a promise in good faith and then discover in office that the situation has changed, and the promise is no longer the best option. An example of this was in our previous discussion of the situation facing President Barack Obama if he failed to withdraw as promised from Iraq. As the situation had potentially changed in Iraq since the promise had been made, Obama faced difficulties. Politicians can lose face when they do not keep their promises. Knowing this, a politician now has a conflict of interest, where the better policy, which is to break their promise, is not in their own best interest. This conflict of interest makes tough decisions even tougher, where personal political survival could be adversely affected if the right decision is made.

While it is possible to gain advantage through broken promises the practice will continue. Where there is a significant delay between policy promises and policy legislative decisions there is always the possibility that promises will become problematic or unwise to fulfil due to changing circumstances. Delivering decisions about policy once, at the time near to that of implementation, would work around one part of this problem. Removing the need to make promises as a part of our government process altogether would address the problems associated with the breaking of political promises.

We will build a democratic process which has no requirement for, and hence influence from, political promises.

Policy packages

In many representative democracies politicians publish packages of policies for each election. Where policies are voted upon as a package there can be major difficulties for voters. Voters may agree with some of those policies, but not all. An individual can disagree with many of the policies of each and every competing party. With every vote there is an inherent compromise for the voter. It is often the case of having to decide which group of policies is least objectionable.

By the time a set of policies is presented to the electorate a whole range of compromises have already been made. Politicians must balance the differing requirements and self-interests of a range of groups, from internal party factions, competing advisers, lobbyists and special interest groups as well as from supporters. By the time policies reach the electorate they often bear little resemblance to what would be the preference in an ideal world. Policy compromise is built into the system of politics.

The current political structure encourages deals and compromises to be made in order to agree both policies and policy packages. Removing the grouping of policies and the deals done to obtain compromise would seem critical improvements. A better democratic process would include no policy packages. A better democratic process would also not allow for the possibility of deals between legislators, where support for a particular policy was dependent on subsequent support for other policies.

We will build a democratic process where all policies are decided independently on their own merits.

Populist policies

Politicians' popularity is improved by giving the people what they want, and yet populist policies may not be best for society as a whole. Politicians will offer tax deductions which cripple government revenue. They will offer superficial solutions which leave in place the underlying causes of problems. They will offer protectionist policies to pander to people's natural xenophobic instincts, even if these are not in the long-term and even short-term best interests of the nation as a whole. Politicians will also offer financial handouts to various groups because these are popular, even if not sensible. The 2016 Brexit decision in Britain is an example of a politician caving to a populist policy in which the leader did not believe.

As Fareed Zakaria has said: "When historians write about these times they will surely be struck by our constant, never-ending search for the pulse of the people. Politicians, corporations and journalists spend vast amounts of time, money and energy trying to divine the public's views on everything from Social Security to the afterlife to carbonated drinks. It is a race actually, to be the first to genuflect before them…Washington today is organized around the pursuit of public opinion. It employs armies of people to continually check the pulse of the American people on every conceivable matter. It hires others to determine the intensity of their feelings on these issues. It pays still others to guess what people might think tomorrow. Lobbyists, activists, consultants and politicians all use this information as the basis for their actions."

Pandering to the people's whims may deliver the re-election of candidates but will not deliver the best policies for the future of a nation. Populism can be a difficult problem to deal with when the majority rules. The human condition can overrule people's higher instincts. However, our current political process also makes this inclination worse since politicians will actually leverage these basic desires of voters in order to gain cheap and easy popularity. Politicians will actively play up the superficial reasons for short-term policies since this is an easy way of gaining support.

We must remove the political incentives from the process. We must make it impossible for our legislators to gain from pandering to populism. As well as this we must mitigate against the natural tendency of voters and legislators to support populist short term policies. We need to find a way to ensure that policy debate is more thorough, more evidence based, more rational and with more consideration of the greater long-term good. However, the risk of support for populist policies remains in all democracies. To deal with this risk we will also include a more robust governance framework.

We will build a democratic process which produces no benefit from pandering to populism, which is less impacted by populism and which is protected through a robust governance framework.

The policy pendulum

On stable government

The Australian political system has been relatively stable for more than 100 years and for another 100 years before that when under British rule. For 25 years up until the year 2017, it had sustained unparalleled and continuous economic growth where other western nations had fallen into recession at least once. However, in 13 years of those seemingly good times, between 2002 and 2015, there were 66 leadership changes in the 9 major governments and opposition parties (State and Federal). Repeatedly, personal ambitions and politics delivered leadership coups. This includes 6 changes of Prime Ministers in around 8 years. Each Prime Minister brought in a new wave of policies, as well as a new wave of unpopularity. This was either through repeated broken promises or because they were put in power by their political party (and not the Australian people) or because they were just considered out of touch. The various governments rarely had the support of the Australian people and invariably could not get their major policies supported by both houses of parliament. There was regular political gridlock and threats of a "double dissolution" of parliament, which is triggered when critical legislation of the government is repeatedly rejected by the Senate. In 2016, a double dissolution was finally triggered. A new election was held, and the government was re-elected. The government still did not hold control of the Senate. The government then needed to do deals and compromises with minor parties. The minor parties, generally unpopular with the majority of the electorate, were able get some of their own policies signed into law. And yet policy movement was still limited for the government.

The structure of our democracies enables an ongoing swing from one government to the next, from one leader to the next and from one set of policies to the next. Much of the change is more about the ambition of individuals than what is best for the nation. Career ambitions of politicians can have a significant impact on the performance and stability of our political system.

The policy pendulum swings continually between governments from one side of the political spectrum to another. This can be a positive thing, as after

43

one government swings too far in one direction this can be tempered by the next government. In other ways this is a waste of resources as one government will legislate a new policy on which much budget is spent to enact, implement and enforce, only for the next government to reverse the policy, spending further to unwind and reverse the whole system. As one example of many, in 2005, the Howard Government established the Australian Building and Construction Commission to monitor and enforce workplace relations laws. The watchdog was then decommissioned by the Gillard government in 2012, and merged into Fair Work Australia, at the behest of its union backers. Then in 2016, the Turnbull Government revived the watchdog and recommissioned it. This costly and inefficient policy pendulum effect is all too common. Laws and policies swing in one direction only then to be reversed by the next government. Swings occur from less regulation to more regulation, from a larger public service to a smaller public service, from more services for the poorer members of society to a reduction in services for the poorer members of society and in many other ways. The cost to nations is significant.

The underlying issue is the democratic process itself, which involves switches between opposing political parties and ambitious politicians chasing career advancement.

We will build a democratic process which is has little requirement for, and is protected from, the influence of adversarial politics and career ambitions.

Voting for policies and people

One of the features of our democratic system is that during election campaigns we debate the capabilities of both the candidates and the policies presented. We are not only selecting a set of policies for our government to enact into law, but we are also selecting people to run the government itself and then to vote upon future policies. So, the character of these people is invariably in question just as much as the policies themselves. This makes for a complicated decision for voters. We must decide between candidates with many characteristics and capabilities and with their own set of policies and promises. Decisions about complex policies can be difficult enough and yet our process makes it even more complicated because our single vote

44

must decide on both current policies as well as on the people to implement them. Good policies can be proposed by poor candidates and bad policies by good candidates. Personal integrity and capability are paramount in politicians and sometimes good policy loses out to this requirement. This complexity makes tough voting decisions even tougher.

To resolve this issue properly we must remove the requirement to vote for both politicians and policies at the same time. Ideally, we should reduce the complexity of decision making for both our voters and for our legislators. We should separate the decisions on each individual policy. It does currently save time to decide on more than one issue at once, and not to have millions of busy and often disinterested voters required to vote on every issue. And yet for decision making to be effective, each decision maker needs to focus on just the relevant information and issues, without being clouded and confused by unnecessary complexity. Any new democratic system must ensure clarity and focus in our decision making process, as well as being efficient and effective enough to allow decisions without the need to ask millions of voters to make every decision.

We will build a democratic process where policies, decisions *and government appointments* are decided independently and efficiently, on their own merits.

The influence of special interests

"I know a little something about soft money, as my family is the largest single contributor of soft money to the national Republican Party." She said, "I have decided, however, to stop taking offense at the suggestion that we are buying influence. Now I simply concede the point. They are right. We do expect some things in return. We expect to foster a conservative governing philosophy consisting of limited government and respect for traditional American virtues. We expect a return on our investment; we expect a good and honest government. Furthermore, we expect the Republican Party to use the money to promote these policies..." Betsy DeVos - Dark Money

On agnotology

Science historian Robert Procter, from Stanford University, first defined the term agnotology as "the study of wilful acts to spread confusion and deceit, usually to sell a product or win favour". He has revealed the tactics of special interest groups in manipulating the limitations of our current democratic processes.

Agnotology was first used widely by the cigarette industry to challenge and discredit the scientific evidence that cigarette smoking was both addictive and harmful to smokers. The industry consciously spread disinformation in order to imply that the scientific evidence was far from overwhelming. A secret memo of the cigarette company Brown and Williamson revealed the tactics: "I think we should give immediate attention to the possibility of running ads stating, in effect, that there is no scientific evidence of a causal relationship between smoking and lung cancer" - J.W. Burgard, Brown and Williamson, 1967. The cigarette industry ran a campaign for decades which dismissed the reasonable scientific conclusions made by medical experts, feeding misinformation and unreasonable conclusions and generally stoking doubt. Future US Supreme Court judge Lewis Powell said in an annual report of Phillip Morris, "We deplore the lack of objectivity in so important a controversy...Unfortunately the positive benefits of smoking which are so widely acknowledged are largely ignored by many reports linking cigarettes and health, and little attention is paid to the scientific reports which are favourable to smoking." There were no reputable scientific reports which documented the "positive benefits of smoking", the evidence at the time was instead that smoking was addictive and deadly. However, politicians and voters find it very difficult to distinguish reputable science that follows a rigorous scientific method, from the less reliable "scientific" conclusions made by biased industry sponsored studies. Science is complex and can be easily manipulated when financial fortunes are at stake. The tactics however, delayed effective government action to reduce the impact of smoking for decades. It also confused the issue for the public, decreasing their motivation to avoid such a harmful addiction. In all likelihood, the tactic contributed to the unnecessary deaths of tens of millions of people.

Since then the same method has been used by the sugar industry to imply that the evidence for the damaging effects of sugar on our health is far from overwhelming. Cristin Kearns, a post-doctoral scholar from the University of California, San Francisco, has studied the history of sugar industry politics. For decades the industry paid for studies whose results were used to influence the political decisions around dietary recommendations. Kearns, Glantz and colleagues wrote "Together with other recent analyses of sugar industry documents, our findings suggest the industry sponsored a research program in the 1960s and 1970s that successfully cast doubt about the hazards of sucrose while promoting fat as the dietary culprit in coronary heart disease". From Marion Nestle of New York University, "Mark Hegsted (a leading sugar researcher at the time) was a kind of nutrition hero, so it was kind of shocking to find out that he was taking very large amounts of money from the Sugar Research Foundation to do what they wanted". Since that time, further work has confirmed that sugar has had a significant adverse effect on the health of millions of people. The evidence from studies that were independent of the sugar industries influence was drowned out by studies whose science was often dubious. A very vocal sugar lobby managed to sway the politics. Their influence meant that there were few warnings about the dangers of excessive sugar and no limits on the dietary recommendations for sugar intake for around 40 years. The media as well as the governments around the world found it difficult to distinguish the respectable science from the industry manipulation. Sugar intake soared over the years as industry found that it was cheap (in the US, sugar has been subsidized by the government for decades). Sugar also made food easier to sell and hence profits soared further.

The incidence of avoidable type 2 diabetes has soared over recent decades. The World Health Organization (WHO) estimates that more than 3 million people die each year globally from conditions as a result of high sugar levels in the blood. WHO also projects that diabetes deaths will double between 2005 and 2030. In the US in 2006, it was reported that there were approximately 65,000 amputations from largely avoidable complications of diabetes. In the UK, amputations from diabetes have grown to around 7000 per year.

Agnotology has also been used with regard to Climate Change by industries that depend on fossil fuels for their livelihood. Robert Brulle of Drexel University investigated, in a peer reviewed study, the recent campaign by

47

special interest groups to manipulate the climate change debate. He uncovered more than half a billion dollars, from 140 different conservative foundations, that went to organizations that countered the confidence in the climate change evidence. The original funding was from, amongst others, various multinational oil and energy industry companies. Even though the scientific evidence that climate change was both real and man-made was solid and getting stronger, due to the repeated doubts raised by special interest group in the US, the public consensus in the US then diminished.

It is quite astonishing given what we know now to hear a future Supreme Court Justice expressing such a view about the "positive benefits of smoking" and claims of how scientific evidence was ignored in the campaign against smoking. As a judge, he would be expected to have the capacity for well-considered and reasoned arguments. Yet his conclusions about smoking were proven so wrong. This does not even seem like hindsight bias as there was clear evidence at the time. This demonstrates the risks of leaving critical decisions to an individual - even highly educated people can make poor decisions when their incentives are askew.

Our democracies should be capable of independently assessing the scientific risk of various substances and issues to society and presenting clear and timely regulations and recommendations to its people. And yet government policy has been unduly influenced for decades on cigarettes, sugar, oil and climate change, amongst many others. The delays in dealing with critical issues have meant that there have been tens of millions of avoidable deaths and enormous adverse impact to society.

On opioids

Opioids are an addictive form of narcotic used for the relief of significant pain. This addiction risk has been known for hundreds of years and has been documented scientifically for decades. Throughout most of the 20th century in the US and Canada opioid use was severely restricted, in part due to its highly addictive nature. In the 1990s in the US however, lobby groups petitioned for the increased use of opioids for pain relief. These lobby groups included both paid physicians as well as US "pain societies", whose sponsors included drug companies which would profit enormously from opioids sales. Arguments were made to include a stronger form of pain relief to help people with a range of health problems. In 1995, the FDA issued its first approval for OxyContin (oxycodone) by prescription. The approval was for a slow release form to deter abuse. The slow release form of the pill was inexplicably easy to abuse by simply crushing the pill to force immediate release. This allowed an easy fix for addicted drug users. Purdue Pharma, the manufacturer of OxyContin, claimed publicly that its product had a 1% addiction rate and was safe for widespread use. Competing opioids from other manufacturers were soon also approved. By the early 2000s, the first reports surfaced of deaths from overdoses. In 2007 Purdue was fined $US 634 million by a federal prosecutor for misleading claims, marketed to the public as well as to health professionals, around the addiction rate for OxyContin. Purdue was also reported to have actively thwarted efforts from the Virginia state government to limit the number of prescriptions and reduce addictions. Purdie had paid a middleman to bypass the system limits that state insurers had placed on prescriptions. In 2008, the manufacturer of the opioid Actiq (fentanyl) was fined $US 425 million for marketing its pain killing drugs for non-approved uses, which significantly increased sales (as well as addictions and deaths). By 2014 the US CDC reported that almost 2 million Americans abused or were dependent upon prescription opioids. The CDC also reported in 2017 that each day 1000 people are treated in US emergency departments for misusing prescription opioids and that at least 15,000 people die each year from overdoses of prescription opioids. There are also reports (and supporting testimonies) that, as addicts sought cheaper forms of the drugs, heroin overdose deaths increased fourfold since 2002, to total more than 13,000 per year in 2015 (National Institute of Drug Abuse, US). In 2015, US Surgeon General Vivek Murthy said that 250 million prescriptions were written for opioids every year.

Similarly, in Canada around the same time, OxyContin was approved for chronic pain. Its slow release pills were also easily bypassed through simple crushing. As in the US, once the easily abused, crushable pills were taken off the market, many addicts turned to illegal drugs, and deaths from those drugs increased significantly. The Canadian Centre for Substance Abuse reports that more than 21% of the population used prescription opioids by 2008. By

2010, amongst those Canadians aged 25-34 years old, 12.1% of all deaths were from opioid use.

Our civilised democratic governments are meant to protect us from the dangers of unfettered greed and runaway capitalism and from intentionally or carelessly inflicted harm. It seems extraordinary that our modern societies, through conscious and deliberate legislation and approvals, would allow such tragedy. Allowing profit making companies to so adversely influence the legislative and approvals process, trusting an easily bypassed slow release method and allowing patently false marketing and advertising to the medical profession and to the public, seems a clear failure of sensible governance. The company in question has reportedly made around $US 35bn in revenue from the falsely marketed drug and has in all likelihood contributed to the deaths of tens or even hundreds of thousands of people. And yet it was given a "fine" that represents, by some measures, about 4% of the total company worth. The responsible company executives were convicted of "misdemeanours" for their part in the enormous death toll. The drugs are still sold today. The drug companies plan to expand sales overseas including in countries where the regulatory controls are even less effective than those of the US. Our democratic process of decision making, which has allowed millions of people to be blatantly lied to, manipulated and become addicted for financial gain, remains unchanged.

The incentive to influence

"In the councils of government, we must guard against the acquisition of unwarranted influence, whether sought or unsought, by the military-industrial complex. The potential for the disastrous rise of misplaced power exists and will persist. We must never let the weight of this combination endanger our liberties or democratic processes. We should take nothing for granted. Only an alert and knowledgeable citizenry can compel the proper meshing of the huge industrial and military machinery of defence with our peaceful methods and goals, so that security and liberty may prosper together." President Dwight D Eisenhower's farewell address to the nation

In "The Logic of Collective Action", Mancur Olsen describes the incentives behind the influence of lobbying in politics. His argument has been paraphrased by Fareed Zakaria thus: "If a group of 100 farmers got together to petition the government to give them $10 million, the benefit to each farmer is $100,000. The cost to the rest of the country is about 4 cents per person. Who is more likely to form a lobby, them or us? Multiply this example by thousands and you understand the central problem of American democracy". This same problem applies to all democracies.

In theory, our democratic system is implemented to reflect the will of the majority of the people and to act in their best interests. In practice, there is much to gain by having influence over the democratic process. Interests may be amongst others, based in religion, ethnicity, geography, or finance. For many there is a greater motivation to do what it takes to ensure that their special interests are met. For some billionaires, potential tax liabilities each year can be as high as tens of millions of dollars or more. Allowing certain expenditure to be considered "tax deductible" can have a material impact on an individuals' tax liability. For others, the spiritual or ethnic impact of certain policies could have a more motivating effect than all other issues.

Companies too can have a significant financial dependence on government policies. The levels of company tax as well as any potential exemptions to tax can be worth billions of dollars every year. The impact of regulatory changes to the whole basis of a company's profitability is extraordinary. For example, if the environmental approvals and regulations around coal production or oil transportation change, then the viability of whole businesses models can be at risk, and the assets that underlie the very basis of a company's valuation can become effectively worthless. Conversely, the renewable industry sector can also gain much from lobbying the government, asking for special treatment, tariffs and subsidies to prevent climate change.

If the government changes the laws around cigarette smoking, then there is the potential for significant wealth destruction. The cigarette companies' lobby group has been active internationally for decades. If policies are changed around the use of prescription drugs, then there is the potential for significant wealth creation. Gambling industries globally aim to ensure that their industry is not restricted by government due to industry's sometimes

51

catastrophic impact on gambling addicts' lives. The banking industry globally has a special interest in ensuring that costly regulation is limited, which can cost billions of dollars and severely restrict profitably. The US Economic Policy Institute estimated that the cost to the US government of the so called "carried interest tax loophole" is around $6 billion dollars a year. To individuals gaining from this it would seem reasonable to spend large amounts of money to protect this tax loophole.

How and what has been influenced

"There are five or six people in this room tonight that could simply make a decision - this will be the next president - and probably at least get a nomination, if ultimately the person didn't win. And that's not the way things are supposed to work" – President Barak Obama during a campaign funding speech, Dark Money

There are some major ways in which political influence has been achieved.

Direct financial support of candidates and political parties
Special interest groups provide funding for political parties. The loss of this support could affect a politician's ability to fund their next election campaign or conversely it could also lead to their direct opponent gaining access to the same funding. The incentive is to keep these donors happy. Even if a politician is not consciously giving any payback to its financial supporters there is always some pressure to be supportive of a donor's needs, otherwise future support could be lost to your opponent.

Lobbying for legislative support

"Corporations now spend about $2.6 billion a year on reported lobbying expenditures – more than the $2 billion we spend to fund the House ($1.16 billion) and Senate ($820 million)" – Lee Drutman, Political Scientist, PhD (written in 2015)

In the US the number of lobbyists has increased significantly over the years; between 1979 and 1993 it increased seven-fold. The sums involved can be staggering. In 2013 alone, the pharmaceuticals industry reportedly spent $US

226 million on lobbying the US congress, with more than one thousand pharmaceutical lobbyists. There are also now reportedly 30,000 lobbyists working in Brussels at the European Union government headquarters. Lobbyists provide reports, information and whatever it takes to influence politicians to modify legislation in support of industry and special interest groups priorities. There is nothing to validate that the evidence provided by lobbyists is correct or that the analysis produced is reasonable. The incentive is for the lobbyists to do whatever it takes to gain advantage for their employers and history shows that there is no requirement for integrity in any influence peddling. The billions spent, and the influence bought, are extremely unlikely to be for the greater good.

Direct Promotion of Issues

"After studying the Kochs' political problems for six months, he (Fink) drew up a practical blueprint ... Called 'The Structure of Social Change', it approached the manufacture of political change like any other product. As Fink later described it in a talk, it laid out a three-phase takeover of American politics. The first phase required an 'investment' in intellectuals whose ideas would serve as the 'raw products'. The second required an investment in think tanks that would turn the ideas into marketable policies. And the third phase required the subsidization of 'citizens' groups that would, along with 'special interests', pressure elected officials to implement the policies." - Jane Mayer, Dark Money

The second means of influence is to pay for your own election campaign impact either through direct advertising or more recently through extensive social media campaigns. Special interests can be promoted to voters either by the presentation of their own side of the argument, or to promote a candidate that they know is favourable to their cause. A regulatory framework to protect truth in advertising has been elusive in many democracies. There are a range of ways that blatantly false claims can be made discretely and seemingly anonymously that support an industry's view. Campaigns based on lies and distortions have proven extremely effective.

Paid up employees of these partisan politically funded foundations can re-brand and re-name policies, when repeatedly appearing in the media as "experts". President Obama's healthcare legislation was misleadingly called a "government takeover" when it instead involved private health companies. There were paid "experts" using the term "death panels" to imply that the new healthcare was going to euthanize old people, which was false. To counter against proposed cap and trade legislation, "reams of faxes" of complaints from "voters" were sent to senators which were all fake. Instead the faxes were generated by a coal industry trade group. The Heritage Foundation published data, later quoted in Congress, which claimed that the new climate legislation would cost thousands of dollars a year for Americans. The Congressional budget office said the figures were not true and yet the damage was already done. To assume that this lack of integrity is limited to the US would seem incredibly naive.

Social media campaigns in the modern world can be just as effective. With no real accountability for factuality, stories can simply be made up. An example is the campaign against Iowa senator Bruce Braley. A video was circulated that he supported building a "mosque at Ground Zero" (after 9/11 in the US). Being from Iowa, he had in reality previously said nothing about this proposal since it had nothing to do with his district. However, an ambush style video interview was heavily edited to claim otherwise.

Much can be achieved by cherry picking evidence to support your point of view. There is also an almost unlimited opportunity to run campaigns that are based on non-sequiturs, twisted logic and irrelevant misinformation. An ad campaign to a busy and often disinterested public can deliver quite significant misdirection and false logic and can be quite influential.

In Australia after the turn of the century the government proposed a new mining tax on excessive profits that were made during the peak of the China based mining boom. The Mineral Resource Rent Tax was initially fairly well received by most Australians, until the mining industry advertising campaign began. Around $AUD 23 million was invested by the industry to convince the voting public that the mining industry - which was claimed to be the backbone of Australia - was being unfairly targeted. Selective statistics and figures were presented that presented the mining industry's case. The government was overwhelmed and backed down to the point where virtually no tax was paid by the industry for years. The debacle arguably contributed to the government's subsequent demise at the next election.

A few quotes from *Dark Money* follow on the scale of donations in election campaigns in the US:

> "On its own, in 2012 the Kochs' network of a few hundred individuals spent at least $407 million, almost all of it anonymously. This was more than John McCain spent on his entire 2008 presidential bid."

> "With a final tally of approximately $7 billion in traceable spending on the presidential and congressional campaigns, it (the 2012 election) was the most expensive election in American history by far. One donor alone, Sheldon Adelson, who had vowed to spend "as much as it takes," had dumped nearly $150 million, $92 million of which was disclosed, and had still come up short. Approximately $15 million of that had reportedly gone to the Kochs' group, Americans for Prosperity."

> "This time, the Koch network aimed to spend $889 million in the 2016 election cycle. The sum was more than twice what the network had spent in 2012. It rivalled the record $1 billion that each of the two major political parties was expected to spend, securing their unique status as a rival centre of gravity."

Funding to influence education and research

"In all, by the time it closed its doors in 2005, the Olin Foundation (John M Olin funded, promoting free market ideology) had supported eleven separate programs at Harvard, burnishing the foundation's name and ideas and proving that even the best-endowed American university would allow an outside, ideological group to build 'beachheads', so long as the project was properly packaged and funded." - Jane Mayer, Dark Money

Special interest groups have directly contributed to US university departments and even to new courses, which inevitably then produce research and education which supports the sponsors policies. Departments and universities need the funding received which inevitably makes true independence difficult. In an open society, where special interest groups can influence the education process the potential is for people's very beliefs to change. The practice of buying research influence is possible in virtually any democratic country.

The new discipline *Law and Economics* was funded largely by the Olin foundation throughout the US, with funding at times more than 80% of national universities' costs. Political scientist and author, Steven M. Teles,in his 2008 book*The Rise of the Conservative Legal Movement*, described Law and Economics as "the most successful intellectual movement in the law of the past thirty years, having rapidly moved from insurgency to hegemony...*Law and Economics* is neutral, but it has a philosophical thrust in the direction of free markets and limited government. That is, like many disciplines, it seems neutral, but it isn't in fact."

The support for and potentially the creation of new political parties
After a research project by Professor Theda Skocpol, Harvard University and the Ph.D. student Vanessa Williamson, it was discovered that much of the organization and funding of the US Tea Party was delivered by foundations like FreedomWorks and Americans for Prosperity, which are in large part funded by large corporations. This funding would not imply that the Tea party is a "grass roots" party as is claimed. Many of the actions of the foundations were to help organize participants in the tea party protest rallies using tactics similar to those of the cigarette companies, who mobilized paid operatives who filled "smokers' rights" groups. Paying for organizations to provide protestors would again not seem like a grass roots movement.

The results of influence

"The influence of special interests is now at an extremely unhealthy level. It's at a point, where it's virtually impossible for participants in the current political system to enact any significant change without first seeking and gaining permission from the largest commercial interests who are most affected by the proposed change" - Al Gore, US Presidential candidate and Nobel Laureate

After the Great Recession of 2007/8 there were many in society that realized that some of the policies implemented, especially around a lack of regulatory control and an adherence to a purer form of free market policies, had contributed to the significant issues that were faced. Even Alan Greenspan, one of the key architects of the move towards less intervention in free markets as head of the Reserve Bank, admitted to the House Committee on Oversight that he had changed his views. Special interest foundations around the US however, worked to reframe the crisis and to avoid a critical lesson, preferring to stay with their anti-regulatory world view. These continual claims by various foundations impacted political views, with Marco Rubio, future Presidential candidate claiming in 2010, "This idea - that our problems were caused by a government that was too small - it's just not true. In fact, a major cause of our recent downturn was a housing crisis created by reckless government policies". The Great Recession had a range of complex causes, but partisan claims to isolate those causes to a particular world view alone, while ignoring any other contributing factors, will likely only lead to a recurrence of the problems.

After Ronald Reagan was elected, he proceeded to distribute a copy of the Heritage Foundation's policy playbook (an industry funded and conservative special interest group) to every member of congress. Edwin Feulner of the Heritage Foundation later claimed that 61% of the policies in the Heritage playbook were implemented by Reagan, including substantial tax cuts for corporations and high income individuals. Reagan also abolished economic controls on the oil and gas industry, which Charles Koch had opposed, as well as cutting taxes on oil profits. Bush similarly enacted legislation that contained some $6 billion in oil and gas subsidies and $9 billion in coal subsidies.

57

After years of expensive promotion by a range of industry funded foundations of the counter climate change views, more than 156 members of Congress had signed the "No Climate Tax" pledge. After lobbying, a number of senior politicians simply reversed their positions and then opposed climate change, including Presidential candidates Lindsay Graham and Mitt Romney. Thus, federal government intervention to reduce fossil fuel emissions has been less common in the US. From Americans for Prosperity's President, Tim Philips, "We've made great headway. What it means for candidates on the Republican side is, if you…buy into green energy or you play footsie on this issue, you do so at your political peril. The vast majority of people who are involved in the [Republican] nominating process—the conventions and the primaries—are suspect of the science. And that's our influence. Groups like Americans for Prosperity have done it". Agnotology and paid influence simply works.

Significant US state and federal government subsidies have been engineered by various special interest groups. These include (amongst many others) subsidies on cotton, wool, shipping, agriculture, airlines, automobiles, farms, oil and energy and sugar. Fossil fuel subsidies also run into billions and reportedly trillions of dollars a year globally. With respect to sugar, the billionaire owners of sugar industries in the US receive billions of dollars in subsidies every year (restricting imports and amongst other things, to create floor prices on sugar). Gary Hufbauer, a senior fellow at the Peterson Institute for International Economics and former deputy assistant secretary in the Treasury Department was quoted as saying, "sugar, dollar for dollar, is the most influential commodity in the U.S.". Many governments have tried to remove many of these subsidies and failed. In 1995 George Bush proposed eliminating around 300 subsidy programs to save more than $US 15 billion. The subsequent lobbying to protect financial interests was intense. When Bush finally ended up passing a bill, the program of savings had been reduced to one tenth of the originally planned amount.

To assume that this issue with special interest groups' influence is a US specific issue is naive. While it is possible to gain leverage over politicians and policies then motivated people will do so. The temptation is too much. A comparable situation is clearly in evidence in Europe. As highlighted previously, the European Union reportedly has 30,000 lobbyists. To assume that these lobbyists are doing nothing and achieving little and yet still being funded would again seem naive. Special interest groups continue to spend and to act because they can further their own interests. Where an electorate is filled with busy people who are generally disinterested in politics, there are options for manipulation. In fact, as society has matured, and democracies have become more stable this arguably leads to greater disinterest in politics from the majority since everything is going so well. Every modern democracy has the scope and potential for special interest groups who have a particular desire to influence certain policy areas. Special interest groups can fund research, fund media influence, fund politicians, fund education campaigns and even fund new parties. As society has seen again and again, where there is a benefit to be gained, smart and motivated individuals will inevitably find a way to achieve what is in their best interests. The influence of these groups is clearly not in the best interest of society as a whole and will continue to occur in every modern democracy.

There is nothing inherently wrong with special interest groups attempting to do whatever it takes, within the law, to fight for their rights. In an ideal world, the influence of special interest groups would be a single source of information and opinion. This would then contribute to form a balanced overall view, from which decisions could be made based on all the information available. Where this becomes a problem is where these groups are able to influence the political and legislative process in ways that do not allow for a sensible and balanced view and in ways that are detrimental to society as a whole.

It is a weakness of our democratic process that those with the loudest voices can often overwhelm and influence a busy and disinterested majority. Those loud voices are not limited to those with money. Motivated individuals and minorities can influence democratic outcomes in many ways, especially with the capabilities of social media and the internet. These weaknesses within our democratic process have clearly led to enormous hardship and untold deaths over a long period of time.

The problem is with our democratic system itself. While money and special interests can influence elections and policy, and while politicians' success depends on a popularity contest, our democracy is weakened. Until this is changed, the problem will remain. The new democratic process will be structured such that it is simply not possible for anyone to exert undue influence over any part of the democratic process.

We will build a democratic process in which you cannot gain advantage through political manipulation or through financial or special interest groups.

Slow (or non-existent) change

On lead in society

In the 1920s, engine knocking was limiting the fuel efficiency and damaging cars produced by the automobile industry. Much effort was made to find a solution. Thomas Midgely eventually discovered that if tetraethyllead (lead) was added to fuels, then knocking was prevented. Any alternatives that he found were either too expensive at the time or ineffective.

There were, however, quite a few scientists who expressed grave concerns for the adverse effects of lead on the public. Professor William Mansfield Clark wrote to the Assistant Surgeon General at the Public Health Service warning of "a serious menace to public health". As a result of concerns raised, a study was commissioned to investigate the impact of lead in gasoline. As was to become a pattern in the future, the subsequent study was funded by corporates who would benefit financially from the approval and subsequent sale of leaded fuels. The incentives were then setup to potentially impact the integrity of the "research" produced. Agreements were made to allow DuPont and General Motors to control the study, and to criticize and even sign off on the findings before release. In an amazing capitulation it was agreed that to avoid negative publicity any discussion around the issue was to include the trade name "Ethyl" rather than the more accurate scientific term "lead" since there were already negative public perceptions on the dangers of lead. This was partly because it had been reported that dozens of workers had been dying from the effects of lead poisoning at various companies' fuel plants around the US, and that hundreds had suffered from lead's effects. Workers had even dubbed one plant "the House of the Butterflies" for the hallucinations that it produced. The companies themselves blamed the deaths on their own workers' unprofessionalism and carelessness. After revelations about the deaths of workers some municipalities and states banned the sale of leaded gasoline.

Subsequently, the findings of the industry funded report on the safety of leaded gasoline exonerated lead as a danger to the community. Fairly quickly though, the industry funded report was criticized by a number of scientists and experts. Criticisms came from the editor of the Scientific American, from the professor of Public Health at Harvard and from the Dean of Harvard Medical School. In reaction, again in a similar pattern that emerged subsequently in 20th Century democracies, advocates of the industry stepped up to blunt the criticism. Some advocates were known industry spokesmen, whereas some experts had industry funding that was simply unknown to the public. A conference was organized to discuss the issue. At the conference, the fuel industry defended the use of lead as being for the greater good and argued that progress always came with some risk. In hindsight, the most hauntingly accurate statements were from Dr Yandell Henderson of Yale, "conditions would grow worse so gradually and the development of lead poisoning will come on so insidiously ... that leaded gasoline will be in nearly universal use and large numbers of cars will have been sold ... before the public and the government awaken to the situation". There were also however, scientific detractors about the risks of lead and given some doubt as to the insidiousness of lead's impact on the human body it was decided that further study was required before a decision could be made. Production was paused until a study could be completed. That "blue ribbon" study was designed by committee to be a short-term study of only 252 people working in and around lead gasoline, mostly garage attendants and chauffeurs. The very limited study found no impact from lead but recommended that further studies on the long-term effects were essential. Leaded gasoline was then approved for use by the government. The government then did no further long-term study, ignoring the recommendations. As happened repeatedly in the 20th century, other nations' governments then followed in US footsteps and lead was used in fuels globally.

By the 1970s, the long-term devastating effects of the accumulated lead in the environment had become obvious. An estimated 7 million tons of lead burned in gasoline in the US alone had leached into the soil, air, water and human and other organisms. Children were particularly susceptible to lead in the environment. The effects on children were known to include lowered IQs, learning disabilities, hyperactivity and behavioural problems. In a 1988 report to Congress, lead expert Dr Paul Mushak estimated that 68 million children had received potentially toxic exposures to lead from gasoline since the 1920s. A 1985 EPA study estimated that as many as 500 Americans could be dying yearly from lead-related heart disease alone. Over the next 20 years or so, lead was removed as an additive in fuel in many nations. The total global health impact of accumulated lead in our living environment – where lead had been used in virtually every country in the world, is extremely difficult to determine.

The democratic nations that subsequently did remove lead sometimes took decades to finally organize an effective legislative process and the final removal. For example, Australia completed its ban on the sale of leaded fuel in 2012, 24 years after the formal reports to US congress of lead toxicity and 90 years or so after the first scientific concerns were raised.

It is a disappointing aspect of our democratic process that the lessons of science can take a long time to be heeded and that lessons learnt in one nation can take quite some time to be translated into effective legislation in other nations. The situation involved inherent delays and obstructions in legislating to outlaw a known toxic chemical - which caused untold damage to society and its people. Recommendations for follow up studies were simply ignored by the government. While scientists had been repeatedly warning of the issue, it took more than 60 years for democracies to respond and remove the lead from its petrol and from its air. Was this the best that our democratic system could do to protect the very air that we breathe?

This is also not an isolated incident. Thalidomide caused tens of thousands of birth defects. Tobacco has killed hundreds of millions of people globally and continues to kill, with the US FDA reporting 480,000 Americans are dying every year. The introduction of the drug Vioxx caused 30,000 heart attacks in the US alone and 100,000 people have developed heart disease from its use. Opioid addiction reportedly causes up to 30,000 deaths a year in the US and Canada alone. These are not merely the consequences of dealing with complex issues. Many in government have shown a lack of understanding and even a disdain for the scientific method. Many decisions by our democratic governments have been extremely ineffectual in managing and understanding the requirement for scientific due process. Politicians have consistently failed to heed the balanced counsel of scientists and of scientific consensus. Politicians have shown an inability to relate well to scientific principles and scientists have found it extremely difficult to gain the attention of politicians in a reasonable timeframe. Millions of people have suffered and died as a consequence. Nothing substantial has changed in the decision making process of our democracies. If nothing has changed in our democratic process, can we really expect different outcomes in the future?

On avoidable infections

In the 1840s Ignaz Semmelweis was appointed to what was effectively the chief resident at Vienna General Hospital. He soon noticed the fairly widely known distinction in death rates between two of the hospital's maternity wards. One averaged a death rate of 10% for mothers and one less than 4%. With one in ten young women dying during childbirth, Semmelweis became obsessed with finding the difference between the two clinics. He painstakingly considered everything possible within reason. Eventually he established the only difference that he could find, which was that the clinic with better survival rates was worked in by midwives and the other by student doctors. Meanwhile, a colleague died of a pathology similar to puerperal fever after he was accidentally cut with a student's scalpel during an autopsy. This was a similar illness to that of many of the mothers. Semmelweis postulated soon afterwards that the problem was caused by poor hygiene. He believed that the medical students were working on dead bodies and then passing particles onto the mothers, causing the deaths of young mothers. He proposed that students wash their hands in a solution of chlorinated lime between doing autopsies and dealing with patients. After this procedure was implemented, the death rates in the troublesome clinic dropped by 90%. At the time, bacteria had not yet been discovered by the medical community and his work was reportedly ridiculed and ignored. In spite of the impressive results, many doctors dismissed his methods and his conclusions, preferring their own "established" views, that puerperal fever was due to "uncleanliness of the bowel". It would take until two decades later, after the publication of Louis Paster's work on the germ theory of disease, that Semmelweis' views would be widely followed. Paster discovered that given the potential adverse effects of germs, hand washing was essential for doctors, not just after handling corpses but between all patients. In the meantime, many thousands of mothers had continued to die, but for a simple procedure.

Centuries later in 2016 in the US, around 100,000 people still die in hospital every year from infections. Healthcare researchers have estimated that up to 30% of hospital deaths happen as a result of infections. Independent research has estimated that up to 70% of those infections could be easily avoided if recommended protocols - including hand washing - were followed. Which means that in the US alone, researchers believe that around 21,000 people die every year from infections which could be avoided with simple procedures. Globally, the estimates for deaths from avoidable infections could be higher than 500,000 per year. This deadly problem continues to this day, 150 years after we first understood the danger of infections.

The cause of this problem has been known for centuries, the ongoing nature of the issue has been documented, and few governments are doing anything substantial about it. There have been some fairly simplistic efforts, with hand washing stations and education campaigns, but these have been largely ineffective, and many flaws remain in the system. While little is done, potentially hundreds of thousands of people die every year. The consequences of which would also cause an extraordinary financial burden on the health system. As bacteria has evolved recently in response to the widespread use of antibiotics, superbugs have emerged in hospitals globally - for which there are no known treatments. The transmission of these newly evolved bacteria could have far reaching consequences as they become more common. With no treatments available the consequences of infection are severe. People have been admitted to hospitals for very minor procedures and have then emerged with life changing and life ending infections. The responsibility for this type of issue can be unclear in our democratic systems. It should not be. Members of the medical community as well as researchers have repeatedly called for decisive government action. But government action can be very slow in democracies. It is extremely difficult to get the attention of politicians when it comes to complex issues that are largely unknown to the populous. While democracy delays, many continue to die.

On multinational tax avoidance

For decades now, multinational corporations have been seeking to substantially reduce their tax liabilities through a range of complicated schemes. Taxation avoidance has become easier since different countries have different tax rates. There are quite a few ways in which companies have manipulated the tax system - to effectively transfer their taxable profits from higher tax countries to tax havens. In Europe for example, computer company Apple, declared much of its revenue in low taxing Ireland. Apple then paid around 4% tax on around € 200 billion in revenue, potentially avoiding tens of billions of dollars in taxation throughout Europe. The OECD in 2015, estimated that conservatively, as much as $US 240 billion is lost every year globally to these tax avoidance schemes. This has had a significant impact on government budgets as in many nations corporate taxation revenue has declined substantially.

In many cases in the past, companies that have been paying significant taxes on profits for years or even for decades have done a simple corporate restructure, and then their taxation liability has immediately fallen to zero. The results have been obvious, significant and in many ways blatant. The corporations themselves have the resources to pay for substantial legal and corporate manipulation since the results of avoidance are so lucrative. On the government side, taxation departments invariably have little funding to deal with the issue in spite of the enormous losses in taxation revenue.

Although some in the media, in government, in taxation departments and in society in general have known about this for a long time, it has been extremely difficult to bring about effective legislation, or efforts to counter the problem. And yet, the issues have always been resolvable with in some cases minor changes to the tax law or greater enforcement powers. In recent years some solutions have been put in place. In the meantime, trillions of dollars in government revenue have been lost globally over decades of abuse.

In an ideal world, positive changes would come relatively quickly. Progress and improvement would be an ongoing and regular occurrence. Yet in the last century we have seen many problems last for extended periods of time.

When individuals in society discover issues, it can take them years to convince the right powerful career politician to take up the cause. Where a new policy is not already popular with the population in general, legislative change involves risk for the politician. As John Maynard Keynes said, it is better to fail conventionally, than to succeed unconventionally. Unless the public already wants change, politicians see only risk in pushing for change. Careers are on the line if they push for something that the public does not want, and there will inevitably be special interest groups that will push back firmly. While our process requires popularity in our politicians, then politicians need to know that the majority of people already support a proposal before they will risk their careers. It can take decades for an otherwise busy and generally disinterested public to become convinced of the need for change. Few in society take the time to research issues, especially complex ones. Politicians ignore the issues and wait for the slow process of convincing millions of disinterested voters before they act. Decades can pass, and unresolved issues can cause enormous risk, financial costs, hardship and death.

Also, the requirement for change can be first discovered by someone whose communication, media and political skills are not great. Scientists, researchers, economists and the public generally do not have the skills to convince large groups and politicians to get behind them. Even if the policy could solve a very large problem, often few will know about it.

We have seen this again and again in society. Scientists were right for years on cigarettes, leaded fuels, toxic waste, infection risks, sugar and many more. Evidence and reason alone are not enough to move a busy and disinterested populace toward a required policy or change. Our current democratic process requires us to do things backwards, requiring widespread knowledge and understanding first, before effective policy change. Meanwhile, millions of people have died and will continue to die.

In the US, the original tax code was 14 pages long, today the tax code is over 2000 pages, with 6000 pages of regulations and tens of thousands of pages of rulings and regulations. Estimates of the cost for Americans to simply comply with this extremely complicated tax system run around $US 100-500 billion dollars annually. That is, a minimum of $US 100 billion dollars spent every year in rather pointless bureaucracy and paper shuffling. There have been many efforts over the years to reform tax laws, all of which have largely failed. Most democratic nations have convoluted and cumbersome tax codes, accumulated over many years which have significant compliance costs. These costs that would be vastly better invested elsewhere. In Great Britain, the tax code reportedly runs to 17,000 pages. In Australia there have been repeated efforts to simplify and reform the tax code all of which have largely failed or have been deferred. The problem is not just that of the billions wasted on compliance costs, the complexity itself helps corporations obscure their tax avoidance. Corporations simply have more money for tax avoidance than the regulators have for monitoring.

When faced with difficult decisions that could cost them politically, an effective tactic of many politicians is to choose to delegate the decision. Instead of making the tough decisions a politician will set up a commission to investigate and to make recommendations. In this way, the politician can delay the pain, possibly even until it is someone else's problem. If a government sets strict and limiting terms to that commission's scope, then they can ensure that difficult issues are not faced. For example, if a commission is set up to deliver proposals for tax reform, the government will specify that certain taxes are not to be considered in the review (as has happened repeatedly). The solutions will then be severely limited. In this way, the political risk for politicians is reduced since the unpalatable options, even though for the greater good, are removed. Politics has many ways of limiting the scope of change.

As well as this, when a commission's recommendations do finally come in the public fervour for action has likely quietened down. The politician can then potentially "consider" the report for quite some time and even quietly shelve the report afterwards, without taking any action. The Wallis Tax Report in Australia is still quietly shelved, decades later, after much effort and expense. The Tax Discussion Paper produced in 2015, was again just quietly ignored. In December 2011 the recommendations of an Australian Government review into a better regulatory framework around marketing by drug companies was arbitrarily rejected. Decisions on the Gonski report into education funding in Australia were delayed and delayed again. These examples are from just one democracy over a few years.

Let's briefly consider the legislative process. When a new law or policy initiative is first proposed to a politician they may first modify or even ignore it. A politician may however decide to act. To move forward the policy must be presented to her colleagues, to factions, to supporters, to special interests and to leadership for support. At some point the new policy may have to be included in a package of policies that will be presented to the electorate in an upcoming election. The policy may also have to be presented to the government's coalition partners for approval by the legislature.

Note that at every stage in the above process the new policy idea may be modified or rejected by any of the long sequence of groups involved. This whole process can make critical changes extremely slow.

The issues are both the challenges faced by an individual in promoting new policies, as well as the structure of our democratic process in gathering support for and implementing policies. Our elections, parties and parliamentary systems get in the way.

The potential for compromise, and for significant delay, is in fact intrinsic to the democratic process itself.

Instead, a democratic process should allow new policy proposals to be openly and transparently prioritized based on their merits alone, without apathetic voters, complex politics and self-interested career politicians getting in the way. Removing these policy obstructions will be essential in our new democratic process.

To summarise our requirements related to policies:

We will build a democratic process which cannot be influenced by short term political concerns. A democratic process which has no requirement for, and hence influence from, political promises. A process which produces no benefit from pandering to populism, which is less impacted by populism and which is protected through a robust governance framework. A process which is has little requirement for, and is protected from, the influence of adversarial politics and career ambitions.

A process where policies, decisions and government appointments are decided independently and efficiently, on their own merits.

A democratic process in which you cannot gain advantage through political manipulation or through financial or special interest groups.

A process which can identify, evaluate and prioritise important ideas quickly, efficiently and effectively.

Elections

In representative democracies our governments are formed from politicians that survive (and thrive) through the election process. The process is designed to ensure that the government is an expression of the will of the people. And yet the process is far from perfect.

Voter limitations

"Political apathy is the luxury of an affluent society where the majority does not feel threatened and people's basic needs are met. Under such circumstances, apathy is understandable, predictable, and perhaps even rational." - Thomas Magstadt, PhD, Understanding Politics: Ideas, Institutions, and Issues

"It is ... far more important to resist apathy than anarchy or despotism for apathy can give rise, almost indifferently, to either one" - Alexis De Tocqueville, Democracy in America

On 89 votes

In 2007 David Leyonhjelm stood for political office as a member of the Liberty and Democracy Party (LDP) in the Bennelong electorate of Sydney, Australia. The electorate contained around 90,000 voters. Voting is compulsory in Australia. He won just 89 votes. In the Senate that year, the LDP overall had won just 7772 votes in the entire state of NSW (or just 0.19% of the total voting population of that state). The LDP was a political party with little support. A few months afterwards the Liberty and Democracy Party applied to change its name to the Liberal Democratic Party. One of the existing two major parties in that state which generally formed government was called The Liberal Party. The Liberal Party strongly objected to the new name. They argued that the name would cause confusion on the electoral ballot paper since it was so similar to its own name. The independent electoral commission however after legal advice, allowed the name change. At the subsequent election, the Liberal Democrat Party was still a tiny party on a very busy ballot paper. Nothing had materially changed for the party or for its popularity between elections. The newly named

"Liberal Democratic Party", was then also randomly selected to be first name on the ballot paper. The party subsequently won 434,000 votes and a huge 9.5% of the overall vote. Their vote increased by around 6100%. Many Liberal Party voters afterwards stated that when they saw the "Liberal Democratic Party" as the first on a very complicated ballot paper, they voted for that candidate assuming it was the traditional Liberal Party. Under the state's proportional representation voting system for the first time ever, David Leyonhjelm was elected to the NSW Government Senate. In the subsequent parliament, the newly elected senator - who in the lower house had previously obtained 89 direct votes, now had the potential to contribute to the balance of power on key national issues.

Voters have busy lives and voting - compulsory in Australia, is seen by many as an onerous duty. The fact that a party, whose name was merely first and similar to a major political party, could then obtain an extra 400,000 votes, demonstrates the level of time spent by many voters on the voting process. The concern is that for voters, it is not just that little time is spent on the process of voting, little time is also spent on the consideration of candidates and policies.

There are many different types of electoral system around the world and each has its own imperfections. Certain types of electoral peculiarities like the one seen above can change an elected government. The consequence is that governments can be both unrepresentative and ineffectual.

In democratic societies many busy people do not spend much time evaluating candidates, policies or parties. The perception can be that one vote does not really count amongst millions of other voters. There is an element of truth to this, the chances of a single vote making an actual difference are virtually nil. Yet voter apathy, when expressed collectively, makes an enormous difference. It is difficult for any society which depends upon the collective wisdom of the electorate to produce capable political leaders and sensible policies when the vast majority of voters spend little time on political decisions. This can be worse in democracies where life is fairly safe and stable. It has been repeatedly claimed that a reasonable portion of voters decide upon their vote in the seconds spent at a polling booth without doing any detailed research into candidates or policies. It has also been demonstrated by researchers that a sizable portion of the electorate will vote for the same political party at every election. It is only the swing voters - those that do change political sides, that affect the outcome of elections. This is clearly not producing the best political decisions possible.

Repeated surveys have indicated that most of the electorate does not know the name of their current legislative representative and certainly does not know their qualifications for the job. Many do not even know which party their representative is from or in which electorate they reside. According to Bryan Caplan, Professor of Economics at George Mason University:

> About half of Americans do not know that each state has two senators, and three-quarters do not know the length of their terms. About 70% can say which party controls the House, and 60% which party controls the Senate. Over half cannot name their congressman, and 40% cannot name either of their senators. Slightly lower percentages know their representatives' party affiliations. Furthermore, these low knowledge levels have been stable since the dawn of polling, and international comparisons reveal Americans' overall political knowledge to be no more than moderately below average.

In fact, the adversarial nature of our political system can entrench viewpoints and stoke partisanship and closed mindedness. A study by Jeremy Frimer, Linda Skitka and Matt Mostly of the University of Winnipeg and the University of Illinois, documented what many suspected already, that voters exhibit what they call "Motivated Ignorance". That is, voters actually want to avoid the opinions which support the opposing side of politics - they prefer simply not to listen. That is, voters would rather keep listening to opinions which back their pre-conceived viewpoint. This can hardly create a balanced viewpoint based on both sides of an argument. Adversarial politics can make open minded collective decisions much more difficult.

If we look to actively increase voter engagement this can only have limited success, since the vast majority of people will still consider their personal lives and interests more motivating and more enjoyable than any political

72

discourse. It is unrealistic to expect that politics would ever be of serious interest to the majority of voters. Conversely, we cannot limit participation to those willing to spend time investigating issues because it violates our requirement for democracy to be representative of all of its citizens.

Rather we must change the implementation of our collective decision making such that it can still produce the best and most representative decisions, even within the limits of time and motivation within our democratic societies. We must also remove the impact of adversarial politics to enable us to come to fair and effective collective decisions. The new democratic process must allow for effective collective decision making which fairly represents the interests of the majority.

We will build a democratic process which can produce the best legislative assemblies and decisions in spite of a having largely disinterested and otherwise busy electorate.

Voluntary or compulsory voting

On rule by 37%

Many in Britain in the late 2000s saw the increasing problems in Europe and were concerned that Britain could no longer control her own destiny. Facing an election in 2015, Prime Minister David Cameron finally relented to pressure and promised a referendum on membership of the European Union. After his election win, Cameron delivered the so called "Brexit" referendum, even though he wanted to stay in the European Union. The vote to leave the European Union won the day, Brexit had managed to obtain almost 52% of votes. However, with a participation rate of 72% of eligible voters, only around 37% of all eligible voters had voted to leave Europe. The majority of voters had either voted no or had not voted at all. A critical national issue had been decided with only 37% of eligible voters actually voting to leave. Brexit had surprisingly been passed.

Less than 50% of all eligible voters had voted to leave Europe and it is possible that of the whole voting population, the majority of voters actually wanted to stay within the European Union. With almost a third of voters not bothering to vote or not thinking it was necessary to vote, it is not possible to

73

know the full voter intention. Democracy is not always an expression of the
view of the majority of voters.

For those people in democracies that enact a compulsory voting system, it
seems extraordinary that a critical national issue could be decided with only
37% of definitive support. Yet for those in Britain without compulsory voting,
the electorate seems generally more accepting of this situation. The
difference between the two perceptions of the results is quite indicative. In
some ways, it represents the effective acceptance and even resignation of
each nation to their existing political structure. No nation really questions
the status quo of the democratic structure that exists, they are all effectively
resigned to their existing democratic implementations. And yet each system
can produce very different outcomes as representations of their electorates.
As we will see in other sections, change in democracies can be slow or in
many cases, simply non-existent.

Under compulsory voting every eligible citizen is required to vote at every
election. Those that do not, without reason, are liable to be fined. In this type
of democracy, typically around 90% or more of the eligible voters decide
each election. The downside to this system is the lack of freedom for the
voting public and that it is necessary to fine your citizens for not voting. The
upside is that the results represent a closer approximation to the whole of the
population.

Voluntary voting systems are less onerous on citizens, but generally involve
much lower voter participation rates. It is common for critical national
decisions to be made with only the most motivated of people, those that think
it is important enough to get out and vote, affecting the result. It can be the
case that the more radical voters, the ones further to the left or the right of a
political debate are more likely to vote, with the majority of voters in the
centre less likely to make the effort. As well, polls taken during an election
campaign can indicate which side of a debate will win and sometimes
indicate that one side will win easily. The risk then with voluntary voting
systems is that voters may choose not to vote at a particular election, because
the polls show that the vote is already won. In this case, this lack of

participation by the confident and less motivated side can actually change an election result - away from the consensus view.

Our democratic system requires a large number of generally busy and often disinterested voters to choose parties, policies and candidates through the registration of a single vote. We need to find a solution that bypasses these complexities and yet still represents the collective will of the people. This seems like an intractable problem, but when addressed in the right way we will be able to construct a simple, workable and effective solution.

We will build a democratic process which can produce the most representative legislative assemblies and the best collective decisions.

Electoral systems

"In fact, given the federal structure of American elections, it's possible to control the executive and legislative branches of government with as little as about one fifth of the vote, if the votes are really efficiently placed" - The Dictator's Handbook, Bruce Bueno de Mesquita and Alastair Smith (both professors at New York University)

There are two major types of electoral systems - majoritarian and proportional representation. Majoritarian is where the winner of an election is the candidate who simply gets the most votes (often called plurality and/or first past the post). In this case, the winning number of votes can be less than 50% (if there are more than two candidates). In another implementation of majoritarian, the winner must ultimately get more than 50% of the votes. In this process, if one candidate does not initially get more than 50%, then there is some run off system - with candidates successively reduced until only two remain. This run off system can involve a system of preference voting or possibly by having subsequent elections with only the most popular candidates.

In proportional representation candidates are elected by the proportion of the votes that they receive in the election. For example, if a party received 30% of the votes, then they get approximately 30% of the elected candidates in the legislative assembly. There are quite a few variations of this system.

75

In some democracies there are several hybrid systems of each of the above, which attempt to deal with some of the limitations of each system. First past the post, where the candidate who gets the most primary votes in the election is directly declared the winner, means that a candidate can win while not getting 50% of the votes. This can mean that a candidate (or party) wins who may actually be the last choice of most of the electorate. It can also mean that in a house of parliament where all candidates are elected on a first past the post basis, a government can be formed while achieving only a third or less of the electorates' support. There are various combinations of preference voting systems that try to clean up this process or even multiple run off votes for Presidential elections, where candidates are eliminated in each phase. However, each has its limitations. Proportional representation has been criticized for over representing minor and even extreme parties and for giving those parties too much influence in the parliament. Proportional representation has also been criticized for producing the likelihood of parliamentary political gridlock.

Dividing the votes up into electorates also influences the value of each individual vote. An individual voter in an electorate which traditionally votes overwhelmingly for one party has little chance of ever influencing the election result in that electorate. In some electorates, the candidate from a particular political party has always won the seat. It is unlikely that any voter in these electorates can truly influence the result of an election since the result of every election is by such a wide margin in favour of one political party. Whereas a voter in an area with closer results has a greater potential to have an impact - as do all of the voters in those seats.

In the Westminster system of government, a structure using electorates means that a Prime Minister can be appointed as leader without their party winning the most votes. Prime Ministers are voted into office through the elected members of parliament. Parliament is filled with delegates who win each electorate. If many voters from one side of politics are concentrated into certain electorates, then a party can gain the most votes but can still gain fewer successful parliamentarians overall. Having your voters distributed evenly gives political advantage.

In the US, the electoral college system which is used for electing the President has a similar issue. A presidential candidate can win the most votes in an election and yet not become president due to the structure of the electoral college system. This has occurred a number of times including recently in the election of President Donald Trump and George W. Bush.

In the US Presidential election of 2000, Ralph Nader ran as a left wing candidate who was considered more left wing than the Democrats. The US has a first past the post form of election and the person with the most electoral votes becomes President. In the key state of Florida - which was the deciding state in the election, Nader received more than 70,000 votes. Most of those people who voted for Nader would normally be expected to have voted for Al Gore in preference to George Bush, since these voters were from the far left and Al Gore was the next closest in policies. Having two popular left wing candidates up against one popular right wing candidate split one side of the votes. George Bush won the Florida vote by just 537 votes. If Ralph Nader had not been running, it would be expected that the majority of the 70,000 of his supporters would have voted for Al Gore ahead of George Bush. Al Gore would in all likelihood have then won Florida and hence been elected as President. The quirks of the electoral system can significantly change the government of the day.

In many democracies one house of parliament is structured so that power and voting rights are more evenly distributed between states and provinces, rather than directly between voters. Historically, this was to ensure that state's rights were not overruled by the more highly populated states. In fact, at the time that nations were formed, it was sometimes the only way of ensuring that all states would join the newly formed nation; if state rights were guaranteed, then the states would come together. The US Senate, through which all legislature is approved, consists of two senators for every state. The population of each state is not relevant. This means that in 2013 (according to US census numbers), approximately 1/6 of the population controlled more than 50% of the senate votes and the law of the land. Similarly, in Australia there are only 6 states in the nation each of which has twelve senators. The smallest three states with only 22% of the population then control half of the senate votes. Democratic rule in this way is not a fair representation for all.

It is quite difficult to design an electoral system which can fairly represent the true majority view of the people without being distorted by the process itself. In representative democracy we vote for politicians, within electorates, within parties and within states or provinces. Any and all of these can distort the process and distort a true representation of the will of the people. The fact that none of these systems are perfect is demonstrated by the number of variations of democratic voting systems globally. No one system has been found to be universally acceptable.

Any collective decision making process must allow for an effective and fair representation of the will of the people, without the many limitations inherent within the present forms.

So, again, we will build a democratic process which can produce the most representative legislative assemblies.

Election funding

"You can get a politician for $2000 a year, a party for $100,000 a year and policy for $200,000 a year" Charles Livingstone, PhD, Monash University, in a submission to an Australian Senate inquiry

Politicians and political parties can be responsible for fund raising to pay for their activities and their election campaigns. Elections are costly affairs - advertising to sell your policies to a large populace is expensive. The more private money that is raised by politicians, the more potential for those donors to consciously or unconsciously influence the democratic leadership.

To deal with the issues around political fund raising, some democracies have implemented limits on overall election spending, limits on fund raising and limits on individual and corporate donations. Many of these options must be balanced for their positive and negative consequences. In the US, funding limits have been imposed on individuals to ensure the integrity of the election process and to minimize the risk of donations influencing policies. Funding limits over time have been reduced to $US 1000 per donor. With many millions of dollars required to fund both elections and political parties themselves, the downside to this limit is that politicians must then find an enormous number of donors, which can be very time consuming. A recent "Model Daily Schedule" was produced for newly elected Democratic senators in Congress. In the schedule, 4 hours was allocated every day to calls for fund raising. This takes away a substantial portion of a Senator's time and limits their ability to actually govern.

In 2016 $US 6 billion was reportedly spent on advertising for the US Presidential election. As well as Presidential elections there are separate congressional elections as well as state elections. Even if direct advertising spending is limited, politicians can still spend vast amounts of money on a range of social media campaigns. As well as this, other special interest groups can spend money to influence election results. There is also the grey area of politically approved government advertising campaigns, which "educate" the public on services that the government has made available to them. In many countries this allows politicians to spend government money advertising their own policies and achievements.

If all election funding was to become directly funded by the government, it would still be possible for political donations to continue to buy further influence on top of government funding. Indirect funding could still be possible, where a political supporter paid directly for campaigns. As regulations become more rigid, smart individuals will find ways around the problem in order to keep their political influence.

The fundamental problem here is not that money *does* influence elections and politics, rather it is that money *can* influence elections and politics. The fact that money can influence the outcome of elections means that the problems of its influence remain, no matter what regulatory framework is imposed. Where we have a small subset of identifiable individuals who can control decisions that affect large sums of money, the incentive for influence is strong. Where those individuals are more likely to be successful with greater available cash, the incentive for corruption or influence is powerful. The solution is to entirely remove the capability for money to influence either elections, policies or legislative outcomes.

We will build a democratic process which has no dependence on politically motivated finance in producing its legislative assemblies or in making its decisions.

Violence and intimidation

There has been political violence in Russia, Ukraine, the USA, the UK, Pakistan, India, Lebanon, Egypt, many countries in South America and Africa, and many other democratic nations over the years. Violence has included physical intimidation of voters to discourage voting and limit their ability to vote. Violence has been committed against journalists who are trying to give a fair and balanced coverage of issues. Violence has been reported against election officials.

In most democracies the threat of violence during or after elections is still a relatively unusual occurrence. There have however been individual assassination attempts against a range of leaders and politicians throughout the years. There have been 4 US Presidents shot and killed while in office, with many more Presidents and election candidates attacked and permanently injured. It is always a risk that disgruntled and unbalanced voters can resort to violence in an attempt to achieve their goals. Our adversarial political system makes this problem worse. Politicians need to motivate supporters, and this is often done by inflaming passions against their opponents.

It is still a significant possibility that human beings would be influenced by the threat of violence, especially where complex policy decisions are concerned. It can be easier to delay critical decisions in certain high risk policy areas and leave those decisions for a later time or for another person to deal with.

This is not an easy problem to solve and to remove the threat of violence completely, especially violence which seizes overall power, is effectively impossible. The potential for electoral violence, even though reduced in recent times for mature democracies, will remain.

The only way to resolve the issue as best is possible is to remove any incentive for violence, just like for the issue of corruption. We can still remove the possibility that violent acts or threats can gain any political advantage. Having a relatively small number of known, long term politicians with great power allows the potential for influence through violence.

We will build a democratic process in which there is virtually no possibility of gaining electoral or policy advantage through violence.

The benefits for supporters

In the book *The Dictators Handbook,* Professor Bruce Bueno de Mesquita and Professor Alastair Smith discuss a practical model for the common workings in government. The mechanisms they describe are present in governments as varied as modern democracies, monarchies and even dictatorships. Essentially, the common mechanisms define the way in which power is attained and retained. They describe three common groups and structures that are used irrespective of the type of government. These are named - the interchangeables, the influentials, and the essentials. It is a simple way of characterizing the critical and in many ways, definitive qualities of government. Interchangeables are those who have at least some say in choosing the leader, even if not directly. For example, an interchangeable would be a voter who chooses their local politician, with that politician then voting for the leader on the voter's behalf. Influentials are those who actually determine the leader of the government – in our previous example, the politician who then elects the Prime Minister. Essentials are those who then maintain the power of that leader, this may be a political cabinet in a democracy.

All forms of government have a leader that needs to obtain and then maintain power. After all, even dictators and monarchs need the support of a group of people to maintain their power. The only difference between the various government types is the relative size of the three groups. For dictatorships and monarchies, generally each of the groups are quite a bit smaller and would include the military instead of voters. All forms of government need to ensure the continued backing of their essentials. Ironically, even in a dictatorship, without the support of the military and the Presidential guards that protect the leader, a leader becomes quite vulnerable. Many seemingly powerful dictators have lost power (and their lives) once their key backers' support has dissolved.

In a democracy, voters are the interchangeables. They have at least some say in choosing the leader. The influentials who actually select the government's leader can be elected members of parliament as in Britain, electors of the electoral college as in the US, the general public as in France (and some would say, the USA as well), or senior members of the Royal family as in Saudi Arabia. The essentials, that maintain the power of the leader, can be the members of an inner cabinet, an inner policy group that controls real policy and candidates as in the former Soviet Union, or they could include key financial backers and those that can control groups of voters.

The key for us here is that in all current forms of government - democracies, autocracies and monarchies - power must be attained and maintained. The distribution of benefits must happen for each of the forms of government. In every form that we know leaders must pay back their supporters. This is a fundamental requirement of the process. It also causes issues since the supporters then get an uneven distribution of assets and policies. The process mandates that we are not governing based on what is best for all, we are instead governing based on what is best for our key backers. The democratic process may not be as poor as an autocracy, which distributes benefits to a much smaller, elite group, but the requirement remains the same.

In a democracy the rewards to ensure continued support must be spread amongst cabinet ministers, financial supporters, people who control large groups of voters, and many key swing voters as well. Key cabinet, committee and leadership appointments will be given to supporters who maintain that power. There will also be key policy compromises to those supporters that can maintain power. Unfortunately, the requirements of maintaining power for a leader in no way guarantee the best person for the job for critical appointments or the best policy mix for the nation. These supporter benefits are rarely in the best interest of society as a whole. Where government resources are not directed based on needs (or efficiency and fairness), this cannot be good for the general public.

There is then a large cost for the maintenance of political power in democracies as well as in monarchies and autocratic governments. Politicians generally repay support for their own personal benefit at the expense of the broader populace. The underlying problem is that there exists a political need to maintain power. To avoid the problem, the new democratic process must remove the need to maintain political support from the democratic process itself. In the new democratic process, resources can then be allocated fairly and equitably, and critical government jobs can be offered based on merit alone.

We will build a democratic process in which there can be no political advantage gained through the rewarding of supporters, and no possibility of payback for political support.

Majority rule

"Give all power to the many, they will oppress the few. Give all power to the few, they will oppress the many" - James Madison

There are difficulties with a multi-party system if each party aligns to a particular ethnic or religious group, since one group can then consistently rule over the others. Scholars Alvin Rabushka (Stanford University) and Kenneth Shipley (Harvard University) have concluded, "democracy - the free and open competition for the people's vote - is not viable in an environment of intense ethnic preferences". This pattern has occurred in many nations where a single religious group dominates the majority political party. The rights and preferences of any minority group can then be largely ignored, and so civil unrest and violence can easily erupt. This has happened in nations like Iraq, Rwanda, Indonesia, Turkey, Spain, Northern Ireland, the former Yugoslavia as well as in the Middle East.

Similarly, in his essay, *The Challenge of Ethnic Conflict. Democracy in a Divided Society*, Professor Donald L. Horowitz documents the consistent problems where ethnicity conflicts with democracy. The rule can lead to persecution, starvation, internal conflict, civil war and even to genocide. He speaks of the "concrete failures of democracy in divided societies". The problems have been repeated in countries such as Rwanda, Iraq, Turkey,

Ukraine, Uganda, Syria, Benin, Nigeria, Sri Lanka, Zambia, Cameroon, Georgia, the former Yugoslavia, Thailand, Zambia, Zimbabwe, Slovakia, Bulgaria, Romania, the Philippines, Indonesia and Afghanistan, as well as others.

Democracy can give a majority or even a minority group consistent and unyielding control. The imperfections of our electoral process itself and its difficulty in aggregating votes into political representatives and political parties can exacerbate this problem. Any new democracy must ensure a fairer representation in its legislative assemblies which avoids the limitations of our electoral systems. This issue also demonstrates the importance of a strong constitution to protect the rights of individuals. However, any democratic process still depends upon the rule of the majority and this rule has risk. To mitigate this risk, the new democratic process will also include a more effective governance framework,

We will build a democratic process with limited potential for groups to gain unfairly through their collectivism, and with a robust governance framework to limit any undue influence.

The Media

"Communications between nations must promote understanding— so went another dream. But the machines of communication can be manipulated. What is communicated can be truth or lie. Communication is a strong force, but also for either good or evil" - Richard Feynman, PhD, Nobel laureate

The media is an essential part of democracy. In most modern democracies a significant proportion of the people will have never directly read any policy documents or have never listened to any party speeches. The media is simply their only view of politics. The majority of voters only experience their politicians through brief sound bites in the media or on the internet. People have busy lives and the popularity of politics is quite low in modern democracies. This gives the media quite a large amount of influence. The media in its various forms, from traditional TV and newspapers, through to the more recent social media and the internet, get to decide what information and stories to present. They set the debate, they control the message, they control what is communicated, as well as controlling the priority given to each message. Transparency of political information has improved through greater competition and with the increased use of the internet. But the majority of voters still rely on largely unregulated private third parties to present information about politicians and policies. The presentation of this information is then open to extraordinary subjectivity.

There is also a difficulty in that individual voters will only get their news from a limited list of sources. Although there may be a variety of competitive sources from which voters can choose, voters tend to have favourites from which they get the majority of their news. These favourites can then have much influence.

The media also has a significant conflict related to their basic requirement to make a profit. Under this constraint it becomes extremely difficult to cover complex policy decisions. A demonstration of this problem occurred in the 2016 US Presidential election where Donald Trump was, essentially, an anti-establishment candidate. Donald Trump was the lead story virtually every day, saying things that were largely populist and headline grabbing, and yet was also reported by fact checking organizations as telling one lie for every 3 minutes of speech. The establishment, of both politicians and media, were facing challenges with the new candidate. Trump's statements were so interesting that he was given significantly more coverage than any other candidate. The CEO of CBS (a key network news company in the US), Leslie Moonves, was quoted as saying, "I've never seen anything like this and, you know, this is going to be a very good year for us. Sorry! It's a terrible thing to say, but bring it on Donald! Go ahead, keep going. Ah, it may not be good for America but it's damn good for CBS, that's all I gotta say". Revenue and ratings must be a priority, and this is invariably in competition with good journalism.

Selling TV, newspapers, internet websites and social media requires a media organization to grab and maintain people's attention. In the modern age of the internet, attention spans are short and click-bait – where the aim is to get people's attention, is highly effective. There are difficulties in the requirement to provide entertainment as well as fair political reporting. Politics is rarely entertaining. To make it so almost inevitably reduces the quality of the debate. The complexities of an evidence based debate between conflicting and detailed policy options does not fit within the need to grab attention in the media. The media cannot capture and keep a busy person's attention when discussing the balanced evidence for and against various complex policy options. Most people neither have the interest nor the time to read these long articles. What is certainly easier and more effective financially is to highlight one superficial, scary, or anger inducing aspect of a story and to tempt people with just this component. Distorting and highlighting a particular aspect of a story simply works. Those organizations that do not follow this successful strategy lose customers. Only the profitable will survive. So inevitably, the media has descended to the lowest common denominator to compete in a tough world. We have seen in the past few years how the profitability of the paragons of quality journalism has just disappeared. Quality journalism struggles to sell. The public does not get to see a balanced and thorough coverage and cannot make informed choices.

In more recent times, usage of media has changed significantly after the widespread use of the internet. Reportedly large portions of society now get their news from social media rather than traditional newspapers or television (multiple surveys and reports of up to 44% of people getting their primary news and information from social media). Social media sources do not have the same levels of scrutiny for factuality or integrity of information. The US government claims of Russian interference in the 2016 US Presidential election, through the use of targeted "fake news" stories, demonstrate the potential risks. Social media and unregulated website coverage can produce the stories and information that people want but are not accountable for integrity. In 2017, independent watchdog Freedom House reported that in the previous year elections in 18 nations were influenced by online manipulation and disinformation.

Social media campaigns have also produced targeted ads which are only sent to particular sub-groups of users who fit certain criteria. Those direct ads and communications not only have little accountability but may not even be detected by anyone else. Margrethe Vestager, the European Commissioner for Competition was quoted as saying, "If political ads only appear on the timelines of certain voters, then how can we all debate the issues that they raise? How can other parties and the media do their job of challenging those claims? How can we even know what mandate an election has given, if the promises that voters relied on were made in private?".

There is an enormous potential for the priorities and agenda of the corporate or government owners of the media to influence reporting. In many democracies there is no significant independent regulator or body which can ensure balance in journalism. Even where a regulator exists, balance has been difficult to monitor, and regulators have little power irrespective.

Bias can also be expressed in an extraordinary number of ways. Objective measurements of bias have proven difficult and forms of bias vary widely. It is possible that bias can be exhibited in a single article in giving a favourable interpretation of a single policy or politician. Or more likely bias can be expressed as an overall pattern of behaviour that comes out over months and years. Over a period of time a particular media organization may well report each new policy differently for each side of politics. Every new policy involves give and take, costs and benefits, winners and losers. Government is generally a zero-sum game since there are limited resources available. Whenever a new policy is announced the media can choose to either highlight the benefits or the costs. For one side of politics, they may consistently choose to highlight the benefits of new policies, and for the other they may consistently highlight the costs of new policies. The choice, conscious or otherwise, can be made to consistently highlight different evidence for each side of politics. Any individual article may not on its own demonstrate bias but when seen as a pattern of behaviour over months and years the bias can be clear. The media may generally give one side of politics the first coverage in each article, delegating the response to the end where few readers remain reading. They may provide more column space to one side of politics. The media may more consistently provide expert evidence for one side of the political debate. The media may consistently explain one side of expert opinion more clearly. They may give one side more direct quote space. They may consistently highlight problems that are of concern to one side of politics more so than they do for the other side of politics. They may endlessly refer back to and reiterate past problems for only one side of the political spectrum. The media may also even portray differently the motivation of each side of politics. For example, they may describe the policies of one side as being primarily designed to buy votes, and for the other side as being designed for the benefit of the nation. It is difficult for a member of the public to be aware of subtle, long-term patterns of bias. While the media is often the only source of information for the voting public ongoing entrenched bias is a serious concern for democracy.

Politicians are so dependent on the media for virtually every public perception that it is very difficult for them to deal with any concerns about the media. If they make proposals which would inevitably reduce media power, influence and/or freedoms, then the real risk for politicians is that of the media's conscious or subconscious wrath. Most politician are currently unwilling or unable to deal with the problems of the media. To propose meaningful changes to regulations or the law around the media is considered politically dangerous and, in some cases, political suicide.

A basic cause of problems is also a freedom that is held dearly, that of the freedom of speech. Our basic freedom of expression - whether that expression is incorrect or filled with irrational thought, is highly valued in our liberal societies. Plurality of all thought is considered a key protection against many ills, including that of a potential degradation to despotism. Inevitably any potential changes proposed around this in our existing democracies will be more about an effective governance process to mitigate risk. Some regulatory framework around our media to encourage more balanced coverage would have positive benefits. However, if we are not careful in looking to mandate better media regulations and standards, which is possible, we may also reduce our basic freedoms. As well, chasing media manipulation with regulations alone is a difficult process since resourceful people will then imagine more creative ways to influence public thinking.

The media has arguably the most influence on our election process as well as on our perception of policies and politicians themselves. Most large industries do have some independent form of regulation. It is extraordinary that what is clearly the single most influential organization in our democracy - the media, can in many nations have no independent and powerful external regulator. The argument that the single most influential industry in our democracy can also be the only industry that is self-regulated, would seem somewhat ludicrous. There is little ongoing evidence to justify our assumption of a trusted and benevolent media.

The issues facing the media in modern society represent a fundamental concern for our democratic process. Without a clear, thorough and transparent view of our political process we cannot expect to run an effective representative democracy. At the moment we assume that our open society will allow this to happen. In reality, there is little to guarantee that voters have a clear view of the issues at hand.

A more effective and powerful regulatory framework would seem essential and worth the effort. However, this cannot be the only solution since it is not getting to the heart of the issue. All forms of media remain an imperfect view of politics simply because it is unworkable to expect the delivery of an in-depth, thorough and balanced coverage in a competitive media landscape, which requires entertainment for profit. The media face an almost impossible task if we expect them to be our only view of politics.

The problem is not that the media *does* influence our democratic process, the problem is that the media *can* influence our democratic process. Instead, we need to improve our democratic process to ensure that we can act reasonably, in spite of this influence in our society. Where the media does inform us, we need a way to clarify and expand our view of the world, with the media being one of a number of sources of information. Those involved in our collective decision making must be fully and transparently informed, without a dependence on the media for information. Essentially, the collective decision making of the new democratic process must be structured to be immune to the influence of the media.

We will build a democratic process which can make the best decisions, and the best legislative and government appointments possible, in spite of any (adverse or otherwise) media influence.

Bloc voting

In some democracies the members of each party are mandated to vote with their party at each parliamentary vote, or risk expulsion from their party. This system has the advantage of ensuring that a voter gets what she has voted for. There can be no mavericks who decide to go against their party's

89

policies and there can be no people who get elected pretending to support a set of policies only then to vote differently in parliament. The downside is that a parliamentarian must then vote for a set of policies, all of which they may not agree with. The politician elected has no flexibility in their voting intentions and cannot necessarily vote what they believe.

The alternative system allows individual politicians to vote their own way, independent of their party's or colleagues' preferences. The downside in this situation is that voters have less idea what policies it is that they are voting for at election time. Special interest groups and others can then influence how each individual candidate votes. Different systems exist in different democracies. No system is perfect.

In some countries political parties are made up of large groups of core constituents, for example labour unions. In Great Britain, Australia and New Zealand, one of the major political parties has been historically made up primarily from the trade union movement. In parliament in these Labor parties up to 80% of their parliamentarians have consisted of people who have never worked anywhere except in politics, or as union officials. This has a large disadvantage in representing a broad base of the community or in having a diversity of views. It also means that one particular special interest group – the unions, will deliver a bloc of votes for itself first. Although some may consider this an advantage for often poorly treated workers, it has caused a range of issues as well. Sometimes what is best for union members is neither best for a country, nor for the unemployed, nor even for other non-union workers in the nation. Whenever a particular special interest group has dominated politics priorities have become distorted. For example, the rights and privileges of existing workers and union members may be protected, at the expense of overall jobs in the country, since those protected rights may make overseas workers cheaper in comparison. If continual privileges are approved by a union dominated government, it can lead to an increase in jobs disappearing to overseas workers who do not have those privileges. In a competitive environment excessive employee benefits can also lead to company failure and the loss of jobs. The globalized world is a competitive place. Protecting your own supporters' interests may not be in the best interests of all.

Bloc voting has also occurred on geographic lines, on ethnic lines and on religious lines. Religious leaders can direct groups who to vote for, clan leaders can do the same. Senior leaders in villages can organize to gain the support of the whole village - for the right payback to the village leader. At times in the past supporters would hand out cash to purchase votes directly. In India and in many African nations whole village's votes are "negotiated" for a particular candidate, from whom their payback is best. This payback may be directly to the village leader or elders. The villagers and voters themselves receive little in return. This can be the case with bloc voting where the leaders of the bloc gain advantage and the members gain little.

The disadvantage with bloc voting is that the support of a particular politician or party is rarely if ever due to their broader policies. Even if the vote is not merely about the corruption of the people who control the bloc, the reason for voting a particular way can be merely about one issue. When a particular bloc votes on one issue alone this is not in the best interest of the nation as a whole, nor even sometimes in the best interest of the bloc itself.

Blocs who vote for the wrong candidate can also be deprived of government support. In Singapore, those that did not support Lee Kuan Yew's government found themselves deprived of the allocation and maintenance of public housing. In Zimbabwe, Robert Mugabe used bulldozers to demolish houses and markets in areas where he did not receive support.

The ability to gain influence in our elections through bloc voting is a key cause of the problem. Bloc voting distorts the general voting preferences and enables individuals who control blocs to gain advantage for a privileged few. It can lead to an unfair distribution of benefits throughout society, especially for those blocs of voters that play the system well. The mechanisms which allow blocs to gain influence over our democratic agenda must be mitigated, and the undue influence, beyond that of any other voices in society, must be removed from the democratic process.

Again, we will build a democratic process with limited potential for groups to gain unfairly through their collectivism, and with a robust governance framework to limit any undue influence of a majority.

Electoral fraud

"The people who cast the votes decide nothing. The people who count the votes decide everything" - Joseph Stalin

There are many ways to distort and cheat the election process and most have been tried over the years. In India, "booth capture" involves party supporters taking over polling places and casting every vote for their party. Ballot stuffing, miscounting ballots, destroying ballots in certain areas and even restricting voter attendance have been effective forms of electoral fraud. In the US in poorer areas where most citizens vote for one party, the lines at these booths can last for most of the day - which discourages voting. More recently, "voter ID" legislation has restricted access to voting for poorer people who are unlikely to hold eligible drivers' licenses or other photo ID. From *The Dictator's Handbook*, "There's no election better than a rigged one, so long as you're the one rigging it. The list of tried and trusted means of cheating is long. Just as quickly as electoral rules are created to outlaw corrupt practices, politicians find other means".

Many democracies have independent bodies that define electoral boundaries. In these circumstances, gerrymandering - where electoral boundaries are set to give one side of politics a distinct advantage, is more difficult. However, this is not always the case. In the US system, the electoral boundaries are controlled by the elected candidates themselves. Every 10 years, the politician in power has the opportunity to reset the electoral boundaries. The surviving politicians then, the ones with the greatest ability to influence decision making, are those that make themselves extremely difficult to be removed from office. Many politicians manipulate the boundaries to ensure that they get the most value from their supporters in each electorate. They concentrate opponents' voters into a small number of electorates and then spread out their own traditional voters to gain the most seats. For example, it was reported that in 2012, the Democratic Party won 51% of the House of Representatives votes in the state of Pennsylvania and yet won only 28% of the seats. In North Carolina the Democrats won 50.6% of the votes and yet lost 9 out of 13 seats. Thus, individual politicians can and do stay in elected office for decades, effectively until they retire. Performance in government is less relevant unless their own party throws them out. Again, from *The*

Dictator's Handbook, "The practice of gerrymandering has made it such that the odds of being voted out of a US congressional seat are not that different from the odds of defeat faced by members of the Supreme Soviet under the Soviet Union's one-party communist".

Many other nations have a non-partisan and independent system for setting electoral boundaries, which works much better for the integrity of the democratic system. However, even this system can be imperfect, where the "independent" managers of electoral boundaries are appointed directly by political leaders.

The issue here is the ability to gain advantage through electoral fraud. If it is possible to gain advantage through fraud, then someone will do so. Elections are extremely complex processes involving large numbers of voters and ensuring fair and balanced practices is a challenging task.

We will build a democratic process where the legislative assemblies can be populated without electoral fraud influencing any outcomes.

Outside interference

External governments have interfered in the democratic process of many nations consistently over the years. Governments of all type have even been deposed and replaced by foreign influence. In the 20th century, CIA records show that the US spent vast sums to interfere in the internal politics of France, Germany, Greece, Egypt, Pakistan, Japan, Thailand, the Philippines, Liberia and Vietnam, as well as in most South American nations, amongst many others. Governments were overthrown, corrupt governments were propped up, regime change became a continual policy. Superficially democratic governments that hold corrupt elections in name only have been financially supported by western democracies for decades, since they align themselves to western policy. While many democratically elected governments were overthrown by western government interference, the replacement governments committed mass murder of political opponents, killing reportedly tens of thousands of people, but quite probably more.

Even supposedly philanthropic efforts in international relations can be vested in self-interest from donor nations. Many nations will quite generously donate to a range of developing nations. Yet donations occur only to those nations that support the donors' global goals or sometimes to those that support the multinational companies that would like access to those developing countries' markets. China and the US have supported nations from whom they can get a supply of reliable and cheap oil. Corrupt regimes and tyrannical leaders that would likely not have been able to survive on their own, have survived simply because of the injection of cash from international donors. Financial support to corrupt and incompetent regimes allows their leaders to pay off their supporters and maintain their power. As well, nations that are on the United Nations Security Council - with the power to vote on key global issues - have been independently measured to receive more aid than those not on the council. Aid is obviously used to gain voting influence on the Security Council.

Many nations will have laws in place to make foreign investment in elections difficult. Yet foreign nations are not beholden to another nations' internal laws. Where the reward for success has been potentially high, wealthy foreign nations have intervened. In the 2016 Presidential election the retiring President, Barack Obama was faced with a dilemma, his security agencies were reporting Russian attempts to influence the election outcome through the production of widely disseminated fake news articles that supported one side of the campaign. Although the evidence of influence seemed strong President Obama felt that he could not interfere with an existing election campaign. If he did go public with the allegations, then this could be seen as inappropriate partisan politics. He then stayed quiet in the face of a quite blatant attempt by an external government to influence an election. After a foreign release of internal and illegally obtained documents, support in opinions polls markedly declined for Hillary Clinton. The election was then won by her opponent Donald Trump. No real conclusion can be made about the effect of the influence - elections are after all complex. But the potential for influence, as well as a history of actual influence, still exists.

The root cause of this problem is the ability of foreign governments to influence the outcome of elections and parliamentary voting. Democratic governments vulnerability lies within our freedom of information, our public election campaigns, as well as the ability of anyone to influence busy and sometimes apathetic voters. While this vulnerability remains, undue influence both internally and externally, will continue.

The new democratic process will remove the possibility of foreign governments gaining influence over legislative outcomes and policy.

To summarise our requirements related to elections:

We will build a democratic process which can produce the best legislative assemblies and decisions in spite of a having largely disinterested and otherwise busy electorate.

A democratic process which can produce the most representative legislative assemblies and best collective decisions.

A process which has no dependence on politically motivated finance in producing its legislative assemblies or in making its decisions.

One in which there can be no political advantage gained through the rewarding of supporters, and no possibility of payback for political support.

One with limited potential for groups to gain unfairly through their collectivism, and with a robust governance framework to limit any undue influence of a majority.

One which can make the best decisions and government appointments possible, in spite of any (adverse or otherwise) media influence.

One where the legislative assemblies can be populated without electoral fraud influencing any outcomes.

One where external government cannot influence either the makeup of legislative assemblies or government policy decisions.

Political Parties

"No America without democracy, no democracy without politics, no politics without parties" - Clinton Rossiter, PhD, US Political Scientist

Political parties organize and run election campaigns, as well as contributing to the basic functions of the legislative and executive arms of government. Yet those parties can have adverse consequences and are far from perfect, as we shall see.

Multi-party government

On multi-party states

In the 67 years between 1946 and 2013, Italy formed 67 different governments. After an Italian election it typically takes months for an Italian leader to form a coalition government. This is partly because of the unique structure of the democratic system in Italy, formed this way to reduce the risk of another Mussolini type seizing power. The result is a democracy of weak and ever-changing government. One of Italy's more recent Prime Ministers - Silvio Berlusconi, served as Prime Minister three times between 1994 and 2011. Independent observers commented that Berlusconi only remained in power because his family owned a significant portion of the Italian media and was hence able influence the voting public. Over time, the controversial Berlusconi was charged with dozens of offences but was only ever convicted of one, that of tax fraud.

The instability of the Italian government since 1946 demonstrates the potential frailties of a democratic system in a large, complex and potentially divided nation. The Italian experience also demonstrates the risks of media influence and corruption in government. It might seem that the Italian system of democratic government is a unique problem for the Italians and that most democratic societies have a more stable form of two party politics. And yet, the ratio and popularity of parties can and has changed over time. In both Great Britain and Australia in recent times, a history of essentially two-party rule has evolved into governments based regularly on multi-party deals and coalitions. Similar changes have happened in many democracies. The stability of democratic rule changes over time.

Our democratic system is an adversarial, party based system of government. Political parties by their very nature gain power through the defeat of their rivals. On some level their purpose is to seek power. To gain power political parties have to create both reasons for an electorate to support them as well as reasons for the electorate to dislike their rivals.

Political party members have a key role to play in the appointment of party leadership positions. Over recent years this membership has declined significantly. Appointments have thus become less a reflection of the will of the generalized populace. According to Ingrid van Biezen, Professor of Comparative Politics at Leiden University, "On average, the absolute number of members (in Europe) has almost halved since 1980". Professor Biezen goes on to conclude, "Party memberships in contemporary European democracies have now fallen to such a low level that they no longer seem to offer a meaningful indicator of party organizational capacity. This inevitably calls into question our dominant way of thinking about political parties as a meaningful linkage mechanism between the general public and the institutions of government". In 1950, 20% of Britons were members of political parties, now the figure is closer to 1%. As membership numbers drop, manipulation of the system becomes easier. Branch stacking, to falsely provide new local party membership to gain political power, becomes much more easily achievable.

Parties can have undemocratic systems for the appointment of political candidates for election. At times these candidates will be appointed directly by political leaders or by factional groups - to maintain a sense of unity to the electorate the party faithful must align with their leader or faction. Candidate appointment can be less about who is the best person for the job and more about who will shore up support for the faction or for the party leadership. To show public dissent would undermine the unity and leadership of the party and hence reduce the chances of winning elections. Political rivals will withdraw from the race so that anointed candidates can be elected to positions unopposed. Unopposed elections have been used for quite some time to effectively remove power from the voting party membership, all the while shoring up support for the current political leadership. Party structures in many political parties can support, via their constitution, the maintenance of power in their leadership through the internal appointment of party leadership and management positions. It is a process which undermines the democratic power of the people and yet is essential in the maintenance of political power. It is ironic, that often the most undemocratic of places are within democracy's political parties themselves.

With declining party memberships many countries' politicians are sourced from an ever smaller proportion of the population. With only 4-6% of the population voting for the politicians who will represent them at elections, the process is not in any reasonable way representative of the whole population. Direct and unopposed appointments avoid the need to vote for candidates entirely. There are many flaws in the process.

We will build a democratic process where we can populate our legislative assemblies with the best possible and most balanced representation of the people.

Policy zealots

"This wasn't malfeasance by Greenspan and Gilleran; rather, it was nonfeasance, the intentional failure to perform a required legal duty or obligation. Even the FBI got into the deregulatory act: In 2004, the FBI warned that 'fraud in the mortgage industry has increased so sharply that an "epidemic" of financial crimes could become "the next S&L crisis""' - *Barry Ritholtz, Bailout Nation*

On the President's men

For decades global banks and their lending practices have been regulated. This ensures the stability of the banking system which benefits the banks themselves as well as their customers. When George W. Bush gained power in 2001, he proceeded to appoint a range of leaders to his executive government as all US presidents are required to do. Many of the appointments in George Bush's government were more of the free market thinking types. They considered regulations to be a restrictive red tape on society limiting both profitability of the banks and efficient market operation of the economy. They believed that the markets were self-correcting and would hence adjust efficiently through competitive pressure to deal with bank risks. The banks were after all, responsible institutions which had sophisticated computer systems and dedicated departments intended to responsibly manage their own risk. People with little belief in the need for regulation were then appointed to run the regulators in the US.

James Gilleran was appointed to run the Office of Thrift Supervision (OTS). The OTS was responsible for regulating savings banks and savings loans associations. He was not a supporter of regulation and stated publicly "our goal is to allow thrifts to operate with a wide breadth of freedom from regulatory intrusion". He famously and literally took a chainsaw to a stack of regulations in 2003. The Securities and Exchange Commission is responsible for enforcement of federal securities law, proposing rules and regulating the securities industry. George W Bush first appointed Harvey Pitt, a securities industry defence attorney to head the SEC. He was a Wall St insider, most known for fighting the regulators, who reportedly called for a "kinder and gentler" SEC. The next SEC chairman appointment was William Donaldson, who had previously founded his own investment bank. After Donaldson, Bush appointed Christopher Cox, a long-time Republican. All three reportedly supported a significant reduction in regulations and were appointed to head up a regulator. During the next few years, many regulations which supported the banking and investment banking industry were relaxed. This included increasing the borrowing leverage allowed for investment banks from 12-1 up to 40-1, which allowed the banks to borrow (and invest for profit) significantly more money. Previously the 12-1 limit was considered sensible to ensure that the banks could handle any crisis. Amid warnings from experts, the regulators also allowed many new unregulated products to be traded by the investment banks and financial institutions. During the three Bush SEC chairmen's tenures there were state government warnings of a lack of regulation. Multiple federal requests to improve regulations on the banks were either ignored or watered down significantly. At the same time under Gilleran's leadership the banks in his area of responsibility relaxed many of the requirements for responsible lending, including credit rating requirements, down payments requirements and the "ability to pay", amongst many others. Many unregulated appraisers who were incentivised to appraise properties generously supported the lending process with high appraisals. This prompted people to warn the regulators of their concerns. The legislative and executive government zealots repeatedly refused to do anything about any concerns raised to their attention, believing that the free market would re-balance itself. Existing regulations were repeatedly not enforced under the more "understanding" regulatory framework.

Appraisers overvalued property since this got them more business. Mortgage applications were fraudulently filled in by the mortgage brokers instead of customers to ensure that loans were approved. Mortgage sellers were selling mortgages to those that they knew could not pay, with complex terms that meant they would soon default. Loans were fraudulently misrepresented to customers. There were referrals from state regulators to ask for action from federal regulators, there were petitions written and complaints were made to the government and to the regulators, but the executive and legislative governments believed in free markets policies. The regulators ignored the breaches of the regulations. Fraud became widespread. Meanwhile the investment banks quickly borrowed significantly more capital and then took on risks with many of the newly created financial instruments, like collateralized debt obligations (CDO) and Credit Default Swaps (CDS). The new and unregulated products were too complicated for the banks' risk departments - especially the systemic risk that other banks and financial institutions would default on the complicated products. There were none of the "norms" of regulated financial instruments - capital requirements, a central clearing house, regular audits. There was no guarantee in the products sold that any counterparty could honour terms or any future payments.

Eventually the housing market inflated to the point of collapse. The bubble burst and millions of people were evicted from their houses. The new financial products collapsed with the housing bubble. Within a few years of the new financial instruments' creation many of the largest banks and financial institutions did default. Under trillions of dollars of debt from unregulated products, three major investment banks (Lehman Brothers, Bear Stearns and Merrill Lynch) collapsed or were sold for massive losses for shareholders. The remaining large investment banks (Goldman Sachs and Morgan Stanley) were given significant government cash injections. More than $US 700bn was initially required to prop up the US banks. Eventually after the resultant housing collapse thousands of home loan lending officers were also prosecuted for their predatory and fraudulent lending practices.

The lessons here are many, the negative influence of special interest groups on government policy, the ignorance of lessons learned from past experience, the poor decision making of politicians and the adverse impact of political zealots dominating decision making. All of these contributed to the global financial carnage. Similar failures occurred around the same time in the banking systems of Europe in Iceland, Greece, Spain and Italy. Globally, billions of AAA rated (highest safety) dollars were lost and written off. The banking perpetrators in the US were generally bailed out. The profits made from the poor recommendations and misrepresentations were generally kept by those most responsible for the carnage.

The ongoing lessons have been swept up in political infighting. Although regulatory requirements were initially tightened after the crisis, by 2017 many have been rewritten and reduced once again by those who stand to gain the most from the system remaining the same. The changes first enacted by the government following the Great Recession to protect the economy from a recurrence were later watered down by US congress. Many of the changes under "advice" from special interest groups from the finance sector have now been reversed by the new Trump administration. The fact that many nations outside of the US may well have kept their sensible banking regulation remains problematic due to the global interconnectedness of the finance markets. Global banks are now dependent upon each other through lending in the money markets and when one collapses, others can face serious difficulties. No bank can tell which other interdependent banks are at risk of insolvency. No matter how well run banks may be in one country, their need to source and supply funding from an international market will ensure that a banking collapse in one location can still have impact all over the world.

The system that led to the financial carnage of 2007/8, largely remains in place today. Having government policy run by a small group of policy zealots who arise from only one side of the political spectrum is a serious risk to any democracy. Yet it is an aspect of our democratic process that the more radical and motivated people are often attracted to government and that our adversarial system allows these zealots to be put in place to run the government all at once. The systemic risk remains to this day, both in our banking system and in our democratic process.

In theory our representative democracies aim for separation of powers between the executive and legislative arms of government. In practice there is currently quite a bit of overlap. After an election, the government of the day controls the legislative arm of government. That same government then also chooses those who will fill the executive arm of government. This allows the government to select political appointments to the executive arm of government with very similar political views to themselves, without any real opposition. This applies to the types of democratic governments that appoint the executive arm from within the ranks of elected politicians. It also applies to those democracies that appoint the executive arm of government from the general public. In both cases, with control of the parliament it is easy for one political party to control both new legislature and its execution through the executive arm. When one side of politics dominates the governing process, policies can swing sharply to that side of the political spectrum. The temptation for a government is to appoint leaders to the executive branch that are unquestioning supporters of the government view. This can lead to many difficulties, as suddenly the checks and balances disappear. If the party faithful control both arms of government then the natural counterbalance of an opposing or even a moderate view disappears.

With the new Trump US government of 2017, the same situation has arisen. Donald Trump has again appointed many right wing, anti-regulation and free market zealots to the executive arm of government, including to head up the government regulators. Scott Pruitt was appointed to lead the US Environmental Protection Agency (EPA), a man who has repeatedly sued the EPA, has publicly called for less environmental regulations and does not agree with scientists and his own department on man-made climate change. He reportedly described himself as "a leading advocate against the EPA's activist agenda". Trump appointed Jay Clayton to head up the Securities Exchange Commission which is the regulator of the finance industry. Clayton is a lawyer who has spent his career fighting for Wall St financial firms against the regulators. Trump also immediately called on his appointee to reduce regulations. Trump appointed Ajit V. Pai to head the Federal Communications Commission (FCC), who is also known to be anti-regulation and was quoted as saying that he wanted to "take a weed wacker to current FCC rules". Trump even appointed Rick Perry to lead the Department of Energy, a man who had publicly called for the dismantling of that very department.

Establishing an effective regulatory framework over the economy and business is a complicated task. Implement too much regulation and the economy can suffer under red tape, implement too little regulation and there can be dangerous consequences, including death and global financial destruction. Getting the balancing act right is extremely difficult when policy zealots and people of extreme views are in charge. The preference should be for clear minded decisions on a sensible regulatory framework, that reduces risk without excessive overhead. Politics gets in the way of this process.

Similar issues occur when the political left is elected to power and they then enact their own pet projects and one sided policy. There have been many instances of excessive red tape over the years. For example, for decades in various US states, politicians on the left have rewarded their supporter base with extremely generous pensions schemes. Unfortunately, many of the pension schemes were unfunded and extremely expensive. Some states have no way of paying the predetermined pensions. For example, the unfunded pension total in the state of Illinois alone in 2015 had reportedly risen to $US 129.8 billion. Many US states are now technically insolvent and have no way of paying their pension liabilities and funding the ongoing operations of the state government. As of 2017, the total unfunded pension liability in the USA is reported to be around $US 1.7 trillion. Future generations are liable for these generous and yet largely irresponsible schemes. At the time, politicians did not seem concerned that future taxes may be required to fund their decisions now. Many of those politicians are still in power today – they survived because they rewarded their supporters. But their policies have caused major problems.

A person with more passion about one side of politics has more motivation to deal with the frustrations of politics. Those in the centre (which are likely to be the majority of voters), are less likely to be passionate enough to face the challenges. Those in the centre may actually support policies from both sides of the political spectrum and so may find it difficult to decide which party to join. Historically, there have been many instances of political zealots who were so convinced of their righteousness that their beliefs were not changed by contradictory facts or reasoning. The political structure of our parties exacerbates the problem. The current system encourages a level of extremism and zealotry and can at times give this unrepresentative group unchecked power.

We need to reduce the adversarial, partisan politics which incentivises political zealotry. We should instead ensure that those involved in executive and legislative decision making will be a balanced group, containing people from all views within the electorate. We also need to ensure that any appointees to the executive arm of government are accountable to an effective governance framework to mitigate risk. These will be essential features of any new democratic process.

We will build a democratic process where we can populate our legislative assemblies *and our executive governments* with the best possible and most balanced representation of the people.

Deals and compromises

After an election a winning political party can either form government on its own if possible, or it can combine with other parties to form a coalition government. Governing with other political parties involves many policy compromises. Even inside of a political party, competing factions jostle for power in a similar way to that of competing parties in parliament. Competing factions lead to many of the same policy deals and compromises as those between parties in a government.

Australian politician Malcolm Turnbull expressed a need for policies to deal with man-made climate change and had personally proposed climate change policies. However, to regain the party leadership and hence control of the government, Malcolm Turnbull had compromised with the right-wing side of his own party. Any climate change policies were then dropped. With the deal he became Prime Minister, but at the cost of many of his publicly stated policies. Malcolm Turnbull had also supported extending marital rights to same sex couples, which at the time was widely supported. However, as a part of the deal to gain power, he agreed to hold a national referendum on the issue. Without the deal, Malcolm Turnbull as Prime Minister could have simply held a vote in parliament, which would almost certainly have succeeded. So, for a policy which he supported, which already had majority approval in both houses of parliament as well as in the greater electorate, the Australian Government was forced to pay a reported $US 96 million dollars to run a costly, unnecessary and non-binding referendum. Malcolm Turnbull had effectively forced the Australian people to pay a high cost simply to protect his position as Prime Minister. Politics is not always efficient.

When parties themselves involve somewhat unrepresentative groups of people, competing for power and influence through an ongoing popularity process with many factional deals and policy compromises, there is a large potential for ineffective policy choices. Conflicting interests of parties, people and factions can dominate the decision making process. Any solution to the many problems caused by our political parties will need to resolve the basic structural problems involved, which are the real cause of the issues. We must ensure that our democratic process is able to make collective political decisions that are in the best interest of all in society, without the inherent conflicts of interest and political compromises.

We will build a democratic process in which you cannot gain advantage through deal making and where each policy, each decision and each government appointment is decided independently, on its own merits.

The politics of opposition

"The two parties continue to go at each other in the conviction that winning political advantage for the tribe is more important than improving living conditions for all" - Peter Hartcher, author and journalist

On government gridlock
For 17 days in October 2013 the US government in many ways ceased to function, as Congress refused to fund its operation. The most powerful

democratic government on the planet was without money. The Republican Party had control of the House of Representatives and refused to fund the budget - without the Democratic government making major cuts to expenditure. As a result of the budget gridlock, more than 800,000 government employees were put on temporary unpaid leave and 1.3 million employees were required to work without knowing when they would be paid. The majority of Americans did not approve of the shutdown. This was not the first time that government gridlock had been threatened, it would not be the last time. Partisan politics and political gridlock had forced the executive arm of government to its knees.

In American politics the threat of government shutdown has been used regularly. Often the budget bills that are finally passed do not even truly resolve the underlying issues but rather just pass temporary funding measures which delay the issue until a further budget crisis arrives later. These budget difficulties and legislative obstructions are not unique to the American political system. They can happen all over the world where there is not an absolute majority or where there are multiple houses of parliament with differing party majorities in each.

After President Barack Obama's victory in 2009, the Republican party's publicly reported policy was to oppose everything that the Obama government proposed. They tried to stop the passage of every new initiative. They would even end up voting pointlessly and more than 60 times for the repeal of "Obamacare" (a healthcare bill) in the Senate, knowing that the votes were meaningless since they did not have the numbers elsewhere to repeal the law. The politics of opposition can seem meaningless.

In Australia a lack of senate numbers has repeatedly stopped key government platforms, on which they won elections, from becoming law. In 1975, the Australian government of Gough Whitlam was actually dismissed after the opposition party which controlled the senate refused to allow the passage of key government budget initiatives. This was an extremely controversial move. Blanket opposition to budget measures are less common in Australia now – after the Whitlam dismissal in 1975 left a long standing legacy.

However, opposition to many "non-supply" policies (which are not critical for basic budget management) are commonplace.

If a political party can enforce legislative gridlock, then the lack of government effectiveness can potentially increase their chances of being elected at the next election. They must decide if this is worth doing at the expense of the current economy or of the functioning of the government. It can be that an opposition leader or party members will regularly "talk down" an economy for political gain. In doing so they risk a loss of confidence in the economy, in trading partners, in investors and in employers, which may make the economic problems worse. Some do say that the short-term pain may be worth the long-term gain, others would abhor the obstruction of a democratically elected government. Neither side is absolutely right or wrong.

While this democratic structure remains, the problems will recur. Adversarial politics, career based infighting, conflicts of interest and ineffectual incentives all contribute to cause issues.

Our solution will restructure our democratic decision making to remove these causes of issues from the process.

To summarise our requirements related to political parties:

We will build a democratic process where we can populate our legislative assemblies and our executive governments with the best possible and most balanced representation of the people.

A democratic process in which you cannot gain advantage through deal making and where each policy, each decision and each government appointment is decided independently, on its own merits.

A democratic process in which you cannot gain advantage through political manipulation or adversarial politics.

Waste and inefficiency

In the US, The Center for Responsive Politics has determined - based on numbers from Federal Election Commission (FEC), that in 2016 $US 6.4bn was spent on congressional and presidential election campaigns. This includes expenditure from all candidates, political parties and independent groups (such as lobbyists). This total expenditure is just for elections, more money is spent later on convincing politicians to vote in a particular way. Around the world, the cost of elections can range upwards from hundreds of millions of dollars. The sum spent globally in more than 100 democracies around the world would likely be tens of billions of dollars per year.

As well as the financial cost of elections, there is the time cost of the process. It has been discussed elsewhere that US congressional candidates need to spend a significant amount of time on fund raising – up to 4 hours a day. Candidates must also spend significant time on campaigning to both the public and to the press. We have seen how election campaigning can impact the time of Presidents, when faced with existential national threats. Politicians also need to self-promote for their own careers. When your own personal career depends on success in elections, any time spent cannot be considered excessive. The costs of personal, party and policy promotion are simply staggering, as well as horribly inefficient.

The purpose of government is to make the right policy and legislative decisions for the benefit of the nation and its people. The vast expense of elections decides which politicians are popular enough to join the legislative assemblies. This process is extremely inefficient by design, given the huge size and limited interest of the voting public.

Imagine a system where the same vast amounts of time and money were instead spent directly on finding and deciding the best possible policies. This will be a main deliverable of this book.

We will build a democratic process which efficiently and effectively determines the best and most representative will of the people.

The problem list is not a small one

"But the political system has never been as dysfunctional. Perpetual campaigning and pandering, money-raising, special interests, and lobbying—most acute in America—have all discredited the system in people's eyes and voter turnouts are shockingly low. Western democracy remains the model for the rest of the world, but is it possible that like a supernova, at the moment of its blinding glory in distant universes, Western democracy is hollowing out at the core?" - The Future of Freedom: Illiberal Democracy at Home and Abroad, Fareed Zakaria, PhD, Harvard

The problems discussed so far are an indicative subset of what regularly happens around the world. Many, many examples have been omitted to maintain some semblance of readability and there are undoubtedly thousands more similar examples from around the world.

We do make poor policy choices in our existing democracy. There is ongoing corruption and fraud. There is little long-term strategy and many ineffectual short-term solutions. There is ongoing negative influence from special interest groups. Voters can be busy and disinterested and are increasingly disengaged from the process. Cynicism abounds. Our voters are unable to effectively vote for change since one vote chooses both politicians and parties as well often choosing whole groups of policies. We often implement overly simplistic solutions - with the difficult issues being avoided and delayed. We waste an enormous amount of money on ineffective and inefficient processes involving tens of millions of disinterested people, merely to decide the best of the politically possible policies, rather than the best overall policies. Our government has difficulty in fairly representing the will of the people and difficulty in deciding on effective change for the benefit of us all. Our democratic system even has the potential for a degradation to despotism with its imperfect independence of the arms of governments.

As it stands, democracy requires largely disinterested, busy and sometimes uninformed people, to vote for conflicted, corruptible and often unqualified strangers. Those elected politicians then run the government on our behalf, while vying for promotion, re-election and popularity, through often the most superficial of policies. Policies are presented to a public through a conflicted media, where often the best and most manipulative salesperson wins. It does not seem surprising that the results are poor.

Clearly these issues with democracies have resulted in trillions of dollars wasted on corruption, wasted on inefficiencies as well as unfair and ineffective policies. At the same time, our poor democratic process has resulted in tens of millions of unnecessary deaths, and probably many more. Tens of millions have also faced unnecessary financial devastation. People have suffered because our political system has been unable to agree upon sensible and timely policies and solutions (more examples will be described later). The consequences of our poor democratic decision making have been avoidable, devastating and far reaching.

As we have gone through the problems and root causes up till now, we have also identified the qualities of a better democratic process (our "We will build" statements). If our new democratic process contains these qualities, then the root causes of our existing problems can be avoided.

Note that the existing functions of democracy need not change and can be preserved. However, those same functions will be delivered through vastly more effective processes. There will however need to be some fairly comprehensive changes to those processes to ensure that we can entirely avoid the long list of issues.

We will soon present an alternative democratic process. That alternative process will be able to produce better results, with minimal risk. The new process will remove virtually all of the causes of problems from within our democratic process, while reinforcing the essential democratic structures.

But first, we'll next look at another critical issue in our democratic process, that is, how should we collectively decide upon change. Without getting our process for deciding upon change right, both as individuals and collectively, we cannot hope to build a better democratic system. This process will be a critical part of our construction of a new democratic process and will deliver an ability to make the best decisions possible for all in society.

Our list of root causes (which need not be re-read) is not a short list.

Root Cause Summary
Incentives to attract legislators are misaligned
Legislators' decision making is complicated by other issues and consequences
Legislators' incentives (for success) are misaligned
Personal ambitions of politicians can corrupt the political process
Upcoming elections can influence policies and government
Much of politicians' time is spent on elections, career and popularity
Policies are grouped together for elections
Politics is difficult and unrewarding for legislators and for their families
The funding of politics is difficult and causes conflicts
We vote for people we don't really know (voting for strangers)
Voters lives are more important to them than politics
Voters can be selfish
Voters are busy, so can lack knowledge and can be misinformed
Aggregating voter preferences to elect politicians is an imperfect process
We must vote for politicians and policies at the same time
It is possible to gain benefits from political influence
Leadership is a single point of failure, is corruptible and has poor governance
Weaknesses and overlaps exist in the separation of powers
Political parties are imperfect representations of voters
Politics leads to poor compromises and deals
Political advantage can be gained through violence
The many can rule the few unfairly
Freedom of speech can be abused and have influence over politic outcomes
Legislators' beliefs and policies may not be representative of their voters
Public debate is invariably not sensible and rational
Policies can swing inefficiently and ineffectively as governments change
An imperfect and conflicted media can influence elections and policy
Election promises are easily broken and can hold negative consequences
Circumstances do change between when promises are made and delivered
Policy initiation by voters can be too difficult and results can be slow
New policies generally require general popularity before political approval, and this can take many years
Deciding the best policies through the engagement of millions of citizens and the election of politicians to parliament, who then vote on voters' behalf, involves enormous expense of time and money and is potentially inefficient and ineffectual

Deciding upon change, as we do it now

"At every crossroads on the path that leads to the future, tradition has placed 10,000 men to guard the past" - Maurice Maeterlinck

We have seen how many problems exist within our democratic process and how many root causes of those problems persist. We have also seen that the process itself triggers these issues and hence we cannot expect better results in the future. Democracy can only deliver the best options if it produces both a fair representation of the will of the people, as well as producing the best collective decision making process for change. A key requirement of government is for decision making, that is, how to make the best decisions about what to change and to improve in our society. To build a more effective democratic process we need to bring together the best practice for our democratic system with the best practice for evaluating and collectively deciding upon change. We'll now consider what gets in the way of effective decision making. By identifying some of the significant issues in our current process we will be able to remove those issues and design a more effective process. Note that this list of issues is by no means comprehensive, rather it is a short list of key issues relevant to the democratic process.

Preconceived notions and false assumptions

"The first principle is that you must not fool yourself and you are the easiest person to fool" - Richard Feynman, PhD, Nobel laureate

"When the facts change, I change my mind. What do you do, sir?" - quote often (probably falsely) attributed to John Maynard Keynes

On political assertions

During the Nixon administration in the US the government repeatedly attempted to solve the problem of drugs in society. The government argued for greater intervention and especially a crackdown on heroin addicts, which it repeatedly asserted were a major contributor to crime statistics. Law enforcement agencies supported the crackdown for quite some time and were set to receive substantial increases in their budgets to deal with the problem. The Institute for Defense Analysis (IDA), which had no vested interest in the outcome, was then commissioned to study the drug problem. The IDA analysis concluded there was no evidence that heroin addiction contributed significantly to crime statistics. This obviously contradicted current government policy, so the report was kept classified. The war on drugs then continued at great expense for decades and, not surprisingly, with insignificant impact on crime figures.

Running major government policy on the basis of predetermined and unfounded opinions can have a devastating impact. Because of the assumption that the best solution was a "war on drugs", other options for dealing with the problem were ignored. The devastating impact of drugs in society continued. The "war" cost enormous sums of cash and created an underclass of dangerous and disaffected criminals whose livelihood depended on selling more expensive drugs.

There are no easy answers when dealing with the complexity of the drug problem in modern society. Yet it is fairly certain that any solution that does not consider all evidence available and does not consider the consequences of any action taken, could make the problem worse. Policy decisions must be debated thoroughly, openly and honestly, especially when the problems are complex and the consequences far reaching.

False assumptions regularly contribute to policies. In 2003, George W. Bush was sure that Saddam Hussain had weapons of mass destruction and went to war based on that threat. The evidence turned out to be as non-existent as the weapons themselves. Robert McNamara was defence secretary for both Presidents Kennedy and Johnson. He wrote in his autobiography (on the Vietnam war), "We failed to analyse our assumptions critically, then or later. The foundations of our decision making were gravely flawed".

Coming into a decision with a predetermined idea for a solution can make an effective decision impossible. Unfortunately, many people will give greater weight to an idea already formed than to any new information or reasoning. People tend to only find and believe evidence that supports their pre-determined positions. Partisan politicians have an incentive to decide an outcome which matches their predetermined political viewpoint. The partisan and adversarial nature of our democratic system effectively entrenches predetermined viewpoints in the minds of politicians. Having passionate and adversarial views is what gets politicians elected. These views also entrench a form of closed minded thinking. Examples of this abound. Any effective decision making process needs to substantially reduce the risk of impact of preconceived notions.

Factual integrity

On 37th place

In the final years of the 20th century Texas had been a state in which there were significant development projects which helped with the state's economic growth and job creation. It was consistently a finalist in a competition called the Governor's Cup, run by Site Selection magazine. The competition rated each state by the number of million-dollar development projects. In 2001 however, it was reported that the state had fallen to 37th place. This critical fall was seen as a perfect example of how the state was losing out to its more competitive neighbours which had new government incentive programs. Subsequently, the decrease in development projects as reported in the Governor's Cup was used as evidence by lawmakers, special interest groups and media outlets to argue for better incentives for local business. As a result of the campaign a new program was approved by the state legislature called Chapter 313. This program gave appraisal value limitations to properties which allowed tax breaks for corporates who built projects of significance in Texas. With the new tax regime many companies approved the building of properties worth hundreds of millions of dollars and were able to make significant profits. The construction industry returned to growth. Those companies also booked enormous tax savings. In total up until 2016, these tax savings totalled $US 7.1 billion in the state of Texas. The next time the Governor's Cup was run Texas was back near the top. Over the years this tax incentive program has reportedly encouraged many large investments. The savings were available to both investments that moved to the state as well as to any investments that would have been in Texas irrespective.

Unfortunately, a subsequent Senate report - "Senate Committee on Natural Resources and Economic Development" of November 2016, uncovered an error. Texas had never actually fallen to 37th place on the Governor's Cup, this was merely a typographical error in the magazine's article. At the time, there was no real vetting of the data. In fact, Texas had maintained its place near the top of the table throughout. The tax cut however and the ongoing billion-dollar tax revenue loss to the state government, remained.

Some may argue that the benefits of encouraging building in the state of Texas were worth the cost irrespective of the initial error. However, when evaluating billion dollar changes getting the facts right seems a fairly basic requirement. The costs vs benefits of change must be decided based upon reasonable analysis. It is very likely that the billions of dollars in tax revenue lost by this scheme could have been more effectively spent elsewhere. In our current democratic process, there is no requirement for politicians to check any assumptions in their campaigns or in their policies.

On CIA assessments

Before the Vietnam war, CIA estimates of the strength of the Saigon government did not match public claims by the government. The government was keen to ensure that general perception supported its political claims. Under government pressure the CIA reports were simply modified. An original comment that described "very great weaknesses" (of the Saigon government) was changed to read "We believe that Communist progress has been blunted and that the situation is improving". The Saigon Government however, quickly collapsed and the original CIA assessment was proven accurate. The political assessment of the government was simply wrong. At a later stage during the Vietnam war the government was again concerned by the CIA estimates for the number of remaining enemy combatants. The CIA assessment seemed too high and did not appear to demonstrate much impact from US efforts in the war. This seemed incongruent with government claims of ongoing success in actions against the Vietcong. The CIA reports were again modified to lower the estimates. In this case also, with hindsight, the CIA reports seemed quite accurate. The government should have been concerned about its lack of impact on enemy combatants since the war was actually not going well for the US government.

Similarly, initial CIA estimates of the threat from the Soviet Union did not sit well with the US Government assessment at the time. Nor did the assessments sit well with the US government desire for action. A key passage was erased from the CIA report on the Soviet capabilities. According to Richard Helms, the head of the CIA at the time, the changes "did not sit well with the Agency analysts. In their view, I had compromised one of the Agency's fundamental responsibilities— the mandate to evaluate all available data and express conclusions irrespective of U.S. policies". Secretary of State Shultz was quoted as saying, "Like a newspaper bent by its publisher's prejudices, the analytical powers of the CIA became one man's opinion…The CIA's intelligence was in many cases simply Bill Casey's ideology". The US eventually ended up spending billions of dollars building up their own military against a Soviet threat that was never as great as the government had assumed.

Government intervention has since repeatedly overruled expert analysis. After the second Iraq war, the US government pushed back on the CIA reports of a growing insurgency. While the government denied the problem the insurgency consistently grew, with devastating consequences.

Even in 2017, US President Trump arbitrarily dismissed the best views and concerns raised by his own government departments on potential interference by the Russian government in US election results.

Deciding upon government policy that is based on "one man's opinion" and contradicts the best available evidence at the time seems a recipe for disaster. The fact that trillions of dollars in defence funding was then approved based on the conclusions made on Soviet threats, demonstrates the concern first raised by Eisenhower: US foreign policy was potentially beholden to the military industrial complex and its influence. Global policy decisions regarding the threats between the superpowers would surely be better decided with all the facts assessed fairly and independently. The risk of getting these policies wrong at the height of the cold war could not have been higher. Our democratic system allowed these political conflicts of interest. Politicians simply need to be seen to be right. Our democratic system has not changed in the intervening years to reduce these risks.

For those whose personal conviction it was that drove the US into the Iraq war, considering the adverse consequences can be difficult. Instead it is easy to dismiss any information which does not support your views. The system allows for personal political opinion to overrule the best available evidence. Of course, the CIA has been known to get issues of significance quite wrong in the past, it does after all work in areas dominated by misinformation and deception. And yet it cannot be a better option to run international policy based on the preconceived notions of politicians and political appointees, whose judgement and experience depends more on politics than on evidence.

Politicians have quite limited time to convince a busy and largely disinterested public. To gain support, it is too easy for politicians to use misrepresentation, lies and irrelevant data. By the time any deception is uncovered public opinion may have already been swayed. In politics the political propensity to lie is well known. One US Presidential candidate in 2016 was reported to have told demonstrable lies once for every 3 minutes of speech. Politicians continue to risk lying simply because it works. By the time they are found out, the discussion has moved on and the public corrections invariably get less publicity than the original false claim. In the mean-time, the lies have gained votes (or the election has already been won).

When issues are debated publicly, live or otherwise, there are significant limitations. Facts cannot be checked in real time and subtle logic cannot be validated quickly. Skilful politicians can get away with quite a lot of political manipulation. Factuality is less important than emotion, anecdote and hyperbole. The public in general will have little idea of the underlying facts beneath the vast majority of claims made by political candidates. Where the political incentive is to win, politicians will also only present evidence that supports their case. Even live moderators are unable to enforce a requirement for factuality in a fast moving live debate. The successful political debaters are invariably the best actors and presenters, rather than those will the best policies.

There is not even a requirement for politicians to know anything about the bills that they sign into law. Time and again, politicians have been caught out not knowing the detail of the bills upon which they have voted.

When designing a decision making process, getting the facts right, and the right facts, would seem important criteria. This is relevant for both the public and for politicians. Factual integrity should be an essential part of any decision making process.

Non-sequiturs

"All who drink of this treatment recover in a short time, except those whom it does not help, who all die. It is obvious, therefore, that it fails only in incurable cases." - Claudius Galenus, 2ⁿᵈ Century physician, whose medical practices were used for centuries

On the Battle of Britain
During World War II when Great Britain was fighting Nazi Germany, the British sent nightly air raids to Europe. There was a high attrition rate of planes over Europe and the British were determined to improve the survivability of the planes and crews that made the long and perilous journey. The Centre for Naval Analysis had researched aircraft returning from the battle and noticed that they were consistently damaged in the same places. If planes kept getting damaged in these areas, then reinforcement was necessary. They recommended that extra armour be placed in those areas to further protect the planes and crews.

However, Statistician Abraham Wald heard of this same situation and recommended the exact opposite. He recommended that extra armour be placed in the areas of the plane that were less often damaged. The British command noticed the different conclusions and went with the suggestion from Wald instead. Wald had reasoned well. He noted quite correctly, that

118

the study by definition had only studied those aircraft that had survived the battle. When these "less often damaged" areas of the planes had actually been hit in battle, he reasoned that those planes simply did not return. If you considered the whole group of planes, including those that did not return, then it was reasonable to conclude that if planes were damaged in the "less damaged areas", then they simply did not survive the damage and make it home. So, the armour was instead put in the "less damaged" locations, which saved many more lives.

This an object lesson in many things, including survivor bias, non-sequiturs, and even in ensuring that all information and a broad range of opinions are included in decision making processes. Too often mistakes, like that of the Centre for Naval Analysis, are made in our society. Sometimes more thought and more opinions should be sought. This is especially the case in the political arena where politicians often follow their own convictions, without regard for the opinion and expertise of others.

On the Space Shuttle Disasters

On January 27th, 1986, Space Shuttle management and engineers met to discuss the risks of the upcoming Space Shuttle Challenger launch. A key issue to consider this time, amongst others, was the temperature at launch time. The launch forecast was for unusually low temperatures and certain key parts of the shuttle had been known to have increased risk of failure at low temperatures. The seals around the fuel tanks had been known to have leaked before and were more prone to these problems at lower temperatures. The seals leakage however, had never caused any problems. The meeting decided that the launch risk was not great enough to justify a delay. As Nobel Prize laureate, Richard Feynman, who worked on the Rogers Commission (the review of the disaster) said, "If all the seals had leaked, it would have been obvious even to NASA that the problem was serious. Only a few of the seals had leaked on only some of the flights. So, NASA had developed a peculiar kind of attitude: if one of the seals leaks a little and the flight is successful, the problem isn't so serious. Try playing Russian roulette that way: you pull the trigger and the gun doesn't go off, so it must be safe to pull the trigger again…". It was not safe, and the Shuttle was lost with all lives aboard.

During the launch of the space shuttle Colombia, it was noticed that a piece of foam insulation broke off from the shuttle and struck one wing. Some engineers suspected that the damage caused could be a problem by causing the shuttle to overheat on re-entry and burn up. But these concerns were dismissed by management. Some simple analysis was done to work out the impact of the damage and it was assessed as minimal risk. Foam insulation had after all fallen off repeatedly in previous launches and had never caused any problems. On re-entry, the Shuttle burned up with the loss of all of the crew.

As Richard Feynman said, "The Challenger flight is an excellent example: there are several references to previous flights; the acceptance and success of these flights are taken as evidence of safety. But erosion and blowby are not what the design expected. They are warnings that something is wrong. The equipment is not operating as expected, and therefore there is a danger that it can operate with even wider deviations in this unexpected and not thoroughly understood way. The fact that this danger did not lead to a catastrophe before is no guarantee that it will not the next time, unless it is completely understood". Obviously, there were a range of causes and contributing factors to the two losses of the Shuttle. But a false security based on previous successes was a contributing factor in each disaster.

It is all too easy in a complex world to fall into the non-sequitur trap, where conclusions are made that are simply unjustifiable. The complexity of life means that the most obvious option may not be the right one. Care must be taken. Our political judgements invariably made with the shortest of consideration in a busy world are regularly at risk.

For example, there were claims that under the proposed Obamacare (US healthcare), that "death panels" would eventually be created to deal with the elderly. This was not a reasonable conclusion based on the legislation, but nonetheless gained significant political mileage. This type of ludicrous "thin end of the wedge" claim, is sadly commonplace. Most people don't have the time to carefully analyse all the options or to consider all of the details and subtleties. Getting to the right answer is not only difficult, but at times can be actively discouraged due to the competing interests of politicians. Detecting flawed logic and reasoning can be especially difficult in the heat of a live political debate.

Our politicians have been shown to be poor at making reasonable conclusions and have a history making the wrong decisions. In our current process, we have no way of minimising this risk and the ongoing consequences are significant. If we can largely identify and eliminate the flaws of logic and reasoning from our democratic process, we will then be able to make substantially better decisions and avoid the many mistakes of the past.

Complex issues (and science)

"Doubt is our product since it is the best means of competing with the 'body of fact' that exists in the mind of the general public. It is also the means of establishing a controversy"- cigarette company executive, Brown and Williamson, discussing the strategy against adverse scientific findings (quote published by Professor David Michaels, George Washington University)

On AIDS in South Africa

When South Africa was faced with the AIDS health crisis the newly formed government of Thabo Mbeki did not have a healthy respect for western governments. After years of the west's support for the previous apartheid regime, quite understandably, suspicion of western governments' goodwill was elevated. The South African government was hesitant to follow the rest of the world and so investigated the risk of AIDS on its own. The government consulted with a number of scientists from around the world. Thabo Mbeki invited specific AIDS denying scientists, including Berkeley professor Peter Duesberg, to South Africa to speak. Those scientists had been discredited by the general scientific community and their research had been widely criticized. However, after consideration, the government then decided that the AIDS crisis was created to sell expensive drugs and that AIDS was a harmless virus. The government ignored the general scientific consensus, refused to pay for AIDS education programs and refused to support health initiatives for its people. Subsequently, South Africa citizens were devastated by a crisis that could have been largely avoided. AIDS infection rates quickly became one of the highest in the world and approximately 25% of the population was reportedly infected. By July 2000, 200 babies were reportedly born every day in South Africa with the HIV virus. There were around 300,000 people dying of AIDS in South Africa every year. It took quite a few years for the government to realize its mistake and to revise its position. In the meantime, the health consequences were devastating for the South African people.

Understanding the complexities of a scientific debate can be difficult for those in government. There are inevitably a range of scientific opinions, the field can require specialist knowledge and involve concepts with which politicians are unfamiliar. Scientific consensus can be difficult to assess. There is no real requirement for politicians to know about or to understand any aspect of the scientific method. Coupling this with a range of preconceived notions and beliefs can add to the difficulties. Yet politicians are expected to decide on policy which can include the appraisals of the most advanced of scientific research. Our existing democratic process allows politicians, without having any skills or understanding, to make arbitrary decisions without necessarily referencing to facts or reason. Getting those judgements wrong can have devastating consequences for the voting public.

On pharmaceuticals

The difficulties with our handling of pharmaceuticals for our health and well-being is comprehensively presented in the book *Bad Pharma*, by Ben Goldacre (MD, researcher, author). The book produces a compelling view of the evidence for how poorly we have handled the relationship with drug approvals globally. A summary of this brilliant book is somewhat difficult here, instead we will look to quote the book's own summary of the current situation from its introduction:

> Drugs are tested by the people who manufacture them, in poorly designed trials, on hopelessly small numbers of weird, unrepresentative patients, and analysed using techniques which are flawed by design, in such a way that they exaggerate the benefits of treatments. Unsurprisingly, these trials tend to produce results that

favour the manufacturer. When trials throw up results that companies don't like, they are perfectly entitled to hide them from doctors and patients, so we only ever see a distorted picture of any drug's true effects. Regulators see most of the trial data, but only from early on in a drug's life, and even then, they don't give this data to doctors or patients, or even to other parts of government. This distorted evidence is then communicated and applied in a distorted fashion. In their forty years of practice after leaving medical school, doctors hear about what works through ad hoc oral traditions, from sales reps, colleagues or journals. But those colleagues can be in the pay of drug companies - often undisclosed - and the journals are too. And so are the patient groups. And finally, academic papers, which everyone thinks of as objective, are often covertly planned and written by people who work directly for the companies, without disclosure. Sometimes whole academic journals are even owned outright by one drug company. Aside from all this, for several of the most important and enduring problems in medicine, we have no idea what the best treatment is, because it's not in anyone's financial interest to conduct any trials at all. These are ongoing problems, and although people have claimed to fix many of them, for the most part they have failed; so, all these problems persist, but worse than ever, because now people can pretend that everything is fine after all...We will see that the bar is very low: that drugs must only prove that they are better than nothing, even when there are highly effective treatments on the market already. This means that real patients are given dummy placebo pills for no good reason, but also that drugs appear on the market which are worse than the treatments we already have. We will see that companies break their promises over follow-up studies, and that regulators let them do this. We will also see how data on side effects and effectiveness can be withheld from regulators, and that regulators, in turn, are obsessively secretive, withholding the data they do have from doctors and patients. Lastly, we will see the harm done by this secrecy: 'many eyes' are often very powerful, to spot problems with medicines, and some of the most frightening harms have been missed by regulators, and only identified by academics who were forced to fight hard for access to data...I am setting out this evidence at length because I want to be

123

absolutely clear that there is no doubt on the issue. Industry-sponsored trials give favourable results, and that is not my opinion, or a hunch from the occasional passing study. This is a very well-documented problem, and it has been researched extensively, without anybody stepping out to take effective action, as we shall see.

The rest of Ben Goldacre's book outlines the significant evidence for the above conclusions. This evidence will not be repeated here. The work of Goldacre has been corroborated by a number of experts globally.

A brief summary of just some the consequences of this situation follows. Vioxx by Merck came onto the market in 1999 and was used by more than 80 million people. It was however discovered that the drug could cause serious heart disease and that the manufacturer had withheld trials that demonstrated this. It was withdrawn from the market, but not before it was reported that around 100,000 people had developed serious heart disease from its use. Other drugs like rosiglitazone have been approved and released by drug companies, only to be withdrawn after there were significant adverse effects. Tellingly these effects have been noticed in small sample sizes by individual doctors, which demonstrates that these issues should likely have been clear in any scientific drug trial process involving large numbers of patients. Yet the drugs have been approved and many people have been harmed. Many other drugs have been simply removed or restricted from the markets after real world harm was demonstrated, including rimonabant in 2009 and rosiglitazone in 2010. The drug reboxetine was approved for distribution, was marketed as a beneficial drug and was prescribed by many doctors. Yet when all of the clinical trials were investigated by other scientists it was clear that the drug was no better than a sugar pill and did more harm than good. Critical trials of the drug which failed were simply not published and not available. Patients were harmed by a drug of no benefit where better drugs were available. Doctors had no way of knowing this. Reboxetine is still on the market (as at publication date of Bad Pharma). Similarly, for the drug paroxetine by GSK which was approved for use with children even though GSK already knew that the drug was both ineffective and dangerous to children. The UK had no law to prosecute for this at the time. Doxazosin was introduced as a new and more effective way to lower blood pressure. It was then measured to be worse than the existing and cheaper off patent drug that had been successfully used for years. Again tellingly, the subsequent drug trial to compare doxazosin was actually stopped for ethical reasons since the people on doxazosin were doing so much worse. The drug is more expensive and less effective and yet the manufacturer Pfizer is still able to market the drug widely. The drug is still in widespread use since in the current system doctors do not easily have access to data on drug efficacy. Midodrine was produced to help with orthostatic hypotension - sudden loss in blood pressure. It was approved using an "accelerated program" - where less supporting data is required, because there was no other effective treatment at the time. To get through the accelerated process the company promised to complete follow up confirmation studies. After 14 years, the regulators demanded that some data supporting its efficacy be finally produced, and the company simply withdrew the drug from sale. The company had already sold significant quantities of the drug without delivering any evidence. Special interest groups (which are invariably industry funded) then stepped in and demanded that the drug be kept on the market (other companies now also produced it), and so the US FDA relented and left it on the market. So, as at 2012, a drug is on the market, with no evidence of its benefit. Celebrex was taken off the market after it was found that it increases heart attacks.

There are undoubtedly more examples and significantly more harm caused. No one knows how many other drugs are in situations like the above because the identification of problems with drug trials and drug companies is extremely difficult. Drug companies protect the data from their drug trials and withhold evidence as a matter of course, making independent investigations difficult. The regulations allow this to happen. There is also rarely any follow up measurement of the efficacy of these widely distributed and government funded drug treatments.

Virtually all the harmful and ineffectual drugs discussed above could have been detected with normal scientific testing protocols. These were not exceptional circumstances. Either drug trial data was withheld, or the drug trials themselves were not effective. Our management of the process is ineffectual. Governments have done nothing of significance in decades to change this situation.

There have been many fines issued to the global pharmaceutical over the years, for a range of crimes, many of which cause significant harm and/or death. GlaxoSmithKline was fined $US 3 billion by the US Justice department for "illegal marketing and failing to report drug safety data". And again, Ben Goldacre has summarized the fines (and crimes) well, "Eli Lilly was fined $1.4 billion in 2009 over its off-label promotion of the schizophrenia drug olanzapine (the US government says the company 'trained their sales force to disregard the law'). Pfizer was fined $2.3 billion for promoting the painkiller Bextra, later taken off the market over safety concerns, at dangerously high doses (misbranding it with 'the intent to defraud or mislead'). Abbott was fined $1.5 billion in May 2012, over the illegal promotion of Depakote to manage aggression in elderly people. Merck was fined $1 billion in 2011. AstraZeneca was fined $520 million in 2010. These are vast sums of money: Pfizer's in 2009 was the largest criminal fine ever imposed in the US, until it was beaten by GSK. When you consider these figures alongside the revenue for the same companies, it becomes clear that they are nothing more than minor issues. For the period of time covered by the $3 billion GSK settlement, sales of rosiglitazone were $10 billion, paroxetine brought in $12 billion, Wellbutrin $6 billion, and so on". And this as well, "GSK bribed doctors with gifts and hospitality; it paid doctors millions of dollars to attend meetings, and to speak at them, in lavish resorts; it used, in the justice department's own words, 'sales representatives, sham advisory boards, and supposedly independent Continuing Medical Education (CME) programs'. It withheld data on the antidepressant paroxetine. It engaged in off-label promotion and kickbacks for the asthma drug Advair, the epilepsy drug Lamictal, the nausea drug Zofran, Wellbutrin, and many more. On top of all this, it made false and misleading claims about the safety profile of its diabetes drug rosiglitazone; it sponsored educational programs suggesting there were cardiovascular benefits from the drug, when in reality even the FDA label said there were cardiovascular risks; and most damningly of all, between 2001 and 2007, it withheld safety data on rosiglitazone from the FDA." Goldacre also reported that, "Over 13 per cent of fraud cases in America involve the pharmaceutical industry, covering either marketing or pricing issues. Pfizer has agreed to pay over $60 million to settle a foreign bribery case in the US courts, and several other drug companies are in the spotlight for similar charges".

Now some may say that the fines imposed on the pharmaceutical industry are actually a demonstration that the regulatory framework is working well and does hold these firms to account. But there are significant problems with this view. The fines are actually generally quite small compared to the profits made from selling these drugs. For those companies, the enormous profits made from the sale of any individual drug generally justify any risk of the relatively small government fines. The incentives for corruption and misrepresentation remain huge. The fines have also not materially impacted the share prices of those companies. Few of the regulations have changed. There are generally no criminal charges for the harm and deaths caused, so the incentive for individual corruption remains powerful. Special interest groups have been able to circumvent many instances of potential regulatory change as we have seen already.

Drug companies can and do mislead the public and the medical community of the efficacy of their products. They can hide data that has shown dangers of their products. Research has shown that billions of dollars are wasted every year in the UK alone through the unnecessary prescriptions of ineffective or overly expensive drugs. Billions more are undoubtedly wasted around the world. Many expensive new drugs are marketed as the latest and greatest but are in fact worse than existing treatments as well as being no better than placebos. Doctors have no effective way of really knowing which drugs help their patients. The only major mechanisms for doctors ongoing education in most countries are effectively controlled by the drug companies themselves. Millions of people have already been harmed by the drugs that have been approved and inevitably will continue to be harmed. The system currently generates vast profits and risks ongoing danger.

Although this sounds like an issue which is primarily due to the complex nature of the process, this is in fact a government issue. There have been many relatively simple solutions proposed to deal with these issues and to vastly reduce our risk of harm. Solutions to these problems have been first proposed many decades ago. In the 1950s, US Senator Estes Kefauver recommended changing regulations since drugs were being approved despite offering no new benefits. He also wanted ongoing reviews (to this day there are no ongoing checks on the efficacy or side effects of drugs that we use).

Our governments globally have shown little capability to get on top of the issues. In fact, there are instances where the regulatory frameworks have actually decreased in efficacy over the years – for example in 2008, the US requirement changed, for drug companies to satisfy the International Conference on Harmonization (ICH) Good Clinical Practice (GCP) guidelines, rather than the previous Helsinki guidelines. The newer guidelines reduced many requirements - including that of using effective alternative treatments in clinical trials, instead of useless sugar pills. This means that trial participants will potentially be harmed through participation in those trials since they do not get good comparison drugs instead of placebos. This use of placebos alone, instead of the best available treatment, will also enable the new drugs from drug companies to seem better in comparison. This will continue to give doctors no real data on whether or not new drugs are worth considering for their patients.

Most of the solutions implemented have been in some way watered down by special interest groups, many times to become wholly ineffectual. While our governments are unable to make effective decisions to solve complex problems these issues will remain.

As Ben Goldacre points out, although the issues that are faced are complex, there are relatively simple solutions. Incentives must be changed and corrected. Creating a regulatory framework, where drugs could only be approved and sold to the public if all clinical trials for those drugs had been pre-registered, with the results of all pre-registered trials made available to regulators - would be one simple system. In this way, all trials for all drugs must be registered up front and nothing could be hidden. Ensuring that data from the results of clinical trials is presented to the government for evaluation would also seem simple (confidentiality could be assured). Creating an independent government view of the relative efficacy of drugs would seem extremely worthwhile. Monitoring the results of drugs released to the public, through a central repository, updated by GPs, would also seem simple. At a minimum, requiring all doctors to update a central repository, any time that they find a drug ineffective enough to discontinue or replace, or where there are side effects, would be of significant benefit. Where billions of research dollars and expense are involved, none of these options would seem excessively expensive.

128

The responsibility for setting up a sensible and risk free regulatory framework for the management of the pharmaceutical industry is clearly a government responsibility. Our governments globally have been unable to implement solutions to these problems for decades. People like Ben Goldacre have been agitating for change for decades – to save potentially untold lives, but few governments have the incentives or the desire to improve the system. In our society, the special interest groups are invariably more powerful and more effective than both our advocates and our governments.

The issue of how our government can handle the requirement for complex decisions is a challenging one. And yet it is not the complexity which is the critical issue. Complex problems can and do get solved if the right process is applied. The problem lies with our process, or the lack thereof. At the moment, politicians are not bound by any requirement to consider evidence, to understand the issues, or to have even checked on the most basic of details. They can make decisions with little information and with influential pre-conceived notions and beliefs. They can be influenced by their own conflicts of interest. Politicians can be influenced by the need for political compromise. The system is set up without any effective controls on behaviour, to be run by people and politicians whose behaviour historically has consistently been problematic. Even where intentions are good, simple misunderstandings and mistakes over complex issues, and a lack of due diligence or time spent, can lead to poor outcomes.

How we handle science in society is a good example of the difficulties that our current democratic governments face when handling complexity. This discussion of the complexities and imperfections of the scientific method may not seem directly relevant to a discussion about the democratic process, but the relationship between the scientific method, as well as the results of science in general, can be extremely important in governing democracies. We currently have no consistent method for connecting the scientific community with our politicians. Science is often not trusted by politicians. There are large opportunities for the manipulation of science as we have seen.

The scientific method itself is difficult on its own and many scientists have gotten it wrong over the years. In an infamous study by Professor JP Ioannidis of Stanford University the title read *Why Most Published Research Findings are False*. He cited a range of issues that can lead to incorrect published results. The complexities can lead to errors even in the most learned of our scientists. Science is a self-informing process. Scientists each work reasonably independently and produce new research, results and ideas, which are then thrown into the public forum. The essence of science is that over time, the good ideas and research will survive on their own merits. Those good ideas will become - eventually, the consensus and hence established widely held views. The scientific method has shown itself to be an extremely effective way of moving forward both our understanding of our world as well as of improving the health and living standards of most of us. And yet, there is little in the way of effective governance of the scientific method. The method can be easy to get wrong.

The only real process that we use to ensure that the process is run correctly is that of peer review. There have been major weaknesses found in the process of peer review. According to Richard Smith, ex editor of the British Medical Journal, "So we have little evidence on the effectiveness of peer review, but we have considerable evidence on its defects. In addition to being poor at detecting gross defects and almost useless for detecting fraud it is slow, expensive, profligate of academic time, highly subjective, something of a lottery, prone to bias, and easily abused". Recently, peer review as a process has been more seriously questioned as new models for published papers arise, like pay for publishing, and non-peer reviewed publishers. It is extremely difficult for society, the media and politicians to keep up with the dilution of scientific method that is produced, with the ever increasing number and type of scientific publishers.

It is possible for scientific evidence to be utilized in many ways that are not a fair representation of the overall evidence and understanding. If politicians take evidence out of context, or take a one-sided view of evidence, or if scientific conclusions are distorted by an industry group, there are few effective governing scientific bodies that can correct the misinformation. The difficulty with a scientific body correcting any government is that the body itself is hopelessly conflicted. National government scientific bodies are dependent of that government for their ongoing funding. Speak ill of the government and they risk the wrath of politicians. When individual scientists do cry foul, they can seem as a single voice in the wilderness. Invariably as well, for every "scientific view" taken by a politician, whether consensus or not, there are always one or two scientists who are willing to extol that view - for the right research price. Science, after all, is not known to pay well.

As a society, our governance over the process has been imperfect and the consequences of these imperfections have been serious. It can be extremely difficult, especially where the underlying science is complicated or requires specialist knowledge, for the media and the general public to ascertain what is a reasonable scientific viewpoint and what is not. In the worst cases, options for change are presented which not only have no basis in logic or reason but defy underlying and established science itself. In spite of our education systems, some people simply do not believe the results presented by science; they distrust the process and will make their own conclusions. We have previously seen many examples of the complexity of science being manipulated for financial gain by groups like the energy industry, cigarette companies, food companies and the health industries. Without having a trusted independent group of people who can analyse the best available scientific evidence to come up with a reasonable view, manipulation is always possible and bad policy, inevitable. Universities themselves work independently, and in fact are in competition with each other. The underlying difficulty here is that in modern society we have few effective governing bodies that independently check scientific claims or conclusions.

The fact that government has done little to deal with these complex problems over the years is only partly due to the difficulty of the problems themselves. The problem of dealing with complex issues has been around for decades, the problems of a lack of governance of the scientific methods have been raised since the 1950s. Governments globally have failed to recognize this as an issue and when some suggestions have gotten through, they have failed to deal with the issue. For politicians, dealing with complex issues raises many risks and few if any, rewards. There have been many reasonable solutions and improvements suggested, but government has been unable to prioritize or decide upon many of them. The difficulty in handling complex problems in many ways is a combination of the many other root causes that we have

131

seen so far. The ability of special interest groups to influence decisions, the misaligned incentives for politicians, the short-term nature of politics, the ignorance and disinterest of politicians, the requirement for deals and compromises and an irrational policy debate, can all contribute to the challenge of dealing with complex problems politically.

The reality is that this issue reflects the inability of our democratic governments to come to timely and sensible decisions when faced with complex problems. What are already complex decisions can be made impenetrable for a government by the influence of special interest groups.

In the future, this inability for democratic governments to handle complex policy environments may become significantly more dangerous. Soon we will have to deal with a regulatory framework for the advent of complex artificial intelligence computers, genetically modified food and drugs, nanoparticle development, self-driving vehicles, autonomous robots and even autonomous weapons. A few years ago, these may have seemed a future based in science fiction, and yet these things are now realistically possible if not inevitable, soon. These new possibilities, if managed well, will be extremely positive developments. Yet each has the potential for huge disaster. Renowned physicist Professor Stephen Hawking was quoted as saying that "the development of full artificial intelligence could spell the end of the human race". If we handle these new developments like we have handled new drugs, or lead in petrol, or infections in hospitals, or opioids, or ulcers, then there may be tragic consequences. The consequences that we face could dwarf the avoidable harm and deaths that we have experienced with previous mistakes. We need to be able to make sensible and timely decisions on these new capabilities soon.

Without a better governance framework, science and its relationship to government policy will continue to be problematic. We must have a way of ensuring that political decisions include sensible scientific evidence and consensus analysis when relevant. We must empower our scientists to raise concerns around current policy without fear of losing essential government funding. Deciding without evidence and reason, and without the inclusion of reasonable scientific opinion is doomed to lead to failure.

When faced with these problems we must improve the democratic process itself. Once we have a better democratic process, without its current limitations, we will be able to improve the relationship between democracy and both science and complex problems. We can then more easily manage and evaluate the consensus on complex problems, including science, within our democracies. This is essential if we are to avoid repeating the devastating issues of the past and avoid even greater potential tragedies in the future.

Deciding upon change, the nontrivial issues

Let's summarize some of the overall difficulties within our current democratic process which relate to decision making. These can cause significant issues. For our existing process, the following summary of the process is true:

Current issues in deciding upon change
Voters often don't know anything about or haven't spent any time in consideration of political candidates, their policies or their party's policies.
Voters and politicians often haven't seen both sides of any policy discussions.
Voters and politicians often haven't used logic or reason in their decision making process.
Voters and politicians often haven't seen verifiable facts in relation to any policies.
The media will often present inaccurate and/or unreasonable information.
Special interest groups can spend large amounts of money to influence voters' perceptions away from a balanced view.
Politicians can successfully present extraordinary lies and misrepresentations to get their way in political discussions.
The requirement for politicians to gain popular support before any new policies are implemented, especially for complex issues, means that the process of change can be extremely slow. There is no real mechanism for getting a reasonable consensus or overview on complex or scientific issues.

While these above limitations are present in our decision making process, we will continue to have significant problems with democracy.

The freedoms of our system of government and the processes of our democracy make it vulnerable to manipulation. Given the incredible financial incentives (and many other incentives), manipulation seems inevitable. Our politicians have consistently shown little integrity in decision making and often have little interest in, and certainly no requirement for, factuality or sensible well-considered decisions. Few people in the general public have the time nor the motivation to monitor politicians and to hold them to account.

Most of the issues above result from inherent parts of our existing democratic process. They cannot be decoupled from our existing process unless we lose freedoms which are generally considered important to our society. But these issues are nonetheless solvable problems. Our best option is to create a decision making process that is structured well enough to work irrespective of the limitations of our free society. This improved collective decision making process can then be incorporated into our new democratic process.

Deciding upon change, as it should be

"Big shots are only little shots who keep shooting" - Christopher Morley

We have now seen the many difficulties that get in the way of effectively deciding upon change. We have also seen the many flawed arguments and processes that inevitably affect our ability to make the best decisions. In the political arena, the process is made even worse through misaligned incentives as well as the undue influence and manipulation of many groups. The list is in no way comprehensive, it is merely enough to highlight the need for change. Let us now look at what should be included in the process to ensure better collective decision making.

When considering change there are a number of essential requirements that must be included in the process to ensure that we evaluate change effectively. Without these requirements our process for change will be imperfect and can potentially produce the wrong outcomes. If these are not present, we will continue to decide on changes that neither move us forward as a society nor solve the problems of our world. With these requirements, we are significantly more likely to decide upon positive change that helps us to build a better society. Again, this is not an exhaustive list, but rather it is a significant start in dealing with the current issues around evaluating change effectively. Considering the list explicitly will also us to produce a process for deciding upon change which will ensure better collective decision making.

Evidence and reason

"I believe in evidence. I believe in observation, measurement, and reasoning, confirmed by independent observers. I'll believe anything, no matter how wild and ridiculous, if there is evidence for it. The wilder and more ridiculous something is, however, the firmer and more solid the evidence will have to be" - Isaac Asimov

On evidence for (and of) policy success

Since the 1980s in the US, many follow up studies have been done on the effectiveness of social welfare programs. They have determined the following, which was presented before a US House Committee by the Laura and John Arnold Foundation, "Of the 90 interventions evaluated in RCTs (random controlled trials) commissioned by the Institute of Education Sciences (IES) since 2002, approximately 90 percent were found to have weak or no positive effects.....In Department of Labor-commissioned RCTs that have reported results since 1992, about 75 percent of tested interventions were found to have found weak or no positive effects". A paper by Isabel V. Sawhill and Jon Baron has stated, "this is the 10th instance since 1990 in which an entire federal social program has been evaluated using the scientific 'gold standard' method of randomly assigning individuals to a program or control group. Nine of those evaluations found weak or no positive effects, for efforts such as the $300 million Upward Bound program (academic preparation for at-risk high school students), and the $1.5 billion Job Corps program (job training for disadvantaged youths). Only one—Early Head Start, a sister program to Head Start for younger children—was found to produce meaningful but modest effects". There were also programs, like *Scared Straight*, which were actually measured to have produced negative outcomes.

Billions of dollars have been spent on these programs, the majority of which have produced no overall positive results. This is not uncommon, and in many areas, results are either not measured at all or measured ineffectually. The results are generally not acted upon irrespective.

Globally, thousands of welfare programs have been implemented for the underprivileged. In all likelihood all have been designed with the best intentions of improving the lives of those in need. And yet the results have been less than ideal. Implementing programs which improve the livelihoods of the underprivileged over the long-term is an extremely challenging task. It is this challenging nature itself which highlights the need to be more careful and measured in our approach. Those billions of dollars spent on ineffectual programs could have achieved greater good if used carefully elsewhere. It is certainly an improvement that some outcomes of these programs have been more recently evaluated using a reasonable methodology. However, the studies on the efficacy of programs are often done separately by academics with little influence over government expenditure. The programs which do not produce results continue to be implemented. Many people around the world (including the Laura and John Arnold Foundation) have been calling for a more effective approach. This would involve the utilization of a more thorough investigation of programs up front using measured evidence of results before vast amounts of government money have been spent. Programs should be independently monitored as they are run to check that the results are what was intended. And yet politicians continue to choose their own unsubstantiated ideas, and waste billions of dollars.

In theory, in modern and relatively well educated societies we should understand the importance of informed and well considered arguments. Without the inclusion of verifiable evidence and sound reasoning we should not move forward on any proposed changes or policies. Yet it is commonly the case where we move forward on change absent these things. There are innumerable examples of politicians proposing and implementing policies with both a lack of solid evidence and with flawed reasoning. It is true that where there is a lack of information it can be reasonable to change things based on sound reason alone if that change is considered carefully. But we must be sure that we do not ignore any existing contrary information.

It is an extraordinary thing that in our current democratic system we require rules of evidence and reason in our courts of law - to protect the rights of individuals, but we have no similar requirement when setting the policies and laws of the land as a whole.

Subjectivity is still inevitably a part of many government decisions. At the same time, where relevant evidence and reason is available it must be included in the decision making process.

Time for consideration

We have seen busy voters who carelessly choose the wrong candidates, who are unaware of political candidates' names and parties and who are unaware of policies or their consequences. Politicians can exhibit the very same problems and can spend more time on campaigning than in carefully weighing the policy options. There is no requirement in our elections or in our parliament for any decision makers to spend any time on the process. And yet it is impossible to get to the right answers in a complicated world without spending time in consideration of the options available. Time for consideration and to weigh all options is essential where we are deciding upon change. We need both informed and well considered decisions.

Root cause analysis

On ulcers

For most of the 20th century ulcers were believed to have been caused by stress and dietary factors. The treatment was the recommendation of certain blander foods as well as if necessary, eventual bed rest and hospitalization. In later years the treatment focused on the reduction of stomach acid production through various medications. Patients were lectured on healthy eating and lifestyle choices. Unfortunately, there was no real evidence for these beliefs nor for the efficacy of the treatments imposed. After treatments the problems would often recur. In 1982, two physicians produced scientific research that demonstrated that in fact ulcers were the result of a treatable bacterial infection. They could be treated with a simple antibiotic and the problem would be resolved. Although the evidence was conclusive, the medical community was slow in accepting the findings. More than 12 years later in the US it was determined that only around 5% of ulcer patients were treated with antibiotics for the infections underlying the ulcers. The vast majority of ulcer patients still blamed their ulcers on stress. It was not until

1996 that the Federal Drug Administration (FDA) in the US recommended the first antibiotic treatment for ulcers. In 1997 a national advertising campaign was launched to educate both healthcare providers and the public about the causes of and treatments for ulcers. Finally, the community began to be treated effectively after decades of ineffective treatments by medical professionals.

When the root cause of a problem is not found the treatments are at best a waste of time and at worst can have unfortunate side effects. It would seem astonishing that in the 20th century we could get the cause for such a widespread illness so wrong and for such a long period of time. Finding the root cause of issues is important not just in medicine but in government as well. Yet preconceived notions, a lack of real measurements of the overall results, as well as an ineffectual government management of the process (and of the science), can allow many problems to remain unresolved. Finding and fixing root causes matters.

It is also interesting that it took so long for the treatment to be widely used even though it was published science at the time. Sometimes lone voices can go unheard for quite some time. Defining who is in charge of documenting new medical treatments or even defining the best existing treatments is a grey area in our democracies. Doctors study medicine, but then have decades of practice often without a clear way of keeping up to date on the latest science. The FDA (eventually) stepped up and delivered in this case. Informing doctors of the best known treatments and incorporating new treatments into this information would seem an essential function of government.

On the Rogers Commission

In 1986, the Space Shuttle Challenger exploded shortly after take-off. After the tragic disaster, the Rogers Commission was tasked with getting to the bottom of the disaster. The principle cause was found to be a design flaw in the O-rings, which are responsible for sealing a section of the rocket boosters. When these O-rings failed to maintain their seal under colder than expected temperatures on the day, pressurized hot gases leaked and led to a catastrophic explosion.

140

The Nobel laureate Richard Feynman was also on the commission. He was determined to investigate further. Feynman understood the criticality of uncovering and dealing with the root causes of issues. Although the actual cause of the disaster was a design flaw of the O-rings and some poor decision making on the day, the root causes of the issue seemed more fundamental to Feynman. He was concerned that if the commission investigated only the issues around the O-rings without checking further, then the problem could recur. Feynman spent quite some time investigating further and talking to many more people on the ground at NASA.

Feynman discovered that there was a cultural breakdown in the management of risks at NASA. The shuttle program faced ongoing risks of failure with many of the components in its design. Managing that risk and mitigating risk sensibly was key to the safety of astronauts. However, senior management at NASA also faced the realistic risk of the loss of financial support from Congress. The public was losing interest in the space program and there was serious concern that Congress would cut funding. This could destroy both the space program and many jobs. Senior management focus had to include the survival of the program itself. It would have been difficult for management to maintain funding in Congress if the true engineering risks of a failure of the Shuttle – for some systems rated at near 1 in 100 - were communicated clearly. So, the risk of catastrophic failure of the shuttle was minimized and glossed over. In this way, a Shuttle that was assessed by engineers to have a reasonable likelihood of failure (1 in 100) in multiple components, was assessed by senior management as a low risk of failure (of around 1 in 100,000). So, in critical meetings where "go-no go" decisions were made, critical questions were not asked and the managers who made the decisions used their own risk assessments, rather than checking in too much detail with the engineers. Under this process and risk assessment incongruity, the shuttle eventually failed twice, with the loss of all astronauts aboard, until the whole program was shut down. The root cause of the problem was that management was not considering and evaluating the real risk of failure, they had long since lost contact with the real risks of failure. Their decisions were more concerned with keeping the shuttle program alive and minimizing the perception of risk. So, when real risks were actually faced like that of the O-rings, they were unable to make effective decisions.

The incongruity between a management assessment of reality and a true assessment can be an issue with science, with business and with government. With a Space Shuttle program this can lead to the death of astronauts. With government this can lead to significant consequences for the whole of society. Without identifying the true root causes of the shuttle failure, which included the competing risks for managers, the shuttle was doomed to fail repeatedly. Nobel Laureate Richard Feynman understood that identifying and dealing with the root causes of issues is essential.

On air safety

In 2007 Garuda Indonesia Flight 200 was landing at Yogyakarta airport. The plane was approaching quickly, up to 89 knots above normal speed. The flaps had been set incorrectly for landing. There were 15 ground proximity warnings that sounded during the approach ("pull up"). The co-pilot had twice suggested that the pilot should abort the landing and go-around. Despite all of the warnings, the pilot decided that he could make the landing and set down the plane, irrespective of the difficulties. Aborted landings cost a lot of fuel, and pilot pay included payments for fuel efficiency. The landing did not go well. 21 people died, and 112 people were injured.

It has been a critical issue to find the root causes of airline crashes - to ensure that people do not die from known issues that could be remediated or resolved. Accident investigation boards have learnt to apply scientific rigor to the process of the investigation of aircraft crashes. Investigators must approach each crash with an open mind and make well considered conclusions based only on relevant information. Investigations can take years to find answers, in large part due to the complexity of the problems that they solve. Yet they always attempt to find the underlying causes of crashes.

For example, Garuda flight 200 crashed due to pilot error. It landed with too much speed. The pilot had set the wrong flaps. The pilot ignored many warnings including those from his co-pilot. Clearly the pilot made some grave mistakes. This was human error. The investigation however also flagged the financial incentives that were in place for pilots to save fuel. The

142

root cause of the pilot's fatal mistake was not the individual mistakes that he made with the landing process. Rather, it was that he was prioritizing his financial incentives over the risk to his passengers. The final decision to continue with the landing in spite of the problems, was actually his fatal error. Up until that point the landing could have been safely aborted. In the moments before landing the pilot made a poor call - that the risks were manageable. It was not a call that a stressed pilot should be making. There should be no conflicts between safety and financial incentives. Until these incentive structures were changed the accident could happen again. After the crash the airline was directed to change its remuneration policy, and this was recommended for all airlines globally.

There are also key lessons that can come from an appreciation of the process involved in air crash investigations. Firstly, is the importance and reverence paid to incentives. The industry's governing bodies realize how much influence incentives have on behaviour. The power of incentives is given the respect that it deserves. There have been a number of airline accidents that have been caused through financial incentives subtly clashing with safety. Safety is now recognized as paramount. On their own, airlines are intrinsically incentivised to enhance profits. The risk is that to ensure the maximum profitability, maintenance, training and critical systems can be compromised, even if only slightly. The regulators simply override and remove the natural incentive through strong regulation, to protect passenger's safety. The regulatory framework is mandatory and so the incentives in certain areas become irrelevant. Maintenance, training and operations must be done in a certain way, to a certain standard, without compromise. If airlines fail in this duty, then planes are grounded, and they are liable to penalties and prosecution. The root cause of the risk is avoided.

The second lesson that can be learnt is around the effectiveness of root cause analysis itself. For every accident in which passengers are injured or killed, a rigorous process is applied to uncover the true root causes of the incident. There can be multiple contributory issues and as best as possible all are identified. Once identified, directives are issued to airlines to remove the causes. This crash investigation process itself can be imperfect and at times, responsiveness has been slower than ideal. And yet airline travel, even though the most complicated and potentially dangerous form of mass transit,

143

is now extremely safe. Even though global airline travel has increased substantially over the years, fatal accidents have been significantly reduced. Acknowledging the power of incentives and dealing with them properly, as well as bypassing or resolving the root cause of problems that do occur, ensures that millions of people can travel every day in relative safety.

Interestingly, in our existing democratic process we still allow politicians to override the success of our airline safety record. Politicians after all, run the regulators. They can reduce the financial support for regulators. They can remove the mandate for some regulations themselves. They could remove regulations because they are seen as red tape or are not cost competitive. They could give in to regulatory pressure applied by an aggressive airline industry special interest group. Or they could say that the airlines will be smart enough to self-regulate (as they have done with the banks). Politicians can do any of this, without due consideration, and even without any understanding of the existing process. They can do this without any knowledge of the lessons learnt from past airline crashes. It is not unforeseeable that politicians could still choose to weaken the support for regulations at some point, for a whole range of political reasons. Thankfully, they have not yet done this. Yet all of these things are possible in our current democratic system.

Three examples have been presented here to reinforce the importance of root cause analysis. It is one of the most critical aspects of problem solving. Problem solving is fundamental in determining what changes and improvements to make in society. In society where we have complex problems and limited resources and capabilities, we tend to identify a problem's symptoms, rather than the true root cause of an issue. Once the symptoms are identified, then we work around those symptoms and sometimes then even believe that we have dealt with the problem. Unfortunately, where we only deal with the symptoms the problems invariably tend to recur in different ways. In some cases, the root cause is not even identified.

In politics taking the time to carefully identify root causes of issues, and then describing the contributing factors in detail, to a public with little time or attention, gains few if any votes. Politicians who take this approach find it difficult to gain support and certainly find it difficult to communicate the real issues through a media that is also seeking to grab a reader's attention quickly. The more successful political strategy is to take an already popular pre-conceived notion and run with it as a solution. It matters little if the notion or policy is wrong. It matters little if the policy is ineffectual or is only dealing with a symptom of the problem. The problems with the solution can take years to surface. This superficial strategy, however, leads to politicians who stay in power. As John Kenneth Galbraith said, "...it is far, far safer to be wrong with the majority than to be right alone", and nothing is truer in politics. We need a better process to ensure that the true causes of issues are identified and effectively dealt with.

The issue and just the issue

Irrelevant information can get in the way of effective decision making. We must exclude irrelevant data, arguments and issues from any considerations. We saw this issue clearly demonstrated in the above example of the Garuda Indonesia Flight 200 crash while landing. The pilot's only issue should have been the safe landing of the aircraft, but he was distracted by concerns of fuel consumption and bonuses. As a consequence, he made a poor decision which cost lives.

In politics, policy decisions can be especially difficult and complex, requiring politicians to decide between many and varied options with potentially far reaching consequences. At the same time special interest groups and political opponents will intentionally include irrelevant information and arguments to further their own agenda. With every policy decision made, politicians must deal with personal career issues, party issues, popularity issues, supporter issues and special interest groups issues, amongst many others. This seriously clouds their decision making capability. We would be better served if decisions were based on the relevant information only – without any spurious issues clouding the process. It would be significantly better if we could separate out the personal consequences of the decision making process and just allow for a decision based purely on merits.

To get to the right decisions in a complex world we need to ensure that our decisions are focussed and simplified, and that we only concern ourselves with relevant information. The process will remain challenging but ensuring simplicity and focus will improve our results considerably.

Cost and risk assessment

For all proposals of change we need an assessment of the relative costs and risks of the change. This includes the relative cost and risk of not doing anything. In many societies, there is a theoretical requirement for politicians to present a thorough cost benefit analysis for any new proposals or developments. And yet, we do see politicians ignoring these requirements for major policy announcements. Or we see the analysis of cost done by politicians in an overly simplistic manner which ignores critical ramifications or outcomes. Getting the assessment of costs right is essential to ensure that large sums of money are not wasted. Getting the assessment of risks right is essential to avoid disasters.

The power of incentives

"Call it what you will, incentives are what get people to work harder" - Nikita Khruchev

On ratings agencies

Ratings agencies in finance markets rate financial products according to certain standards, so that individuals and companies can purchase complex financial instruments with a level of safety. Each financial product is rated by the 3 major global ratings agencies into a range of fixed risk ratings so that buyers will know their level of risk when making purchases. Products (and companies) are rated into ratings like AAA (best quality, lowest risk), AA (slightly higher risk), etc.... right down to a rating of "junk" status. Higher risk products generally earn a higher yearly return since by owning them you are taking on an increased risk of losses. Without understanding all of the complexities of financial products then, investors globally can more easily compare products. There is a quirk however - the rating agencies are not paid their fees by those purchasing the products, they are paid by those selling the products. This quirk has quite far reaching consequence. For ratings agencies to make money they must generate repeat business. Their paying customers are the companies that sell the rated products not those that buy them. So, the incentives have been set up such that for the ratings agencies to increase their income they have to please the investment banks and the finance companies that sell the complex products. The buyers of the products want accurate risk assessment but have little influence over the process. The investment banks want their products to be rated as low risk, so customers will pay more for them. Before the financial crisis of 2007/8, the ratings agencies worked with the investment banks to construct complex mathematical models of those products. These models, not surprisingly, tended to rate the products well. When products received high ratings more business was booked. The financial incentives were set up to encourage the agencies to rate products "generously". Fees for the ratings agencies skyrocketed, with *Bloomberg* reporting that between 2002 and 2007 the ratings agencies earned fees of $US 3.2 trillion. The revenue flowed when the process delivered a low-risk rating for complex and often highly risky baskets of mortgages. Many products that contained highly dubious mortgages were sold globally by the major banks. *Bloomberg* reported that "Of all the securities classed as investment-grade by *Moody's* (Baa3 or higher) in 2007, for example, 89 percent were subsequently downgraded to junk". Many governments, corporations and even charities invested their capital in a range of products believing that they were buying the least risky investments products available in the market. Eventually the complex mathematical models which underpinned the ratings agency assessments were shown to be fundamentally flawed by poor assumptions. The products imploded and many billions of "safely" invested dollars were lost globally.

Nobel laureate Joseph Stiglitz, economics professor at Columbia University, observed: "I view the ratings agencies as one of the key culprits. They were the party that performed that alchemy that converted the securities from F-rated to A-rated. The banks could not have done what they did without the complicity of the ratings agencies". The Financial Crisis Inquiry Commission concluded that "the failures of credit rating agencies were essential cogs in the wheel of financial destruction".

It seems extraordinary to have ratings agencies' profits provided by their investment banking clients, rather than by the customers who purchased and actually depend on the risk ratings. If you had to design a system for estimating the risk of products issued by banks and for purchase by third party organizations, this would clearly not have been it. It would seem an essential and potentially simple thing to fix, to change the incentives around so that the purchaser's pay for the risk ratings of the products that are purchased. Or to have any other simple framework separating the paying banks directly from the ratings agencies, through a third-party system. Sadly, in spite of the catastrophic failures of the current ratings system in 2007/8 the incentives have largely remained unchanged. In January of 2015, it was reported that "S&P paid $58 million to settle claims it had loosened its standards to win business in commercial-mortgage bonds three years earlier; the SEC ordered S&P to suspend significant portions of that market for one year". Although there may be an increase in some scrutiny evidenced in the short-term, governments have generally left the same systems in place, which incentivised disastrously, and created the basis for a large part of such a catastrophic failure.

You cannot blame the ratings agencies alone in this since they are merely working within the system. Given that it is government requirement to have ratings agencies as a part of our economic system, then getting the structure and incentives right is clearly a government responsibility. The system should be fixed to improve our ability to reasonably and independently rate financial products and to remove the misaligned incentive structure. There are many ways in which this can be achieved. The risk remains of another catastrophic failure, which next time could be much worse.

On investment banks

Investment banks offer a range of incentives to their staff in order to induce them to work harder and to earn more money for the firm. These incentives are generally financial in nature. Staff are offered options over company stock and direct bonuses which increase as the money made for the firm increases. Staff are incentivised to earn as much as they can for their companies so that they will earn more money themselves. The system has a few quirks. The incentives are for income earned in the current calendar year. Commissions for sales, profits for products sold and profits for trades made, all record income in the current financial year. Staff bonuses rise if that income improves. In the complex world of investment banking products sold have risk associated with them. The risk for products purchased and sold is reflected in subsequent years, not the current year. Profit is actually increased in the short-term by investing in riskier products which adds to long-term risk. This means that those riskier products may lose significant money for the banks in later years. The bonuses depend on the current year's profit alone and yet by the time a risk is realized, the staff member has already pocketed his bonus. If the product results in losses in subsequent years, then no bonus is returned by staff. People are then incentivised to take risks in the future to earn profits this year. In recent times, short-term financial employee incentives have allowed unaddressed long-term risk to destroy company worth in a range of different industries. This became a key issue in the lead up to the Great Recession and financial crisis of 2007/8 and cost many banks billions.

In the same way, bonuses for senior management are based on the current year's revenue or profit. If the current net profit increases well, then senior management makes significant bonuses. However, running a business is a complex endeavour, especially in investment banking. Making management decisions to gain a profit this year, by cutting down growth investments, costs or staff, may have serious consequences for future years' profits. Management can quite easily get a few good years of profit numbers and subsequent bonuses, before leaving the company to greener pastures, and before the consequences of those bonus-delivering decisions take effect.

Companies such as Enron (energy market derivatives), Bank of America (mortgage backed securities) and Bear Stearns (collateralized debt obligations) have all collapsed and failed spectacularly under the weight of risky products that they have bought and sold. Managers in those firms however had long since received their large bonuses, before the collapse for shareholders. The system works for company management and a range of high paid staff but is not designed to be in the best interests of shareholders.

There seems little motivation at this stage to improve the alignment of incentives to outcomes in the business world. The incentives themselves

149

*motivate senior company officials to serve their own best interests. The lack
of alignment of the employees' incentives to the interests of shareholders
creates significant risk. Shareholders bear the consequences of the risk.
Governance in business involves a select group of board members, who are
senior leaders of business, and whose own incentives are also askew. Board
members currently have little alignment of incentives to that of their
"employers", the shareholders. Their pay is generous and pay often
continues irrespective of the share price or the companies' profitability. So,
their concerns are not generally with the long-term welfare of shareholders
but rather with shoring up their networks of fellow workers who can support
them in getting other lucrative board memberships. Board membership
encourages individuals who unflinchingly support the initiatives of the CEO
- this keeps the board members in well paid work.*

*A better system would align both the CEO and the majority of board
membership pay directly to the long-term increases in earnings per share of
the company. Then all would want to ensure that the initiatives of the CEO
would truly be in the best interests of shareholders. It is no surprise that
some of the most successful firms are those where CEO's have a significant
personal stake in the business.*

*Incentives matter and do influence behaviour in material ways. Getting them
right is critically important in finance, in industry and in government.*

Pharmaceutical companies are privately owned firms whose priority is to
make money. They speak of corporate purposes that mention the welfare of
their clients but at the end of the day they need to make money. They are
little different to any other firm in their primary purpose. The actual
incentives of individuals throughout drug companies from the CEO, through
management, down to individual salespeople are about sales and revenue.
The incentives paid encourage the maximization of revenue and profits.
Getting approval for individual drugs is slow and expensive, so maximizing
the sales per approved drug ensures higher profitability. Finding drugs that
can cure a disease quickly and with a single dose will not help your long-
term profitability. If instead you can find a way to sell a drug in an ongoing
sense for a lifetime, then your earnings will be the greatest for the longest
period of time. To keep selling the same drug to the same person is a simple

thing - do not cure the disease, but rather treat the symptoms. If the disease goes away, so does the ongoing revenue stream. The best option is simply to find a drug that merely treats the symptoms. Choosing to investigate drugs and go through long-term drug trials and regulatory approval has a significant cost. If there are two options for new drugs, one which can cure quickly and one which can treat symptoms for a lifetime, the smarter financial move is to spend your money investigating the one which will earn long-term financial security through a lifetime revenue stream. If a firm does not generate the maximum cash from the sale of its approved drugs, then it will have less cash available to research more drugs to sell. It will simply lose out to its competitors who have more money for research. The incentives encourage companies to find solutions to treat symptoms for a lifetime. Not surprisingly, the vast majority of drugs on the market treat symptoms and many diseases remain. The incentives simply make finding cures less likely.

There is another example which is raised briefly in the book, *Bad Pharma*. An issue which has uncanny parallels to the issues that we have previously seen in the finance industry which contributed to the Great Recession of 2007. The parallels will likely have severe consequences. Pharmaceutical companies have begun to outsource the testing of new drugs to what will be called here (for simplicity), "drug trial companies". These companies often operate in the developing world to reduce costs. This is similar to how the banks outsource – to the ratings agencies, for the validation and rating of products that banks have sold.

Both the drug trial companies, and the ratings agencies are paid directly by the companies who manufacture the products, to vet that those products are OK. Drug companies pay the drug trial companies. Banks paid the ratings agencies. At the moment, pharmaceutical companies globally pay drug trial companies to deliver those drug trials in various low-cost locations globally. The drug trial companies are incentivised to deliver good results (similar to ratings agencies incentives to deliver good ratings). Gaining more business is then dependent on getting great results in the drug trials delivered (like for ratings agencies). As in the finance industry it is in the best interest of the drug trial companies to skilfully deliver consistent good results to their

151

clients - the global pharmaceutical companies, who will then give them more business and bigger fees.

So, both ratings agencies and the many drug trial companies gain more business by giving better results (ratings and testing) to their clients, so the incentive is - to do what it takes to pass the tests. In the case of the ratings agencies, this askew incentive system eventually produced nonsense ratings, and led to a global destruction of wealth in the Great Recession of 2007/8. In the case of the pharmaceutical companies and the paid drug trials system, this could eventually produce drugs that are rated as safe but that actually have catastrophic consequences. We have already seen many harmful drugs produced which, due to poor testing, have impacted millions of people's health. In the future this could get significantly worse. Whereas the misaligned incentives with ratings agencies costs billions of dollars globally, the poor testing involved with drug trials – which has already been experienced repeatedly, could in the future cost tens of millions of lives.

A system allowed to continue in this way, where companies will make more money if they manipulate the testing of drugs, will likely lead to carnage. It is especially risky if the drug trial companies operate in locations which have less regulatory control and less of a history of ethical standards. A system of the testing of drugs must incentivize testing and trial quality above all else. Like for the airlines industry (discussed earlier), which overcomes the problems of cost vs safety incentives through a strong regulatory framework, the pharmaceutical company drug trial process must mandate and enforce quality and rigorous scientific method in drug trials and testing above all else to ensure safety. Many more lives could be lost unless the regulators (government) improves the process.

The responsibility here lies with our governments globally and yet, in our current democratic process, do we really expect delivery of a solution to this problem?

In our modern democratic world, the alignment of incentives to outcome is often and almost invariably askew. Politicians who survive the longest will influence society the most. But what is our politicians' success aligned to? They must win elections. Simply that, they must gain more votes than their opponents. They do not directly need to have better policies or have better skills in choosing policies, they must be more likely to be voted in by thousands of complete strangers, with busy lives, who often spend little more than a few minutes deciding who to vote for. The skill is actually in convincing voters to vote for them for whatever reason, whether for self-interest, for fear, for short-term gratification or for many other reasons. The skill that politicians most demonstrate is that of manipulation of the political process using whatever means possible to gain the most votes.

The surviving politician is not necessarily the smartest or most capable of governing but rather the one who is more able to achieve an election result. Capability, integrity and judgement (and other qualities), in theory are important characteristics which contribute to electability, but the key success factor is an ability to be voted for in larger numbers than your opponents. In reality this is what counts most for success. Is this the correct alignment of incentives if our desired outcome is for the best policies for our future?

We must ensure that misaligned incentives are removed from any process, especially those of leadership and decision making. Ideally, we would also prefer for the incentives to be better aligned to produce better decisions. Any new system that we create for the new democratic process will then need to remove the possibility of the influence of misaligned incentives.

Collective decision making

An essential part of democracy is the process of decision making through broad consensus. We currently favour the results produced by using the collective wisdom of society. This allows for the inclusion of the interests of all people in society. In our electoral system all citizens can vote, not just the experts on politics, law and government. In our governments all politicians can vote on all issues even if they have no expertise in those issues. This is not necessarily a flawed model, as is discussed in the book *The Wisdom of Crowds* by James Surowiecki. The book shows that making decisions through the collective wisdom of a large group of people using the "wisdom of crowds" can be extremely effective. His work is useful here since in a democracy we prefer to decide on our policies and governing laws through collective decision making where the majority rules. Surowiecki describes

153

how utilizing the collective wisdom of crowds can make decisions and obtain results that are in fact better than even the best of our expert decision makers. He also describes how when utilizing collective decision making it is not necessary for the decision makers to be experts. In certain circumstances the wisdom of crowds can produce results that are more accurate than even the best results of every individual involved in the process. This not only allows for the consideration of every citizens' rights, but it also seems to be a good way of coming to more effective collective decision making.

But just as importantly for our use here, as Surowiecki emphasizes, there are 4 key components which enable a consensus decision to be effective. Without these key components our collective decision making can be quite poor. They are described as follows:

Decentralization - people are able to specialize and draw on local knowledge
Diversity - each person should be different enough that they have different opinions
Independence - each person should be able to decide independently, without the influence of others
Aggregation - some effective mechanism exists for turning individual judgments into a collective decision

As Surowiecki says, "If a group satisfies those conditions, its judgment is likely to be accurate. Why? At heart, the answer rests on a mathematical truism. If you ask a large enough group of diverse, independent people to make a prediction or estimate a probability, and then average those estimates, the errors each of them makes in coming up with an answer will cancel themselves out. Each person's guess, you might say, has two components: information and error. Subtract the error, and you're left with the information". Drawing on varied opinions, from knowledge across a wide range, from those whose opinions are free from influence, should inevitably produce a better aggregate view. For collective decisions to be the best possible it seems eminently sensible to ensure that any group of people is decentralized, diversified and independent. These criteria are a great

154

summary of the requirements. With these criteria satisfied we should undoubtedly produce better results.

For example, if we have a group of people who do not have diverse opinions, then it is possible that the best opinions are not included in the group. If the group is not decentralized, then the local knowledge of individuals may skew the results in a poor way. If the group is not independent, then a number of people may influence the whole group, which nullifies the collective wisdom of a broad range of experiences and intellects. Surowiecki presents a range of examples of the importance of his criteria as well as some compelling arguments in support. We will not delve into too much of the detail contained within Surowiecki's book, but rather simply gain from the experience and use the useful and insightful analysis to our advantage in our decision making process. It does seem obvious as well, simply from a perspective of common sense, that the criteria are important in collective decision making.

So, let's consider whether or not our current democratic decision making systems satisfy these requirements for better collective decision making. We have two decision making processes to consider in our democracies. Firstly, our decisions during elections in order to populate our parliaments. And secondly our decisions made inside of parliaments to vote upon laws. Both shall be considered for each of the above requirements. We shall not be too concerned with the degree of satisfaction of the criteria. These are broad brushstrokes and once the criteria are not satisfied in some material way, then there will inevitably be issues.

Let us first consider the requirement to be decentralized. We can easily satisfy the decentralization criteria for our process of elections since voters come from all over a given country. Inside of parliament it would also be expected that in most democracies the houses of parliament would be a decentralized representation of the people since politicians are elected from all over the nation as well. Our democracies are designed in this way. Decentralization is generally satisfied.

There is a different story for the independence of decision makers. As we have seen elsewhere many people always vote for the same political party.

155

These voters, often reported to be up to 60% overall, invariably support the same political parties every time. Although the membership of political parties has declined, the inclination to vote for the same party remains. There are also difficulties when it comes to bloc voting groups who definitely exert influence upon each other. As well, it does seem significantly more difficult for our parliamentary voting system to satisfy any criterion of independence. Almost by definition, the elected delegates are related to each other by party. Within parties there will be an assumption that delegates will actively influence each other. There are also factions and groupings inside political parties. Politicians will also work together to support their leaders. Parliamentarians will certainly be able to influence each other's voting intentions, especially in the Westminster system of government where party members are mandated to vote along party lines. It is then impossible for a group of parliamentarians to satisfy the criteria of independence when voting. Our independence criterion is not satisfied.

On diversity, again this is a difficult criterion to satisfy within democracies. In the voting population for elections there should be a diversity of opinions, although those opinions may be influenced somewhat by, for example, the media and political parties. Without getting too pedantic, for elections, diversity should generally be satisfied across a whole population, within some limits. Elected parliamentarians on the other hand are generally formed from within political parties. By definition then, this means that they all hold many similar views and positions - which are the basis of the parties. Our representative form of democracy generally leads to unrepresentative politicians because of this party structure. Although there are a number of parties within the elected parliament with one side of politics invariably holding the balance of power, many opinions will be suppressed with every vote. Each party is not diverse internally. This is not the ideal of a collective decision making process and diversity is not satisfied.

Next, let us look at the requirement for effective aggregation. We have seen elsewhere that there are problems with the aggregation of votes both in how we elect candidates and where a majority must be formed to pass new laws. There are many systems and approaches to the elections of parliamentarians. Aggregation of the people's will – especially where electing parliamentarians, is not as simple as would be hoped. In the same way our

156

aggregation options inside of parliament also present some difficulties within the party structures. The reality of the aggregation options that we currently use in democracy is that they all have their own weaknesses and imperfections. They do create a combined view that in some ways represents the view of the people. It could be said however, that we can only partially satisfy the aggregation criterion.

Thus, our democratic processes do not include a diverse and independent group of people and aggregation of votes does create some difficulties. Our criteria for consensus decision making are not fulfilled. The degree by which we miss the requirements is less important than the fact that it is missed. Without diversity and independence in the collective decision making of our current democracies we will inevitably produce poor decision making. This should not seem a surprise, we have already seen this in the many examples of problems presented so far. The key here, however, is to ensure that any replacement decision making system includes these four essential criteria and will then be able to make better collective decisions.

Deciding upon change, a sensible process

"To improve is to change; to be perfect is to change often" - *Winston Churchill*

Up until now we have listed the many issues and problems within our existing democratic process that invariably produce poor decisions for our society. We've also considered a range of requirements that would inevitably produce better decision making, and that would certainly avoid many of the mistakes of the past. It is time to put this all together into a sensible process for deciding upon change. This new set of requirements and qualities of the decision making process are designed specifically to produce better collective decisions. This new "Deciding upon Change" process, listed below, will then be incorporated into the democratic process itself.

We start with a summary of the essential requirements in our decision making process to ensure that it is best practice. These qualities must be included in any implementation of a *Deciding upon change* process. The qualities are a sensible combination of the things that we have considered so far. The qualities of the process are then followed by a simple decision making criteria that is essential for producing the right decisions.

Deciding upon change

Qualities of the process

- Decision making must be free of conflicts of interest and misaligned incentives. It should not be possible for a decision maker to directly benefit from the results of their decisions more so than any other person
- Decision making should be free of any influence other than the relevant contributing information – it should not be possible for individuals and groups to adversely influence those that make decisions

- Those involved in decision making must be capable of applying the right time and diligence to the process
- Those involved in decision making must be presented with all sides of the debate with both the evidence and the reasoning being independently verified
- Those involved in decision making must be open minded and educated in effective decision making skills
- Any collective decision making group must be large, diverse, independent, decentralized and equipped with a fair and reasonable process for aggregating the collective opinions into an overall decision

Decision criteria

A worthwhile change satisfies the following:
- The proposed change is enough of an improvement on the status quo that it justifies the costs and risks of making the change itself
- The proposed change is the best available option for dealing with or removing the root cause or causes of the critical issues or problems

This process does not make our decisions for us. Instead, the *Deciding upon change* process makes it significantly more likely that we will get to the right answers.

At the end of the day the vast majority of our decisions do remain subjective. It will still be up to individuals to make the tough calls and this is difficult. What we add with our criteria is help in clarifying the issues and the process, while removing the things that get in the way of good decision making. Importantly we will be able to avoid many of the mistakes and pitfalls of the past where many of these criteria have not been properly considered.

Critical criteria here are what can be summarised as, well informed and well considered decision making. Well informed means that we have removed the misinformation and irrelevant information from our considerations and have only included relevant facts. Well considered means that we have taken the time to remove any false or manipulative reasoning or thoughts from our process, while ensuring that our thinking is reasonable. Any process that we follow needs to be constructed to be well informed and well considered.

159

Our new democratic process will include this Deciding Upon Change criteria to ensure that our democratic decision making is substantially improved.

Let's quickly look at our examples - our "Ons" if you will, with regard to decision making. We can use these as a simple vetting of our process, to demonstrate that it can produce better results. So, we shall consider if these difficult decisions would have been likely improved if our decision making criteria and process had been applied. We won't go through the whole decision making process for each, but rather, highlight how the decisions would have been improved in these cases.

On global conflict(soviet submarine), On political assertions (drug related crime), On 37th place (Texas incentives), On CIA assessments (government overruling the CIA), On the Battle of Britain (aircraft damage), On AIDS in South Africa, On pharmaceuticals (Bad Pharma), On the Space Shuttle Disasters (it has worked in the past), On ulcers (antibiotic solution), On the Rogers Commission (management risk assessments), On air safety (pilot incentives), On ratings agencies (AAA rating for junk), On investment banks (short-term staff incentives)

For these past situations, even simply asking the above questions themselves would have helped with the issues. Specifically requiring a vetting of the facts and a comparison of the benefits and costs/risks before and after a change – as a part of the decision making process, would force the consideration of problems that may not have been analysed. For each of the issues presented at least one of our criteria would have helped to get to a better decision and outcomes. If each is considered in turn, then it can be seen that one aspect of the criteria would have helped with the decision making required. For example, this is seen for independent verification and fact checking for "On 37th place", for "On AIDS in South Africa" and "On CIA assessments", for a lack of conflicts of interest for "On air safety", for alignment of incentives for "On investment banks", and for "On ratings agencies".

One of the key issues with many of these problems is that even if we know the right process it can be difficult in our current democratic system to ensure that the process is followed by our political leaders. So, our new democratic process will need to deal with this risk. It must involve a range of checks and balances to ensure that we are required to apply a thorough process in all of our government decision making.

Note that many of the qualities and processes described here will allow our decision makers to more effectively deal with complexity. If decisions makers have the time available, if they have vetted evidence and reason available, if they are better educated in decision making skills, and if they use the decision making criteria, then they will be more able to deal with complex issues. We have not yet specifically dealt with the issues relating to the difficulties of dealing with complex decisions in our democratic process and our government. Also, as a society, we could certainly do more to improve the relationship between government and science. But this will be possible after we first improve our democratic process. Once the democratic decision making process is improved then it will be possible to implement a better relationship between government decision makers and science (and to complexity in general).

Some changes proposed so far

"We cannot solve our problems with the same thinking we used when we created them" - Albert Einstein

There have been many people who have analysed democracy over the years looking for a range of improvements to our process of representative democracy. A great deal of analysis has been done on many ways to improve the current process. It would be remiss not to consider these proposals as well and to evaluate them according to our change criteria. Those that have been found are listed below.

We'll consider each of them in turn to discuss what benefits they would give and then do a quick evaluation against our change criteria above. Note that we will not delve into all of the details of our *Deciding upon change* process, but rather just highlight the key considerations. For most suggested changes although there may be some benefit the underlying issue remains unresolved.

Abolition of anonymous political donations, improving political donation transparency
Limits on political contributions, both for individuals and for corporations and groups
Limits on campaign finance contributions
Limits on campaign finance spending
Government funded elections through an automated process (and potentially political parties)

We group the first proposals together for simplicity. Clearly these proposals will each give some benefit as they will both limit the ability of individuals and groups to influence politicians financially, as well as to potentially allow better scrutiny to monitor for influence. They may however, also mean that more time must be spent by politicians on fund raising as we have seen in the US after similar changes. A situation where politicians spend a large portion of their time fund raising is far from ideal. Government funding of elections and political parties would certainly remove a range of issues with the process, assuming that there was a fair system defined for allocating funds between parties. Certainly, bypassing the problem of funding through a direct government funding approach would avoid many issues.

Unfortunately, the proposals will still allow for the possibility of the influence upon politicians. Special interest groups could still supplement the funding – if government funding was selected. They could still advertise directly to the electorate and run social media campaigns, as they do now. Also, the value of seeking influence (financial or otherwise) will still remain, and hence the incentive to influence will still be strong. Hence, smart people, with powerful incentives to do so, will still work out ways to circumvent any changes made. It would be potentially better to remove the possibility of influence altogether, or at a minimum to remove the incentives. That is, to remove the potential advantages gained. It is possible then to conclude that although these changes may give some benefit, more change is required to deal with the root causes of all issues around election campaigns, politicians and funding. The options only at best, solve a part of the problem.

Limitations on politicians subsequently taking jobs with policy affected industries
There have already been a range of limitations proposed (and some imposed) on appointments of politicians to jobs where those same politicians have made previous critical financial decisions. Limitations such as time limits before politicians can become lobbyists or limits upon working in related industries. This process has been improved in many places. The limitations and restrictions have made it more difficult for this type of reward for political decisions to have a potential impact on the decision making process. The difficulty is in the number of ways that rewards for decisions can be made. People are smart and where motivated by large sums of money, will find a way to sidestep laws and restrictions even after they have been improved. Where known public figures are alone in charge of critical decisions there is always the potential for subtle forms of corruption as well as subtle forms of payback for support. When laws and rules have been tightened in the past, smart people have found ways around them. Again, although these proposals can potentially lessen the risk of political decisions,

163

they do not eliminate the risk. Rewards will inevitably be paid for supportive decisions until the possibility of corruption is removed completely.

Change to compulsory (or to non-compulsory) voting
Modifications to the proportional voting processes
Remove the electoral college voting system in the US presidential elections
Again, the pros and cons of the various methods of tallying and allocating votes to various politicians and political parties have already been discussed. At the end of the day as many democracies have experienced, none of the systems are ideal. If there had been a system which dealt with the many limitations of the election process, then you would hope that that system would have been implemented widely. This of course, has not happened. Each of the potential changes proposed have their own limitations. Any system where often disinterested, busy and uninformed people have to vote for strangers, who then make critical and significant decisions on their behalf, is prone to problems. Inevitably, in any electoral system in our current form of representative democracy it is very difficult to avoid many of the aforementioned limitations.

Senate number variations – more fair representation across states and populations
Implementing a fairer system of allocating the number of senators per state which also depends on each state's population size would certainly improve our representative democracy. There could be difficulties of some states then being ruled by the more populated states, but this issue already exists again and again for many minority groups in representative democracy, so would not seem catastrophic. Protecting the rights of minorities, include geographic minorities, would seem more of a constitutional responsibility. There are certainly potential benefits from this change.

Fix electoral boundary allocation rules, remove political control
This option where not already done, would clearly improve the electoral process. Removing the power to control electoral boundaries from politicians has little downside and much upside. In some states in the US the system has already been changed to take the electoral boundary allocation out of the politician's hands. In many countries politicians already have no control over

electoral boundaries. It seems eminently sensible to have an independent body in control of electoral boundaries. As mentioned elsewhere, it seems quite indicative of the problems within our democratic process that such a basic flaw in the electoral process should take so long to fix.

Increase people's interest in democracy. Re-engagement of citizens. E.g., internet activism campaigns

Many options have been proposed for this, to increase awareness and engagement of the voting public. A number of these activist campaigns have already been tried globally. Increasing awareness and engagement would clearly be good for the overall process as the voting public would be able to make more informed decisions. The difficulty faced is to maintain the interest of the voting public. This would require a continuous effort and may have severe difficulty in succeeding. It would seem to be up against an ever increasing tide of disinterest and cynicism. After all, as society becomes more stable and democracy brings more success the irony is that the disinterest potentially becomes more prevalent. And where people have become disinterested in democracy it would be expected that they would also soon become disinterested in any new campaign to increase democratic participation as well. Any campaign to improve people's disinterest will fail unless it can deal with the causes of that disinterest, which would be extremely difficult. Politics matters little to normal people especially when compared to their everyday lives, family, work and interests. At the same time, the limitation is not just the people's lack of interest, it is the need for people's time as well so that they can sensibly and thoroughly consider the options available. People will inevitably continue to have busy lives and the time spent on politics will inevitably be limited.

Changes to media laws to promote and enforce balance

Improving the quality of the media coverage of elections could only really be a good thing for the democratic process. Ensuring that policies and politicians are presented to the public fairly and clearly is essential for the running of a democracy. And yet, with the media run by private companies this can be difficult to enforce. Balance has shown difficult to measure and even more difficult to enforce. Even if the major media outlets could be mandated for some level of balance there is always the possibility for smaller companies and new media communication types to circumvent controls. Like for other controls in society, where intelligent and determined people have an incentive to influence any controls put in place around the media will be able to be worked around in due course. Although maintaining a balanced media may be both desirable and beneficial, while incentives exist to gain advantage through the influence upon voters, problems will continue. Again, under the existing democratic process it is hard to remove the root cause, which is the ability to gain advantage through the influence of the media. So, the catch up through any system of controls while potentially beneficial, cannot truly deal with the root cause.

Have non-partisan committees deal with difficult policy areas, and produce a single unmodifiable policy proposal, which is voted either up or down
This option has been used in the US on number of occasions to deal with the political gridlock and bypass any conflicts of interest of politicians. It is based on a similar acknowledgement that partisan politics, conflicts of interest and special interest groups' control can get in the way of real policy implementation. It would actually seem a significantly better system to have a smaller group of people in charge of critical decisions and somehow avoid some of the politics. Yet politics will remain since the group is still composed of politicians and there will still be compromises and deals done. Although potentially of benefit the root causes of many issues remain.

Make more government departments run and manage areas of government - independently of government, for example environment, healthcare, tax - Alan Blinder, a Princeton professor's essay in Foreign Affairs magazine in 1997
This proposal would give more autonomy to many government departments to run independently. It does deal with some of the causal issues in our political system. Some of the politics of decision making is removed – this proposal basically decreases the responsibilities of the legislature and delegates more decisions to the public service. However, the head of the executive government will still be a political appointment and is still potentially aligned to the government and will have the same political zeal. There is also the possibility of major mistakes by the public servants and executive government leadership. Just like those of Alan Greenspan as

discussed earlier. It does seem like a quite potentially beneficial option if it is incorporated with a more comprehensive governance framework, which will be a part of our proposal.

A movement towards a unicameral system to avoid legislative deadlock (have only one legislative assembly/house of parliament)
This would certainly simplify the democratic decision making process. Many issues would remain but generally it could free up the decision making process. The downside is that it frees up the process to allow political and partisan zealots to more easily implement their one sided politics. It also increases the risk of populist policies slipping through the electoral process.

Epistocracy - only allowing those with a certain level of knowledge to vote in elections
In this system, at the ballot box, voters are given a questionnaire to test their knowledge, along with the ballot papers. Only those votes whose voters demonstrate the required knowledge will count. This option does potentially violate our criteria for an inclusive democratic state. Although in some ways, if you do give all people an *option* to freely and easily gain the required knowledge to participate in elections, then theoretically all citizens can still choose to participate in the democratic process. Yet the potential with this option is that the apathetic majority may be less likely to participate and so any results would no longer be a good representation of the people. There have been a range of statistical checks and balances proposed for this process to ensure inclusion of all demographics. The solution presents potential benefits (that of less voting in ignorance) as well as some risks. However, this option deals with only some issues with the process of elections and still leaves many of the other issues and certainly their root causes, unresolved.

Deliberative democracy, Participatory democracy, Sortition
There are in fact a range of theoretical models for a democratic system. In investigation of these models, there seems to be less consensus about how they would work in practice. Although it seems obvious that many of the qualities of these models deliver significant value, finding one which would work as a complete solution has proven difficult. Irrespective, many of the better features of these models will be included in our aggregated system for

167

the new democratic process. The solution presented, Governed Democracy, will be a more practical solution which is specifically aimed at solving virtually all of the identified problems within our current democratic process.

Overall, many of these above options will definitely improve the democratic system and will be measurably better than current implementation choices in our existing democracies. So, in the absence of any alternatives, for many democracies these are valuable changes to the status quo. Most of the changes that have been proposed however are not sufficient to get to the heart of the real problems. Many of the changes may have short-term positive effects but because they don't remove or fundamentally change the true incentives or causes, then after any changes, ingenious people will work out better ways to manipulate the system to their own advantage. This has happened in the past and it will happen again in the future. We cannot suddenly hope or expect for the human race to develop a collective level of integrity that stops them finding effective ways to manipulate the system to their own benefit. It is an extremely strong imperative in our human makeup to work towards what is best for yourself and for your family. Instead, we need a solution that fundamentally bypasses or removes the root causes of our problems with democracy. We will however combine some of the elements of the above options with the decision making criteria already defined. In this way we can build a more effective and more complete democratic process.

What works well in our democracy

Our current democratic states have fundamentally changed the living standards of billions of people who have been lucky enough to live in the right countries. Those democracies have followed a range of different paths. To demonstrate key features and potential success factors we'll group these democracies into broad categories. While these groupings may not be perfect, the broad categories will help us to discern which components are more likely to lead to an ongoing and successful democratic state.

Original western

Initial democratic societies in the west were the first to achieve modern democratic statehood. This includes countries like the US, Great Britain, France, the Netherlands, Norway, Iceland and Switzerland. These states have gradually, over hundreds of years, moved from a government controlled by a rich and select subset of all citizens, into states where all citizens can contribute to the democratic process. Initially, they contained many of the features of constitutional liberalism including a strong public service to support the population and gradually moved towards a fully inclusive democratic state.

Autocratic conversions

A subset of democracies began as autocratic states. Over several decades individual liberties gradually increased and this led to constitutional liberalism. New legal rights were given to citizens including freedom of speech and religious association, greater economic freedoms and the allowance of opposition parties. Eventually democratic elections were held, and power was handed over from autocrats to democratically elected leaders. These states include Greece, Spain, Brazil, Chile, South Korea, Taiwan, Thailand, Singapore and Malaysia. This gradual move from autocracy to democracy has actually led to some quite successful and affluent states, the process of which has also led in some cases to an astonishing leap forward in standard of living, economic success, education levels and life expectancy. In some ways the growth for many of these nations, from developing world nations to successful economic nations, has eclipsed the advances that have been made through democracy in the developing world.

British colonials

Another group includes the ex-British rule democracies including those of India, Canada, New Zealand, Australia, West Indies, Egypt, South Africa, Qatar and Bahrain. Although being an ex-British colony is the defining feature of this group, there was another common quality. According to Fareed Zakaria, "British rule meant not democracy - colonialism is almost by definition undemocratic - but limited constitutional liberalism and capitalism".

French colonials

An alternate group of previously colonized countries were those that were handed over from French colonialism. The overwhelming majority of these nations did not recover well from the handover to self-rule. Chaos struck many which included famine, civil war and the failure of the government itself. Again, from Fareed Zakaria, "France, by contrast, encouraged little constitutionalism or free markets in its occupied lands, but it did enfranchise some of its colonial populations in northern Africa. Early democratization in all those cases led to tyranny".

Non liberal

Another grouping is those that moved towards democracy without many of the features of constitutional liberalism. The new democratic government may still control the people's freedom of expression including the media, it may still control the judiciary and the courts, and may infringe upon the basic rights of citizens. In many circumstances for these states there have been claims of significant electoral fraud and the constitutional rules have been circumvented. This type of democracy includes Russia, Venezuela, Ukraine, Argentina, Bangladesh, Thailand and Cambodia.

170

Collapsed democracies

These nations started out as democratic states but then at least temporarily, collapsed into tyranny. These are nations such as Germany, Spain, Portugal and Italy. Generally, the collapses into tyranny were facilitated through violence and subterfuge. After a period of totalitarian rule (or war), they then transitioned again back into democratic states.

Let's first consider the groups of democratic states that transitioned from colonial rule into democratic states. It has been noted by a number of researchers that the result of colonial rule has been quite different for the countries ruled by different states. That is, for those countries ruled by the British the transition to democratic self-rule was generally successful, but for those ruled by the French the transition to democratic self-rule did not work so well. Virtually all of the ex-French colonies ended in civil war, chaos or starvation. As political scientist Myron Weiner stated, "every single country in the Third World that emerged from colonial rule since the Second World War with a population of at least one million (and almost all the smaller colonies as well) with a continuous democratic experience is a former British colony". The difference between the two results has been said to be based on the differing focus of the two colonial rulers. The British focused on setting up public service institutions and the basics of constitutional liberalism, which allowed the former colonies to transition to self-rule more seamlessly. Under French rule there was little focus on setting up constitutional liberalism or the many public service institutions which defend and implement those rights. Instead, there was more of a focus on extracting resources, which only required the creation of private enterprise and some basic infrastructure. The stability of the resultant democracies was starkly different.

In the autocratic states representative democracy emerged last as the nation matured. In most of western Europe and the US, the democratic states emerged over a period of centuries where gradually people's rights increased over time and more and more people were included in the voting process. At first, the electorate consisted of just the rich and gradually this voting class expanded to include more and more people, including eventually, the working classes, the last groups to attain full rights as citizens (ex-immigrants, indigenous peoples or even slaves), and women. Although a

171

fully inclusive representative democracy did come later, this was generally after the implementation of constitutional liberalism.

A range of analysis has been done on the parts of democracy which has correlated with a successful and long standing government. Amongst each of the successful groupings above, there was a single underlying consistency. Those states that contained the features of constitutional liberalism generally succeeded. Generally, most of the nations that failed did not contain the features of constitutional liberalism. This is certainly the pattern in our simple categorizations above. This indicates that constitutional liberalism itself may well contribute to success. This already makes sense to many since in western democracies the value of these principles has been learnt. It is interesting and indicative to see it play out in experience. Constitutionalism liberalism does seem to be one key difference between the former colonial states of Britain and France. Where this has been absent in recent democratic states the failure rate has been high. In the first western democracies which have had a high success rate, constitutional liberalism was often instituted even before voting rights for the entire population.

There has also been a call from some, after the seeming failure of the so called Arab Spring, that although these states were supported to seek democracy, they have done this in the wrong order. It is difficult for them to succeed if they start with elections before they have constitutional liberalism. After all, ironically, there is no correlation between representative democracy and successful outcomes. Many states have had representative democracy and have failed. In fact, the original western democracies did not actually contain full representative democracy until the 20th Century, well after they obtained constitutional liberalism. It took centuries to allow all of their citizens to vote. The Arab Spring nations may well be another example of the lack of correlation between representative democracy and success as many of these nations have faced significant difficulties after democratic elections. Now some may say that even though representative democracy does not correlate to success, "well run" representative democracy would correlate to success. But clearly, in and of itself, representative democracy does not correlate to success and hence it cannot cause success. From the overall experience of the nations that we have seen, the "well run" aspect is significantly more likely to be the constitutional liberalism component.

There are exceptions. In the collapsed democracies grouping above there was a form of constitutional liberalism. The decline of these democracies often began through a process of the legislative removal of controls. In those fallen states, a key failure was that of the separation of powers. An elected leader was able to gradually increase his control over all three arms of government and hence turn the state into an autocracy. These democratic failures of state would seem based on an imperfect implementation of constitutional liberalism, more so than problems with constitutional liberalism itself. These states then serve to remind us of the importance of shoring up the separation of powers in our democracy to significantly reduce the risk of this collapse. Of note here also is that the same weaknesses in the separation of powers that existed in states like Nazi Germany, continue to largely exist in modern democracies to this day. We still effectively allow both individuals and groups to control both the legislative and executive arms of government.

In the judicial branch of government, Justices can currently be appointed by a process involving the head of state, the parliament and in some cases by independent commissions set up specifically for judicial appointments. Of these options, an independent commission for appointments ensures there is a significantly greater chance that the legislative and judicial arms are themselves independent. Appointing the judiciary independently of the legislative assembly has significantly less scope for undue influence. This process works reasonably well in a number of democratic states around the world.

It does then seem reasonable to conclude that constitutional liberalism is an important component for any democratic process. We also note that independence of each of the arms of government is important, and that an independent appointment process for the judiciary has worked well.

What works less well in our democracy

"Zhang Weiwei of Fudan University argues that democracy is destroying the West, and particularly America, because it institutionalizes gridlock, trivializes decision making and throws up second-rate presidents like George Bush junior. Yu Keping of Beijing University argues that democracy makes simple things 'overly complicated and frivolous' and allows 'certain sweet-talking politicians to mislead the people'. Wang Jisi, also of Beijing University, has observed that 'many developing countries that have introduced Western values and political systems are experiencing disorder and chaos' and that China offers an alternative model. Countries from Africa (Rwanda) to the Middle East (Dubai) to South-East Asia (Vietnam) are taking this advice seriously" - Quote from the essay "What's gone wrong with democracy" in The Economist

On sports governance

The International Olympic Committee (IOC) was created in 1894. It is responsible for the running the modern Olympics and for deciding which cities are entrusted to host each Olympic Games every four years. It consists of up to 115 members from various groups including current athletes, international sporting federations, national Olympic committees and up to 70 unaffiliated members. It is the supreme authority of the modern Olympics. The President of the IOC can choose the IOC members. Cities bid for the right to hold each Olympic Games which can bring billions of dollars in potential revenue for a hosting nation and city. An election process from the IOC committee members decides on the successful city. In many ways the governance process is similar to the decision making structure in many representative democracies – a small group of appointed representatives make decisions on behalf of all that can have substantial financial implications for some. Governing members from representative countries are selected by an elected President, with the members then voting upon key decisions. The IOC has many similar advantages and disadvantages to representative democracy. Every four years, as few as 58 individuals can

174

decide which city will win the bid to host the next Olympic games and potentially reap billions of dollars in investments and benefits.

Over the years opportunities for graft and corruption have arisen. With enormous sums of money at stake and only a few publicly known individuals who control the process, power is quite concentrated, and corruption is rife. There is quite significant evidence of corruption as well as the purchase of influence over many decades of the Olympics. For the US Salt Lake City Winter Olympic Games, millions of dollars were spent on entertainment, bribes, scholarships, real estate deals and jobs in order to win the event. After the games ten IOC members were removed or resigned, and ten others were reprimanded. Two of the leaders who ran the Salt Lake City bid were prosecuted for bribery and fraud. Generally, it is not uncommon for bidding cities to ensure IOC members are lavished with entertainment and gifts - the successful Japanese city of Nagano spent over $US 4.4m on entertainment. The IOC candidates from smaller, poorer and less developed nations have been significantly more likely to be influenced by financial incentives. Even though there have been apparent crackdowns on corruption in recent times independent investigations have subsequently claimed that IOC votes are still available for purchase.

Similarly, with FIFA, the world governing body of soccer, the location of the World Cup is determined by a vote of FIFA's executive committee. Hosting a World Cup means that billions of dollars of revenue can feed into that nation's economy. Before the 2010 World Cup hosting vote one member of FIFA's executive committee was caught in a sting asking for $US 800,000 as a bribe to secure his vote. With another member of the committee also having been suspended for alleged bribes, the December 2010 vote only required 12 votes for success. The billion dollar outcome was then decided by the vote of 24 publicly known members of the executive committee. Over the years there have been consistent and significant allegations of bribery and corruption of the executive committee. In 2015, dozens of officials were arrested after Swiss and FBI investigations into corruption involving hundreds of millions of dollars in bribes. In the same year, IOC head Sepp Blatter was sacked after a 17-year reign, following a corruption scandal.

The people may have changed but the potential for corruption remains. Any member country who rocks the boat, by publicly calling out the bribery or by calling for change, risks losing the support of the committee in future bids. So, though the incentives for corruption are huge, the system remains.

Where there are a small group of publicly known individuals who, based on their own personal preferences, decide outcomes worth billions, the temptation for corruption is enormous. Where other people have a significant financial interest in the outcome, an interested individual or group can then spend a portion of their potential gains to influence those known decision makers. Over the years there is an ongoing incentive for corruption. The decision making processes of the global sporting bodies are directly relevant to our democratic processes because they both include the same incentives and decision making structures. With the system designed in this fashion it would seem reasonable to expect that there will be problems regularly.

To work out which parts of our democracy are worth improving we will revisit the root causes of the many problems that have been described so far. These root causes have been broadly grouped into: decision making, politicians, political parties and elections. Of course, there are some overlaps. The important thing to note is that they almost all fall somewhere within one of these categories and not somewhere else. The groups nonetheless demonstrate which areas of our democratic implementations produce core problems. The remaining cause which cannot be listed within one of the categories is listed at the end.

1) Decision making

    It is possible to gain benefits from political influence
    Political agreements inherently involve compromises and deals
    Freedom of speech can be abused and have influence in
    representative democracy
    Public debate is invariably not sensible and rational
    Policy initiation by voters can be too difficult and results can be slow

An imperfect and conflicted media can influence elections and policy outcomes

of Deciding the best policies through the engagement of millions of citizens and the election of politicians to parliament, who then vote on voters' behalf, involves enormous expense of time and money and is potentially inefficient and ineffectual

2) Politicians

Incentives to attract legislators are misaligned
Legislators' decision making is complicated by other issues and consequences
Legislators incentives (for success) are misaligned
Politics is difficult and unrewarding for legislators and their families
Leadership is a single point of failure and corruptible power, with little governance
Legislators' beliefs and policies may not be the same as those that elected them
New policies generally require general popularity before approval, and this can take many years

3) Political parties

The funding of politics is difficult and causes conflicts
Political parties are imperfect representations of voters

4) Elections

Policies are grouped together for elections
We vote for people we don't really know (voting for strangers)
Voters lives are more important to them than politics
Voters can be selfish
Voters are busy, so can lack knowledge and can be misinformed
Aggregating voter preferences to elect legislators/parties is an imperfect process
We must vote for legislators and policies at the same time
Political advantage can be gained through violence
The many can rule the few unfairly

Policies can swing inefficiently and ineffectively as governments change
Election promises are easily broken and can hold negative consequences
Promises must be made in advance of decision time

Other problem areas
Weaknesses exist in the separation of powers

Firstly, let's note that the majority of our issues are within our implementation choices for representative democracy. Most of them are problems associated with politicians or political parties or with the running of elections. The root causes are contained within these requirements and processes.

Another key difficulty is that of weaknesses in the separation of powers of the three arms of government. Where one person or political group can effectively control more than one arm of government there are significant risks. This can lead to corruption and poor choices in government or in a worst case, this can even lead to the failure of a democratic state. A lack of an effective governance process over imperfect individuals can make this worse. Where a single person or party can hold unchecked power, there is a potential for poor decision making in government.

So, the causes of problems involve either our implementation choices around having elections or the need for politicians and political parties. There are also problems with our decision making and a lack of separation of powers.

Each of these will be addressed in turn. We can now begin to replace some of the implementation choices of democracy, while delivering the same functions within the same essential structure. We can strengthen the separation of powers, implement a better governance framework, and implement a better collective decision making process. In the next sections we will start to see the details of the new democratic process.

The functions of democratic government

"Although political scientists have disagreed on some of the details of defining and measuring democracy...the eight criteria proposed by Robert A. Dahl...still command widespread support: (1) the right to vote, (2) the right to be elected, (3) the right of political leaders to compete for support and votes, (4) elections that are free and fair, (5) freedom of association, (6) freedom of expression, (7) alternative sources of information, and (8) institutions for making public policies depend on votes and other expressions of preference. These requirements are already implied by Lincoln's simple definition of democracy as government by the people (or by representatives of the people) and for the people." - Arend Lijphart, PhD, Yale University, from Patterns of Democracy

We need to look at the detail of our existing democratic governments as any new democratic system must deliver the same functions. We can see an example of a current definition in the quote from Robert A. Dahl. This definition fairly well defines societies' understanding of our existing democratic process. Our aim in this section is not to define our democratic system, but for an overview of its critical functions. Some aspect of the definition given by Robert A. Dahl will be discussed in the next chapter on constitutional liberalism, to highlight and separate the essential components of our democratic system. Our goal here is to describe the functions first here, and then separately describe the qualities of our democracy. The functions define what our democracy does, the qualities define the features of our democratic process that make it acceptable to us. For example, something like "freedom of expression", will be included as a quality of democracy, whereas "holding elections" is considered a function of democracy. This section will focus specifically on the functions of democracy.

Each democracy is assumed to include a constitution and an ability to change that constitution through a well-defined process. For each of the three arms of government - legislative (parliaments and the approval of law), executive (running the government) and judicial (the courts), we'll present the basic functions. These functions can then be analysed with respect to the underlying problems.

The three major arms of government, legislative, executive and judicial, will each be considered specifically.

Democratic functions

Legislative - To manage the laws of the nation. This includes the following:
- Vet ideas for changes to laws or to the constitution
- Propose and prioritize those ideas for change
- Formally construct each new law
- Present a case for the new change
- Collectively decide whether to proceed with changes to the law
- Collectively decide whether to proceed with constitutional changes
- Appoint individuals to run areas of the executive arm of government
- Appoint (or approve) justices to the supreme/high courts (note that in some democracies, this is part of the executive arm of government)

Executive - To enforce the laws of the nation, including the management of the administration of the laws of the nation and the public services.
- Appoint members of the legislative assembly
- Implement any laws approved.
- Run the executive arm of government
- Appoint justices to the supreme/high courts (in some democracies, this is part of the legislative arm of government)

Judicial - to adjudicate and interpret the laws of the nation.
- Adjudicate on constitutionality of new laws
- Adjudicate on citizens and corporations under the law

Note that we have removed any implementation choices from the above. Essentially, we have separated "the what" from "the how". For example, we have stated "Appoint members of the legislative assembly", without

180

necessarily saying how to do this - there are many ways of currently doing this in many democracies around the world. We have also said "Present a case for the new change", without saying how to present that case (or even who will do this). This allows us to replace those implementation choices later with new processes which deliver vastly more effectively.

To be clear, a requirement like the "defence of the realm", is assumed to be included in the function of running the executive arm of government - the appointed leader of the nation is implicitly responsible for this. These broad functions have been categorized here since the process of these functions is really all about decision making, including the prioritization and allocation of public service resources. Our executive leaders must manage the government to decide if something needs to change and if so to what, which has been described here as "Run the executive arm of government". This description is sufficient for our purposes.

There is a common set of core democratic processes which are largely consistent, certainly in the western styles of democratic system. We wish to investigate the common components of our democratic processes to find opportunities for improvement. Much of the discussion will be of the common processes - even where some implementation choices differ. Arend Lijphart studied the differing implementation choices in detail in the book *Patterns of Democracy*. He analysed 36 major democracies and documented the major areas of variation. He categorized a range of areas where they generally differed. The majority of the variations are in the legislative arm of government. Some can potentially be quite significant in their influence on the legislative process. Some can be a significant influence on the power of the arms of government. There are variations in how the head of government is appointed and dismissed. In some democracies, the head of government is elected from within the elected party members of the lower house of parliament (often called Prime Minister). For others, there is a process of direct election (Presidential style).

The executive arm of government can be selected in varying ways - by the Prime Minister from within the ranks of the elected political representatives (often called a cabinet), or directly by the President from outside the elected political groups. The powers and responsibilities of Prime Minister can also vary, with some favouring more power to a Prime Minister and some favouring power shared with a Prime Minister's cabinet. Variations in our democracies also affect the relative power between the legislative and executive arms of government.

Although there are many variations in the implementation of democracy, the variations indicate that the core components do generally remain the same and certainly implement the same functions listed above. The variations listed are around changes to the implementation choices for the processes of democracy. One of the reasons why there are so many different implementation choices across our representative democracies is that none are perfect. However, most of the variations deal with specific symptoms of the imperfections of our democratic system, rather than resolving the root causes of problems. As stated, our aim is to remove the root causes of problems with our democratic process, and then define a new process. Next, we'll move onto the qualities of our democratic process. By defining the ideal qualities of our democratic process, we will be able to find replacement processes that contain those qualities and hence deliver the best results.

Constitutional liberalism

The qualities of modern democracy are less about the things that are done and more about the defining characteristics that make democracy worthwhile and the best system that we know. They are the essence of most of the things contained in Robert A. Dahl's definition above. This is the concept of what has often been called constitutional liberalism, which is essentially a set of qualities of our western democracies. This involves a range of concepts that essentially assume the rule of law and the rights of individuals. Fareed Zakaria, in the book, *The Future of Freedom: Illiberal Democracy at Home and Abroad*, has described this well:

> Constitutional liberalism, on the other hand, is not about the procedures for selecting government but, rather, government's goals. It refers to the tradition, deep in Western history, that seeks to protect an individual's autonomy and dignity against coercion, whatever the source— state, church, or society. The term marries two closely connected ideas. It is liberal* because it draws on the philosophical strain, beginning with the Greeks and Romans, that emphasizes individual liberty. It is constitutional because it places the rule of law at the centre of politics. Constitutional liberalism developed in Western Europe and the United States as a defence of an individual's right to life and property and the freedoms of religion and speech. To secure these rights, it emphasized checks on the power of government, equality under the law, impartial courts and tribunals, and the separation of church and state. In almost all of its variants, constitutional liberalism argues that human beings have certain natural (or "inalienable") rights and that governments must accept a basic law, limiting its own powers, to secure them.

And further information about liberalism from Francis Fukuyama in *The End of History and the Last Man*:

Liberalism and democracy, while closely related, are separate concepts. Political liberalism can be defined simply as a rule of law that recognizes certain individual rights or freedoms from government control. While there can be a wide variety of definitions of fundamental rights, we will use the one contained in Lord Bryce's classic work on democracy, which limits them to three: civil rights, "the exemption from control of the citizen in respect of his person and property"; religious rights, "exemption from control in the expression of religious opinions and the practice of worship"; and what he calls political rights, "exemption from control in matters which do not so plainly affect the welfare of the whole community as to render control necessary," including the fundamental right of press freedom.

We've listed the key features contained in western democracies below - whether this is the strict definition that may have been applied to constitutional liberalism is not the major concern. In this way however, it will help with the construction of the new democratic process.

Constitutional liberalism

- Protection and equality under the law (by an independent judiciary) of the constitution, individual rights and liberties, property rights, corporate rights (e.g. patent rights). These rights include citizens' rights to participate in all democratic processes, e.g. decide upon legislators, participate in the government
- Freedom of speech (including of the press), freedom of expression, freedom of association and freedom of assembly
- Separation of the powers of church and state
- Independence and separation of powers of the three arms of government

The above features will be incorporated into our new democratic process.

The fourth democracy

" ...that this nation, under God, shall have a new birth of freedom, and that Government of the people, by the people, for the people, shall not perish from the Earth" - Abraham Lincoln

We have presented a long list of the problems with our democratic process as well as with the decision making within modern democracies. We've also seen that the problems with democracy and its decision making are inextricably linked to the current implementation of those democratic processes. To enable us find effective solutions to those problems, let us propose a new overview of the qualities and functions of our democratic system. By directly considering the essential qualities of our solutions, we can make sure that any solutions that we choose contain those qualities and hence deliver the best results. We will bring together our previous qualities and functions of democracy, our new requirements for a better collective decision making process, our requirements for an improved separation of powers as well as a governance of those powers.

So here, we propose the new form, a fourth democracy, which will build on the lessons of each of the preceding three democracies (Greek, Roman, Western), and will remove the ineffectual implementation choices from its functions. The name – the fourth democracy - is a convenience since it will be referred to repeatedly. Critically the fourth democracy will include the qualities that are both essential for democracy's success as well as being essential for it to make the right collective decisions. This fourth democracy brings together the most effective criteria from which we can build a vastly improved implementation of its key processes.

The fourth democracy is an extension of what was originally described in the American system. The essence of democracy was most eloquently captured by Abraham Lincoln with: "of the people, by the people, for the people". Although this phrase described more of the qualities of a democracy than an actual definition, it is an extremely useful starting point.

185

The fourth democracy - a government of the people, by the people, and for the people. That is, a government which is representative of all of its people, a government in which all from society can participate and a government which acts in the best interests of its people. Constitutional liberalism is included as a defining set of criteria. The processes of democracy will effectively define, decide on and uphold a set of laws. It will also run a set of government bodies for the effective management of its society and of its people. Responsibilities will include the protection of its citizens' basic rights as well as the support for and improvement of its citizens' well-being.

Constitutional liberalism is as follows:
- Protection and equality under the law (by an independent judiciary) of; the constitution, individual rights and liberties, property rights, corporate rights. These rights include citizens' rights to participate in all democratic processes.
- Freedom of speech (including of the press), freedom of expression, freedom of association and freedom of assembly
- Separation of the powers of church and state
- True separation of powers and independence of the three arms of government
- The power of individuals and groups is governed effectively

Our requirements for citizen involvement:
- All citizens can participate equally and are represented fairly
- All citizens can propose and contribute to legislation and policy
- All citizens can be involved in the prioritization of legislation and policy
- All citizens can be involved in the decision making process for legislation and policy
- All citizens can be involved in the decisions to choose the leadership within government

Qualities and requirements of the democratic process:
- Power is contained in the process itself and not in the hands of individuals or groups

- The process is protected by a sensible governance framework (including against populist policies)
- Policies, decisions and government appointments are decided independently, on their own merits
- Important new ideas can be identified, evaluated and prioritised quickly, effectively and efficiently
- The process produces the best and most representative members of the legislative, executive and judicial arms of government (and the best decisions from them)
- The process preserves and benefits from the lessons of the past
- The process efficiently and effectively determines the best and most representative will of the people
- A process which is free from all adverse influence including from
  - misaligned incentives
  - conflicts of interest
  - corruption
  - political manipulation
  - adversarial politics
  - deals
  - money
  - special interest groups
  - short term politics
  - policy promises
  - populism
  - career ambitions
  - the media
  - external governments
  - a largely disinterested and busy electorate
  - special rewards for political supporters
- Those involved in decision making must be capable of applying the right time and diligence to the process
- Those involved in decision making must be presented with all sides of the debate with both the evidence and the reasoning being independently verified
- Those involved in decision making must be open minded and educated in effective decision making skills

187

- Any collective decision making group must be large, diverse, independent, decentralized and equipped with a fair and reasonable process for aggregating collective opinions into an overall decision
- The imperfections of individual decision makers must be mitigated and governed

Democratic functions

Legislative arm
- Collectively decide whether to proceed with any changes to the law
- Collectively decide whether to proceed with any constitutional changes
- Appoint individuals to run areas of the executive arm of government
- Approve justices to the supreme/high courts

Executive arm
- Vet ideas for policy proposals and changes to laws and the constitution
- Propose and prioritize those ideas for change
- Formally construct each new law
- Present a case for the new change
- Appoint members of the legislative assembly
- Implement any laws approved
- Run the executive arms of government
- Appoint justices to the supreme/high courts

Judicial arm
- Adjudicate on constitutionality of new laws
- Adjudicate on citizens and corporations under the law

Note that we have included enhancements to constitutional liberalism to include both a true separation of powers and independence of the arms of government, as well as limits and governance on the powers of individuals and groups. These requirements arise directly from issues that have been experienced in our democracies. We have also moved some functions from the legislative branch to the executive branch (around prioritisation and analysis of new proposals/laws and changes).

If our democracy has the above qualities and functions, then it will be equipped to deliver the best possible decisions and outcomes for all of its citizens. We have the potential to avoid the pitfalls of the past, including virtually all of the issues that we experience virtually every day in democracies around the world. Critically, by including all of the above qualities we can be sure not just to define a better form of the democratic process, but rather we can get to the best form of the democratic process.

We will next bring together the lessons so far as well as deciding what can potentially change about our democratic processes. This will allow us to choose a new set of processes that will implement the fourth democracy requirements and deliver better outcomes for us all.

The lessons so far

We now have a description of both democratic functions as well as of the ideal qualities of the democratic process. This includes an effective and representative collective decision making process. We have removed the implementation choices from our description to enable us to replace the flawed choices in the current democratic process. We've described some features of our democratic process that generally seem, both from experience and from basic analysis, to lead to better and more stable democracies. In this section we will work out what can be learnt from putting this all together.

Representative democracy has been a key component of virtually every single democracy in the 20th century and yet many of these democracies have failed. If representative democracy itself led to great national outcomes we would expect a correlation between the two within our experiences of democracy. But the evidence is simply not there. There has been no correlation between representative democracies and successful long-term outcomes for those societies. Yes, many have succeeded very well and many also have failed. It is reasonable to conclude that representative democracy in its current form, does not directly lead to success for a given society. As mentioned previously, the better correlation to success has been the feature of constitutional liberalism. The data supports the success of democracies with constitutional liberalism and also it makes more sense to believe that the features of constitutional liberalism contribute to successful outcomes.

Filling our legislative assemblies through the process of elections is an implementation choice. It is also an implementation choice to have a permanent class of politicians who fill those legislative assemblies. Many of our current problems with democracy are issues within the process of elections, and within the requirement for a permanent class of politicians within political parties. The key here is that the problems are with the implementation choices, not with the functions required. The functions required for our democratic process do not inherently produce problems. For example, there is nothing implicitly wrong with a requirement to fill our legislative assemblies or to collectively decide upon laws. Our implementation choices however - to have largely busy, disinterested and often uninformed electorate vote for conflicted, corruptible and often unqualified strangers, and then have those elected politicians run our democracies, have produced many problems. Where we base our system of government on a popularity contest, voted upon by time-poor and disinterested people, we get neither the best politicians chosen, nor the best policies produced. We have seen the consequences already - poor policy choices, slow policy changes on critical issues, ongoing corruption and fraud, little long-term strategy, many poor short-term solutions and the negative influence from special interest groups, amongst many other issues. Complex issues are avoided, and voters have little time nor interest in policy decisions over which they have little power or control. The lack of separation of powers also creates an ongoing risk of power being subverted and the subsequent decline of democracy itself.

We also have the issue of the inefficiency of our existing representative democracies. Requiring many millions of people, and sometimes even hundreds of millions of people, to participate in the process of helping analyse and decide on our best policies and legislative assembly members, creates enormous overhead, cost and waste. The current process also ensures significant time delays for critical legislative and policy changes.

Our requirement for our democracy is for our government to be representative of all of its people, while allowing all to participate and have their say. If we can fully deliver our requirement for fair representation and participation in a more effective way – without requiring the direct participation of millions of disinterested and busy people, then we could achieve extraordinary savings in time and money, while improving the process itself.

A part of the design of representative democracy was to deal with the risk of runaway populism in government. It was assumed that elected leaders would be more capable of making the hard choices and avoiding populist policies. It was also a sensible way to practically enable collective decisions to be made, where it is impossible to expect all citizens to vote on every policy. The problems that representative democracy intends to deal with are quite real.

191

Yet although representative democracy attempts to deal with the right problems, as we have seen, it is clearly not the best solution to those problems.

We must find a better way, which delivers effective collective decision making while avoiding the risk of populist policies. Alternatives to these implementation choices must be considered. We will propose a way to fill our legislative assemblies without elections, political parties or politicians.

In our collective decision making the four requirements of diversity, independence, decentralization and aggregation must also be satisfied. These will give us the potential of making inclusive, informed and well considered decisions. Decisions that are both the preference of the nation as a whole and in the best interests of the nation as a whole.

We also want to deal with single points of failure. Decisions should not solely be dependent on the thoughts of a single person. Again, there are too many imperfections within us as human beings. However, when it comes to ruling in a crisis or emergency, having the decisiveness of a single leader can be advantageous. An individual leader can still be more effective and efficient in a range of circumstances. Which means that there are potential benefits as well as potential issues, the issue of a requirement for a single leader is quite debatable. And yet, a key aim of our new democratic process is to ensure that power is contained not within the hands of individuals or politicians, but rather that power is contained within the process itself. So, instead of removing power from individuals directly, we will then propose a simple governance framework which includes checks and balances on any individual leader's decision making and power.

We must ensure that the three arms of government are fully independent. There can be no common political parties or linkages between the executive and legislative arms, as there are now. Each arm of government must be appointed independently and must then execute their powers independently. The arms can and should work together, but not from a structure of predetermined relationships (of political parties). For example, an executive leader may request a legislative change to help improve her area of responsibility, but once this request is made the legislative assembly must run with the change independently. There can be no direct influence over the process by the executive leader who made the request, instead only participation. The executive leader would be one contributor to the process of legislative approval. This is an essential feature of effective government, to mitigate the single greatest democratic risk, that of degradation to despotism. With no individual or group able to control any more than one arm of government, there is little risk of a breakdown in the essential controls on our democratic process.

In the new legislative process decision makers must be free from the influence of any ineffectual incentives, conflicts of interest and special interest groups. We need a process where decisions can be made without fear of personal consequences. The system must also ensure that decision makers have the time, motivation and the capability to make informed and well considered decisions. Time for consideration is critical. Without being willing and able to spend the time to consider all options, we cannot hope for our decision makers to choose better solutions.

A key requirement is for our collective decision making to be well informed and well considered. In our democratic societies where free speech is assumed, this is potentially difficult. Any policy debate will inevitably include individuals and special interest groups fighting for their rights and beliefs, activists making a range of claims and the media presenting a selection of often unqualified views. Free speech means accepting sensible debate, along with statements and claims of nonsense. There is no way to reasonably stop this in modern society, it will always be the case that speech can be expressed without any reasonable limitations for truth or rationality. And yet we must find a way to ensure that any debate is fact checked and based on rational arguments, and that the people involved in deciding on our laws and policies consider the right information, to counter any possible misinformation. We cannot stop the noise of open debate, so instead we must include a system where, within reason, legislators have access to a reliable process which can vet information for factuality. We must be able to make sensible decisions without being unduly affected by the public discourse. It must be a system which faithfully can correct flaws of reason and which can call out manipulative arguments. We need a way to ensure that we present information and ideas in a way that both encourages and mandates balance.

For us to implement all of the above requirements, in Governed Democracy we will re-engineer and improve the following:

- The process to populate our legislative assemblies
- The individuals who participate in our legislative assemblies
- The appointment of the executive arm of government
- The process of debate upon policy and legislative change
- The governance and control of our executive leadership

Simply removing elections, politicians and political parties from the process entirely would seem a much more effective possibility than finding solutions to each and every one of the root causes within our long list of problems. We will remove almost all of those root causes at once by simply removing elections, politicians and political parties from the process. These processes do produce virtually all of the problems.

Any replacement processes can be sourced from known working solutions which already exist in our society. If we also enforce a true separation of powers and include an effective governance framework over the process, then we can actually deal with every single root cause of problems within our democratic process. All of which becomes Governed Democracy.

Governed Democracy

"That government is the strongest of which every man feels himself a part"
Thomas Jefferson, 3rd US President

"Politics ought to be the part-time profession of every citizen who would protect the rights and privileges of free men" - Dwight D. Eisenhower, 34th US President

We now have all of the criteria required to build our implementation of the fourth democracy. We have listed the set of functions that must be delivered by an improved democratic process. We have an idea of what processes must change to deliver a more effective democratic system. Plus, we have a detailed set of democratic qualities to be included, that will allow us to choose the best and most effective processes.

But before we go further, we will briefly mention some generic but essential qualities. Any effective process must be simple, efficient and practical. The more complicated our solution for the democratic process, the more likely it will be to introduce problems. So, we will aim for the simplest and most elegant solution that will allow us to collectively decide on changes and improvements, and that will also govern our democracies with minimal risk. An elegant simplicity of our democratic process is an important quality. We would also prefer a process that is fully transparent. These qualities will clearly lead to better democratic outcomes.

Note that each constitution will obviously need to change to reflect our proposed implementation choices. These constitutional changes however, albeit potentially significant, are beyond the scope here. They can be enshrined by constitutional experts.

Any proposals presented here for changes to our existing democratic processes are based on the re-use of working processes from within society. Nothing proposed is completely new, every process presented is based on the re-use of an existing, working model in society. A key benefit in choosing from existing processes is that our risk of change is minimised.

In our proposal there are many details that are open to debate, please do not be concerned with the low-level details, the purpose here is for a high-level design. For example, details like the sitting length for a legislative assembly, the number of members of governance panels, the size of a legislative assembly, voting percentages required for constitutional changes - these are all open to debate. The details of these however will not materially affect the benefits of the overall implementation. Although the choices below do seem the most sensible at this stage, these details can be debated and finalised afterwards. And of course, one benefit of our new democratic system will be that it can more easily change and grow as it matures.

Our new democratic system: Governed Democracy, will guide our democratic collective decision making process, while adding processes to help govern the leadership team more effectively (the term Guided Democracy was actually preferred, but already taken). Our aim here is to bring together a system which includes all of the qualities of the fourth democracy. Yet the collective decision making will still be free to choose its own path. The guiding hand will be the qualities and the processes that help to produce better decisions.

Governed Democracy moves away from a guaranteed right to vote in elections (of politicians), since elections and politicians will not exist. The essence remains that voting for conflicted, misaligned and often unqualified strangers, by a population of busy, disinterested and often uninformed voters, will be removed from the process. Instead, as citizens, we would have the new right to directly propose policy, and the greater right, although not a guarantee, for more people from the general populace to actually participate in the legislative assembly. As well as this, there will still be opportunities for participation in advocacy groups, which can directly propose changes and improvements to the democratic system. There will also be a range of other opportunities for people to contribute directly to the new processes, which will become clear soon. Governed Democracy will be more about having a range of opportunities for citizen participation, instead of allowing every single busy citizen the opportunity to tick a box and vote for strangers.

196

Each of the proposed changes presented here will be one piece in a larger set of changes which will together form the new democratic process. Each change will complement the other changes. The new implementation choices will combine to improve the overall democratic process and deliver our required democratic qualities, but they cannot make the process perfect. We cannot expect any process to be perfect, rather it must remove the underlying causes of our current problems and significantly improve the democratic outcomes for all in our society. Our process must have benefits that justify any cost and risk of change. And yet, we will also improve our governance to reduce the impact of both any imperfections as well as any human errors.

As we go through the presentation of Governed Democracy, we will consider a number of existing processes from within our society. These processes are used every day and are generally seen as effective. Like most things in life they are not without imperfections, there are opportunities for improvement within each which can be capitalised upon for our purposes. These existing processes will be used as building blocks for Governed Democracy. We will consider each of these in turn and consider their weaknesses as well as ways in which we can improve them when utilised.

Trials in our courts of law +
Juries of our peers (useful existing processes)
In our existing democratic societies, we already have a process for making difficult decisions and for vetting evidence and reason in a formalized process. We do this in our courts. Both sides of a case get to present evidence which is vetted by the court, with rules for that evidence, and rules for the presentation of arguments within the process. The decision makers in the courts (judges or jurors), must hear all evidence and reason presented from both sides of the case, and must then spend time in consideration of the cases heard.

The benefit of this process is that we have a way of vetting information and arguments, we can hear from qualified and independent experts, and all decision makers are mandated to hear both sides. There is an opportunity for all claims and arguments to be questioned and clarified or corrected. We also

197

require the decision makers to spend time in consideration of the merits of the case.

There are weaknesses of course. Judges, lawyers and juries can be imperfect. With only 12 jurors, determined individual jurors can potentially affect the decisions of others. Evidence and arguments can be ignored, prejudice can prevail. Sometimes, individual jurors can simply want to go home, and so will yield to the belligerence of others - there are some ineffectual incentives. As well, there is no guarantee that both sides of a case have access to the same resources for the trial or to the same quality of legal skills. In a trial of spoken arguments, lawyers may miss key opponent flaws of fact or reasoning in the moment. Even so, there is an appeal process which can mitigate some of these risks.

Of course, it is possible to deal with many of these issues. We could deliver equal resources and capabilities for both sides of a trial. We could eliminate the incentives that make quick decisions preferred for jurors. We could have a larger group of decision makers, which would reduce the impact of individual prejudices and imperfections (and follow the requirements of the Wisdom of Crowds). We could give each side enough time to assess and deal with any opposing facts and arguments. There are options to deliver a process even better than that of our courts. If this process is reused, it could be made to work much more effectively.

So, let us consider the debate process for policy and legislative change in our democratic process. Again, it seems astonishing that we require rules of evidence and reason in our courts of law but effectively have no such requirement when publicly and privately debating the laws of the land as a whole. There are some rules in parliamentary debates, but this is generally not where decisions are made. It would then seem sensible, without changing any aspect of our overall freedom of speech, to mandate some court-like controls over the whole legislative consideration process (and not just that of parliamentary debate). Public debate can continue unhindered as it is now. But when an issue is put forward for legislative consideration, we can mandate that cases be prepared for and against any legislative change - as happens in a court of law. Rules can be applied to the formal legislative process. If we prepare the cases for legislative change in advance of any time for consideration, then we have the opportunity to take the time to validate the information and ideas in each case. Unlike with our current live political debates, where the better salesperson or manipulator can win, if we take the time to prepare cases for and against, then we have the time to consider options sensibly. The rules would ensure a formalized presentation of all vetted evidence and reason for the consideration of all legislators. All public misperceptions and claims can be clearly corrected. This vetting process could produce a documented case for change. A reasoned case both for and against could then be presented to the legislators, and critically, all legislators would be mandated to hear both sides of the issue before deciding (as is currently the case with jurors in our courts). Having a formal structure around the process with rules and regulations similar to that of a court of law will ensure greater integrity in the decision making process.

In Governed Democracy the process will be absent politics, political parties and conflicted politicians. Legislators are then left with only the influence of the advocacy groups and the media to sway their views and this can be mitigated through a formal process to present a solid case for and against change, which can also correct any misconceptions. This ensures that each legislator can come to an informed and well considered decision. More on this in a moment.

That is, for each new law, an independent group would produce a formalized case, both for and against the change (how this is done will be presented in a moment). The document could include input from anyone in society who wants to contribute. Each contribution is fact checked and vetted for flawed reasoning. Consequences, risks and costs are considered. A "Deciding on change" like process is completed. We apply a formalized approach to the information and arguments which our legislators consider in their decision making.

Once this case for and against change is produced, we then require each member of the legislative assembly to hear it. This is not optional. We put some controls around it - making informed and well considered decisions is essential in the new democracy. At the moment, jurors cannot decide innocence or guilt without physically appearing in the court to hear the evidence - the same should apply to our legislators when deciding the laws of the land. They must hear the case. We implement controls to ensure this. There are a range of ways of doing this and all should be considered - digital technology gives us many possibilities here. Again, the sensible requirements that we have in our courts of law should be reasonable, as a minimum, for our legislative decision making process.

Note that any formal dispute to the prepared content of each case could be decided upon by a court of law. These rulings would require potentially a specialized court whose purpose is tailored to our requirements around balance, evidence and sensible reasoning.

Even when a formalised and vetted case for and against is presented there is still the possibility that some of our legislators simply choose not to trust that information. Some may prefer to believe otherwise. This is a risk in any process. We are after all, a free society and ultimately decision making is a subjective process. The presented information is then one consideration in a broader decision making process (including emotions, personal views etc). As a free society we present a vetted case for and against a proposal and then let the legislators decide. However, the size of a legislative assembly (discussed later) can reduce the risk of influence from those that choose not to trust the process itself. This is also one of the aspects of our collective decision making criteria (from the Wisdom of Crowds), where the errors of judgement of individuals can act to cancel each other out. The process of decision making is inevitably subjective, all we can do is to ensure integrity in the process. Irrespective, as will be described later, there will also be an effective and independent upper house, which can counterbalance any potential legislative folly (which is an ongoing risk in any democracy).

Note also that we can potentially produce a process for the formalised debate of policy which could be better than that of our courts of law. We will not be limited to only 12 jurors. Without the involvement of politicians, legislators can be impeded from influencing the decisions of others. We can overcome the incentive for jurors to decide quickly and then go home sooner in a number of ways (more on these in a moment). Also, in a formalised legislative process, we can easily mandate that similar resources (and skillsets) be applied to the presentation of a case for both sides of the argument. We will then be able to substantially improve upon the process

200

that already exists, and largely works, in our courts. Again, why would we not put effort into the improvement of our democratic legislative process?

Employment panels for our judges, public servants and industry leaders. (useful existing processes)

Already in our society we utilize key experts for the appointment of senior positions, for example of judges, senior public servants and for the leaders of industry (CEOs). A team of experts take the time to consider the integrity, experience and capabilities of candidates for available positions.

The benefits of this system of appointment of senior leadership is that the required time can be taken to source better candidates based on some predetermined and agreed criteria. Having a group of experienced experts appoint senior positions is used widely throughout society.

The downside can be that this is currently a subjective process and there can be a lack of an independence between the employment panels and any potential candidates. Often in industry (and government) today there can be "jobs for the boys". The process must rather be objective.

To improve this process, we would need to ensure that there is no relationship between the appointees and appointers. We could also ensure that we vet the full history of candidates while interviewing a whole range of people that have worked with them, including employers, peers, and employees. Where these employment panels were in the public service, we could broaden the people involved and regularly second outside experts from private industry onto the panel. This would ensure balance, integrity as well as the inclusion of a broad range of experiences and opinions. We could define standard and formalised criteria, that is consistently applied to vet the integrity and capability of candidates.

Let's next consider appointment of the executive arm of government. At the moment, in various governments, leaders are appointed either by a President – from the whole of society, or by a Prime Minister, from her legislative assembly members. One leader and their political teams appoints the executive government team. Whenever a new government is formed the newly elected politicians get together and use their expertise and experience to find the right candidates for the whole executive team. Or, in other words, the executive leadership is appointed by a conflicted, corruptible and often unqualified political class, who were themselves elected by generally disinterested, busy and often uninformed strangers. The appointment process is often based on political alignment, support and deals over capability and skills. As we have seen, this process reduces the independence of the arms of government since one has a relationship with, and/or is dependent upon the other. Both arms are effectively related by their common political allegiances and political parties.

For our executive arm of government, the system of appointments needs to significantly improve the existing system. We must have an independence of the arms of government, and capable, unconflicted candidates must be appointed, whose incentives and goals are that of making the right decisions for the greater good. We must also have the time to analyse any potential candidates and to thoroughly vet their experience, capabilities and integrity. Politics must be removed from the process.

The legislature should also approve any appointments to the executive arm of government and to do this, we need a short list of thoroughly vetted potential candidates, not a list of politically aligned candidates as we do now, but a real list of validated, qualified and experienced people.

Thus, for a better executive leadership to be appointed we propose a minor, but critical modification to the existing process which would remove many of the problems. As said above, in our current democratic process after an election, the new leader and his/her advisers appoints the new executive leadership team. We propose to simply change the group that appoints the executive leadership, from a group of politicians and advisers, to a group of independent experts. Instead of appointments through politics, we empower an experienced group of experts to do so, as is already done in quite a few areas in society. We then appoint our executive leadership team in the same manner as the judiciary - through a specialist appointment panel. This avoids any relationship between the legislative arm of government and the executive arm since they would then be appointed independently of political parties, and independently of each other. We gain independence and use an existing working process, albeit expanded. A group whose sole responsibility and expertise is to source quality independent candidates for executive leadership appointments would be able to do a significantly better job than a newly appointed President or Prime Minister currently does. The appointees can be validated through an ongoing formal process, which takes the time to vet candidates past skills, integrity and experience, including to interview people who have worked for and with the potential appointees. These appointees will have no prior relationship to the elected leader, so are much less likely to blindly agree with policies to further their own needs, and more likely to be independent voices. These expert appointment teams would not have to work within the political constraints which limit a President or Prime Minister, whose choices for appointment candidates can be seriously limited. Having a specialist team whose job it is to find and vet the most capable candidates would be much more likely to produce qualified candidates than our current ad hoc approach by politicians and political parties. As happens already for the existing, working process of judicial appointments in many democracies, an Independent Appointments Panel, could appoint qualified candidates to the executive arm of government. The legislature (without politicians, discussed in a moment) could then make final selections and/or approve these candidates as a final check. This process avoids the conflicts of interest, misalignment and politics, while gaining true independence, and properly vetted candidates. We avoid some of the issues of policy zealots and of policy pendulum swings from one side of politics to the other. The legislative approval of vetted candidates is already a feature of many democratic systems. More details on this in a moment.

Company Boards of Directors (useful existing processes)
Company boards of directors govern the actions of company executives. The purpose of those boards is to, amongst many other things, define the company strategy and to monitor the activities of the company to ensure that sensible options are chosen for the greater good of shareholders. They also appoint the company Chief Executive Officer (CEO).

These work fairly well and are widely utilised throughout the western world, although there are certainly issues. There can be a lack of independence of those company board members. As we have seen, a lack of effective governance has been a problem for many companies around the world, where the CEOs have made inadvisable decisions without being held to account. Many times, board members are chosen since they are unlikely to question the decisions of a CEO. Lucrative positions on company boards are more likely to be given to those individuals who are unflinchingly supportive of their CEOs. These issues are caused by a lack of independence of board members as well as through ineffectual incentives. Both of these parts of the process can be improved upon.

A governance panel must be independent from those people governed. In a democratic process we can choose completely independent governance panels (as should be done in company boards). We can also use governance panels to ensure the integrity of the decision making process of an individual leader. A governance panel acts as a check and balance against an imperfect leader's decisions. Most of the time they do little except to monitor but they are available just in case there is a major issue with a leader's decisions. As well, the profit and career motive that produces poor incentives with company boards, is not relevant when considering potential governance panels within a democracy. Positions can easily be made a once only appointment, so we can remove the potentially misaligned incentives for further positions or for career advancement.

The key to the success of governance panels is for them to be independent from those leaders that are governed. We then need to consider the independent appointment of those governance panels. We have previously discussed the need to appoint judiciary and an executive leadership team. The preference is to expand upon the appointments process that is already used for the independent appointment of judges in many western democracies. We also do see independent appointment panels used in the public service and industry. An independent group of experienced officials whose job it is to find suitable, vetted and capable candidates.

To facilitate all of these requirements for appointments, the following groups will be proposed in Governed Democracy:

Independent Appointment Panels

As we have already discussed we need a range of independent appointments. These will include appointments to governance panels as well as appointments of judges and members of the executive arm of government. There would then also have to be a permanent group whose job it is to recommend names to be appointed to the Independent Appointment Panels themselves including to evaluate any proposed appointees as recommended by the public. Again, these groups already exist in many areas of society, including to help with selections of candidates to government appointments.

Appointments would be a formalized process (unlike the existing executive leadership appointments), to identify the best candidates. These appointments would have to be signed off and approved by the legislative assembly to ensure integrity. The key criteria for these appointments will include a demonstrated capability to make effective and sensible decisions. The proposal here is that a department is created to properly and thoroughly research candidates. Full background checks can be done, validating experience, capabilities and integrity. Previous employers, co-workers and staff can be extensively interviewed to check the character of the candidates. For important roles impacting the leadership of the land we should thoroughly check past behaviour, as well as skills and capabilities. Creating a department who specialize in vetting candidates for capabilities would be an effective way of filtering out the poor choices. A key feature is that these appointment panels can identify an ongoing list of qualified and capable candidates, from which to choose when the time comes. For those in the executive arm of government a key requirement would also be an ability to execute a long-term strategy. These panels would inevitably produce better results than using conflicted, corruptible and potentially unqualified politicians for the process.

Independent Governance Panels

An Independent Governance Panel is responsible for ensuring that the decisions of key leadership are made in the best interests of society as a whole. These panels are appointed independently (by the Independent Appointments Panels), approved by the legislature, and have no prior relationship with the person over which they implement a governance framework. They could have fixed terms of three to five years. The panel, generally of five people, would meet regularly with a leader to discuss and approve the major management decisions made. They vet for evidence, reason and integrity. They can escalate to ensure that a leader comes back with the required information or justification. In serious circumstances, they can overrule a leader's decision and in certain circumstances even dismiss a leader. For a five person panel, to overrule a decision (or dismiss a leader completely) would require a unanimous decision. Governance panels are the ultimate power, but that power is intended to be used only in exceptional circumstances. Much of the time, the panels monitor major decisions and behaviour and only escalate where serious issues arise.

Independent Policy Assessment Department (IPAD)

This is a new and independent government department of specialist policy evaluation personnel. For each new legislative change, they produce a Legislative Change Proposal document. This document provides a formalized and vetted case for and against any legislative change. The purpose of this department is to provide a source of trusted information and sensible reasoning, which may counter any public perceptions in the media, or those opinions put forward by conflicted special interest groups. This department is quite similar to, but an expansion upon, existing government departments in many democracies, which currently produce independent costings for new policies, e.g. the Congressional Budget Office in the US or Parliamentary Budget Office in Australia. However, they do more than just cost any new policies. They take input from any or all from society who want to contribute to the policy and legislative analysis process. It is then their job to research the pros and cons of any new policy. They follow the established rules and guidelines, to propose a case for and against each policy. They assess the potential costs and the risks. They establish if there are other known or potential solutions. They also check historically for any evidence used previously or for any similar policies which may be of relevance. In many ways they act as the "lawyers" for the legislative process and produce a formal case for change or otherwise. Their responsibility is to present a comprehensive case inclusive of all views and opinions. They assess any public submissions to the process for factuality and for any flaws in reasoning. There are no recommendations made or any evaluation of the ethics or the morals associated with each policy - those appraisals and decisions are made separately by the legislative assembly. The IPAD is policy neutral and presents a separate case, both for and against, for each appraisal. Essentially, the case presented becomes a "trusted" source of information for our legislators, which follows certain rules of evidence and presents a reasonable and balanced view. It is expected that the people involved in this process would be specialist staff with specific training, who bring together the skills of the legal profession, of judges as well as of rationality and the scientific method. The government and IPAD could second professionals from society, who could contribute to the IPAD process as a way of ensuring representation and balance in the process. These seconded individuals could also work in key decision making areas, like the independent fact, reason and balance checking group, which would enable a balanced representation from society. For those professionals who contribute to IPAD, this may be their contribution to the democratic process and may even exempt them from responsibility for any requirements for legislative assembly participation (discussed later). The idea with the fourth democracy is to encourage citizen participation in the governing process. These responsibilities would add a key value in democratic society, by feeding verified information and reasonable, balanced analysis into the decision making process. Decisions in the legislative assembly would then be more likely to produce informed and well considered results.

So on to the actual implementation choices for our existing functions of government. What we need to deliver is the same set of government functions as set out previously. Each will be considered in turn.

Appoint judges

As discussed, we would use an Independent Appointment Panel. This type of panel already exists within many instances of our modern democratic process, for example the United Kingdom and Australia.

There are existing governance bodies in most democracies which rule over the actions of the judiciary. What is proposed for the judiciary in Governed Democracy is the same as that which exists in those democracies today.

Adjudicate constitutionality

Adjudicate legality

Adjudicate Legislative Change Proposal documents for the legislature (new)

Any actual adjudication on the constitutionality of law, or on legality, is done by those appointed judges, according to the normal legal processes and frameworks. Western democracy judicial supervision and appeals processes still apply.

There would be a new requirement to adjudicate any objections to the content of a Legislative Change Proposal. A Legislative Change Proposal is a document produced by the Independent Policy Assessment Department (IPAD) to formalize the case for and against any new legislative change. It would be used as a way of ensuring a fair and accurate representation of the case for and against change, for the consideration of the legislative assembly. Any member of the public could appeal a new Legislative Change Proposal document. For example, some people may disagree with the case presented, including the thoroughness of evidence, or its balance. The judiciary would be responsible for deciding those appeals.

Appoint the executive arm

As discussed, our requirement is for true independence (a separation of powers) and for quality of candidates. The executive arm would be appointed by an Independent Appointment Panel. Instead of these positions being appointed by any newly elected politicians, an expert and experienced panel could vet candidates in a much more thorough and comprehensive way, as well as to maintain a list of capable candidates. There would be no politics, no deals, no compromises, no conflicts of interest and no payback for support. This is a minor change from the existing process and can and does work already in many areas of society. There would also be no need to appoint the entire new executive leadership at once after a government is formed. Leadership appointments could be phased in so that new leaders could gain from the experience of others already serving. An Independent Governance Panel would be appointed for each appointed leadership position. Each candidate is appointed for a single term only. Thus, with no concerns around re-appointment or political career advancement, decision making is freed from many potential conflicts.

The President

Note that Governed Democracy includes the use of the Independent Appointment Panel process for the head of state. A short list of candidates, including a report on each individual, could be presented for a final decision by the legislative assembly. All candidates presented to the legislative assembly would be considered capable and qualified for the job, due to the extensive vetting by the Independent Appointments Panel. The candidate that gains the most votes from the legislature becomes President. The candidates for President are voted into office without campaigning, without politics and without political parties. As for the executive arm of government we do not currently question having a *single* head of state, especially since there will be both increased governance and the removal of politics. An appointed head of state would make decisions critical to the future of the nation (including on potential conflict). Even where a head of state does not have to concern herself with politics, or re-election, or career advancement, or conflicts of interest, it is still possible for critical errors of judgement. Ensuring integrity through an overriding governance panel would seem prudent. So, over the head of state would be an Independent Governance Panel to ensure power is used responsibly. In this way, the true power lies in the democratic process itself, and not the hands of individuals or politicians.

Run the executive (including the implementation of laws)

Once candidates are appointed to the executive it is up to those individuals to run the executive effectively. Having an Independent Governance Panel for each member of the executive government is an essential element to ensure integrity of government decisions. There would be no politics, no career concerns and no dependencies or undue influences between the executive arm of government and the legislative arm.

Propose ideas for law

Our democratic requirement is that any member of society is able to propose changes or additions to law (and public policy). The public service then needs to create a process through which proposals can be presented.

Presentation of proposals for new or amended laws could happen from all areas of society – from individuals and companies as well as from a range of advocacy groups. In the fourth democracy the existing political parties would probably transform into new structures, more akin to advocacy groups. Those advocacy groups would then lobby for their own ideas to be presented as policy and legislative proposals. Any new proposals by advocacy groups would be vetted by an Independent Policy Assessment Department. Similarly, the same special interest groups as now would still lobby for their own preferred policy changes, but they would then have significantly less influence on the deliberation process. Advocacy groups and special interest groups would each be one voice in the process, having no more influence than others. A key advantage to this process is the removal of politicians from the process.

At first, a smaller group of independent experts must be convinced of a new proposal's merits, then the requirement is for the approval of the legislative assemblies themselves, who act without politics as we will see. As we will see next, new ideas could be more quickly and effectively vetted and presented for analysis and approval, without the potential for decades of delay required to convince the majority of busy and disinterested voters.

Vet and prioritize law ideas

Write laws

Present case for laws

It would be the responsibility of a new public service department to initially vet and prioritize ideas for change. Each idea from the public will go through a series of stages of approval. Firstly, a fairly brief and informal ratification than it makes sense to be considered further (there may be quite a few ideas to consider and many may be filtered). A very simple *Deciding upon change* process can be applied, and expert opinion can be sought. Then each idea can move up to more detailed and formal consideration, as it passes each stage. Original ideas would need to be taken from initiation, through prioritization and vetting, towards construction and presentation for legislative approval. Prioritization could depend on a range of things, including the initial supporter base for the proposal (sponsor numbers), as well as a determined sense of urgency based on the issue at hand, or even a high level *Deciding upon change* process. It would also be possible to engage with the legislative assembly to help with prioritization decisions if needed. In many democratic governments, a part of this requirement already exists, especially that of writing laws, since a range of new laws are currently created for our elected governments.

The executive arm of government must ultimately present the case for and against any law via the Independent Policy Assessment Department (IPAD). This would include obtaining input from the general public, including any special interest groups. This input would then be vetted by a specialist independent group within the IPAD, who validate any facts as well as reasoning and balance. Essentially the government would include a group of public advocates, in some ways akin to judges, whose responsibility is to ensure an accurate presentation of verifiable facts, sensible reasoning and conclusions, as well as a fair representation of both sides of the debate. These people, whose responsibility it is to ensure integrity of the process, would need to be at arm's length from those others inside IPAD who actually present the Legislative Change Proposals. Independence and balance could be protected by Chinese walls. Again, those vetting the integrity of the process could include both career public servants as well as seconded individuals from society. We do already see this type of independent vetting used regularly in society - speech writer David Litt described how in the Obama administration all speeches were independently (and frustratingly) fact checked by a separate group. When it comes to decisions which can affect the livelihoods of millions of people, spending the time to verify the integrity of the process would seem essential.

We cannot remove the ability of the public to speak freely and to push their own agenda. Rather, over and above this, we allow a formal presentation of vetted reasoning for and against any proposals. In this way, the legislators, who are mandated to have read (or heard) and understood the arguments for and against, can have any misconceptions corrected. We create the best possible platform, from which to make informed and well considered decisions.

Polling our collective opinions (useful existing processes)
Over recent decades, opinion pollsters have needed to check the pulse of the electorate. They have surveyed the electorate to estimate who will win elections or to work out what was the majority view on a range of issues. To do this they have used some basic statistical analysis to determine how many people they needed to interview to obtain a reliable representation of the majority view.

Basic mathematics tells us that there are a number of requirements in order to ensure that any subset of a population is likely to be a representative sample of the whole population. Firstly, the sample must be randomly taken. Secondly, if the sample is above a certain size, probability tells us the likelihood of that sample being representative of the whole population. For example, for a population size of 250 million voters, a random selection of about 2500 voters will give a 95% probability of those voters' opinions being within 2% of the overall population's opinion (actually 2401 voters exactly, but we have rounded up). Let us say that you can accurately survey 2500 randomly selected people on their opinion of a certain policy (more on this in a moment). This means that the opinion of those 2500 people, will have a 95% chance of being effectively the same as the whole group (or within 2%). The interesting thing about the mathematics, is that as population size increases the required representative size does not really increase. A group of 2500 can fairly accurately represent a population of 20 million or 300 million. A sample of 2500 is large enough for both. As the size of the population increases the probability of accuracy changes by only a small amount. This means for populations of 20 million or 300 million, a sample size of about 2500 will still give an accurate insight into the overall view of the population.

The benefits of this are that with only a relatively small sample size you can fairly accurately determine the broader view of a large group of people.

Opinion polls are not perfect however, and they have been criticized. It can be difficult to achieve a truly random selection of voters. Some people refuse to participate, and methods of contacting people have varied over the years. A geographically diverse sample across all areas of a nation is difficult to achieve. Some people want to hide their true opinions from survey takers.

The accuracy of surveys can be a problem as can the honesty of those surveyed. Also, the accuracy of polls can be undermined in the time between a poll being taken and the election itself – much can happen in voters' minds in the mean-time. Nevertheless, even allowing for survey selection shortcomings, opinion polls have been a reasonable predictor of voter outcomes - within their margins of error. Many of these problems can also be minimised or overcome.

If we can ensure that the selected subset is truly representative of the broader group (as in the criteria from wisdom of crowds), and if we can ensure that the individuals surveyed will be honest in their opinions, then we can get a great measure of the view of a very large group, by engaging with a smaller minority.

Appoint legislative assembly

Our requirement for a legislative assembly is for no elections, no politics and no political parties, since these processes are so flawed. We want our legislators to have the time and the capability to make informed and well considered decisions. We also need the legislators to be a fair representation of the population.

The above discussion on opinion polling demonstrates that we can use a subset of individuals - around 2500, to get a fairly representative view of the preference of the overall population (4000 would be even more accurate). In fact, if those individuals have no incentive to hide their opinions and can be truly randomly selected, then we can be significantly more accurate than our recent polling experience would indicate. The margin for error can be reduced to quite small levels. This will be useful inside our new democratic process.

Based on the work of the Wisdom of Crowds, our requirement for a legislative assembly, is for a group of people that is fairly large, diverse, independent and decentralized (aggregation as a requirement is satisfied in the simple process of voting upon laws). If these requirements are satisfied, then we can achieve an effective collective decision making process that will produce better results. The best representation of all of these above qualities, the most likely group to attain such diversity, independence and decentralization, would be a group in which the fewest and simplest choices are made in the selection process.

At the moment, we fill our legislative assemblies with politicians through elections. We know that this process is significantly flawed and produces many poor results. We also have a mature process - that of jury selection, which works well for our courts. This process ensures that the individuals contained in juries are a fair representation of the accused's peers. People are chosen randomly to appear on juries. They are mandated to appear. They serve in juries for a period of time, taking time out from their lives, get paid for their service and then return when done.

The proposal is that we expand upon this working process. That is, we apply the same process that we use to fill our juries, to fill our legislative assemblies. We replace the politicians who sit for a longer fixed term, with randomly selected people, who sit for between one and three months at a time. Through this random selection we are guaranteed to have satisfied our criteria for diversity, independence and decentralization. Our previous analysis would also suggest that we can represent society with a high degree of accuracy with a representative group of around 4000 truly randomly selected people. There have been objections and difficulties with our existing jury process. Most of these existing difficulties appear because a jury is a very small group of people, only 12 jurors or so. We overcome these difficulties because our legislature would have a large group of 4000 individuals. We also mitigate the risk by having an effective and thoroughly researched case made by an independent body (IPAD). Interestingly, with the resources and time available to IPAD, it would seem possible to actually be more thorough and effective than our existing judicial process. After all, equal time and resources can be allocated to investigate and present both sides of the debate (equal time and resources are not guaranteed in our existing courts). Legislators will have the time to make an informed and well considered decision, based on a fair and balanced view of both sides. The legislative group will have no political concerns, no deals or compromises, no career pressures, no influence of special interest groups, no conflicts of interest. Each issue can be decided on its own without other issues or politics getting in the way. What does seem clear here, is that a legislature of 4000 diverse individuals, mandated to hear a vetted case for and against, will be significantly more likely to produce effective decisions than our existing and flawed political process.

Those individuals on the legislative assembly could be paid fairly. They would be educated up front about the entire process. The process would be like that of existing jury allocation in many nations, with all of the same checks and balances, exceptions and supports (although there is no vetting of legislators - all people that are randomly selected, would be used). Each individual could serve for up to three months at a time (the ideal length of service required is quite debatable), with two legislative assemblies formed each year. The size of each legislative assembly would vary depending on the population size, but statistically a group of 4000 individuals would give a statistically relevant proportion of society, as well as not being too cost prohibitive for a nation. The cost of the process must be measured against the enormous savings made through the discontinuation of very expensive elections and the removal of the requirement to have thousands or tens of thousands of permanent politicians and staffers. Note that with a legislative assembly of this size, we know that it would be a great representation of the political will of the people overall. Mathematically, we would have a 95% confidence of any voting result being within 2% of the overall population's view. As well, if we do also require a 60% majority for legislative approval (discussed further in a moment), then we know that any approved legislation does represent the will of the majority. Other checks and balances that we would have in place, like automatic sunset clauses on legislative change, and the inclusion of a governing council (an upper house - discussed soon), would give us a more assured and effective way of deciding policy. The policy decision process would be vastly better than any existing decisions made by our legislative assemblies filled with unrepresentative, sometimes uninformed and self-interested politicians. Note also that individuals would only serve on the legislative assembly once in their lifetimes and it would be illegal to approach or appeal to legislators directly at any time during the process, as per our existing judicial system.

Having such a large group of "unknown" legislative assembly members, would significantly reduce the possibility of any special interest group, or foreign power, gaining control of the process. The process will still have some limitations and imperfections. But it would undoubtedly be vastly superior to our existing democratic process, which involves conflicted politicians as well as having an often busy, disinterested and uninformed public, voting for strangers. The essence here is that with the combination of our proposed democratic process changes, then we can deal with the vast majority of our current problems. The removal of all of the following: politics and political parties, conflicts of interest, deals and compromises, undue special interest group influence, the election of strangers by busy and disinterested voters, an imperfect separation of powers, the risk of individual leadership mistakes. By implementing this new legislative appointment process as well as using our formal Legislative Change Proposals, we gain from the removal of all of the problems just listed, as well as allowing legislators the time for an informed and well considered collective decision making process. With a 60% approval requirement, we can be sure that any new legislative proposal has the approval of the majority, even allowing for statistical glitches in our selection process. We also reduce our risk of problems due to the addition of a more effective upper house process (presented in a moment).

Decide upon laws

For each new law we have a formalized Legislative Change Proposal produced, for and against the proposal. Because the legislators are specifically seconded to the assembly, they only have one job, for which they are assigned full time. They must hear or read and consider the proposal. They have the time available to spend on this since they are dedicated to the task, for which they are being paid. There could be a range of support staff to answer any questions and help in any way needed. Without an unstructured and chaotic public debate as in our current democracy, we can enforce the verification of evidence and the removal of unjustifiable reasoning. It would be similar to our existing judicial process. This will remove a significant proportion of our existing problems with democratic debate, without impacting public free speech. Free speech on all issues of policy is then still possible, however when it comes to the presentation of a case for change to our law, there would be some controls to ensure integrity in the process. As well, individuals in the legislative assembly who have a vested interest in the outcome of a particular legislative decision more so than any others, could be removed from any vote.

Once the legislative assembly has been appointed the process for the approval of laws would not need to materially change. The legislative assembly can vote to approve or reject the new or amended law. The legislative assembly could collectively and individually request more information, or it could even request amendments. A majority vote is then required. It would also seem sensible to require more than a majority for the passage of legislation. After all, if a new policy does not have the support of more than 50.01% of voters then is it really worth implementing? That is, if 49.9% of people disagree with a new proposal, then surely, we can find and present a better option for approval. It would then be sensible to choose an approval ratio of 60%. A higher percentage approval requirement also mitigates the small risk of the legislative assembly not being a perfect representation of the broader electorate (the 2% statistical error mentioned previously). As well, requiring a higher approval percentage mitigates more risk of the legislative assembly getting carried away with populist or short-term policies (there will be other checks presented on this possibility).

After any votes have been taken, the case for and against can be made public for all to see and understand. A highlighted summary could be prepared for those in society who have little time. In this way the broader community could understand the rationale for any changes made. Unlike in some jury trials, after any legislative service, legislators would be encouraged to talk, if they wish to, about their experiences of the legislative process and the decisions that they made. Full transparency of decision making would be considered an important feature within Governed Democracy. There are no back room deals or compromises, all experiences of the process are documented and publicly available.

For constitutional changes, a super majority of the legislative assembly would be required. Our proposal would be for an 80% approval rate for constitutional change. It would also be expected, as a matter of governance, that any new law would automatically require re-approval in say, 5 years' time, as a matter of sensible governance (sunset clause). After 5 years, new laws would be re-approved, to check that they are working as expected. If the

217

law as presented cannot achieve another tick of approval, then it would have to be modified and resubmitted. These sunset clauses, as already used in some democracies, can be used to effectively mitigate the risk of unforeseen circumstances, and would often not need to be applied a second time. But having a single and automatic sunset clause would seem a prudent option. The aim here is to do what it takes to ensure the integrity of the legislative process.

Governing Council – upper house

The risk with any democracy is the same as that which apparently occurred in the Greek democracy, where the people choose what is beneficial to their own interests in the short-term. Some of this risk of self-interest is mitigated by the new process itself, where all assembly members must be presented with and then consider a verified case for and against, as well as having members of the legislative assembly assigned full time. In this way, the members will have the time for informed and well considered decisions and to consider any risks and consequences that have been presented. But the risk nonetheless remains in many ways, people still have an instinct for self-interest and may be swayed by the possibility of short-term benefits at the expense of a better long-term solution. To deal with this risk there needs to be a governing council (an upper house). The idea with a governing council is similar to the reasoning for many of the existing upper houses globally, it is a control on unchecked populist policies or on bad policies that slip through. The difference with a governing council in Governed Democracy is that the members would not be elected through public elections. Like the executive arm of government, the members of the governing council would be appointed directly through an Independent Appointments Panel, through pre-determined selection criteria, and then ratified by the legislative assembly. The aim is that these members would be esteemed and experienced members of society, who could be trusted to be responsible for the greater good in society. Members could be appointed for 5 year periods. Again, the only requirement for them is to vet any new laws for verifiable evidence, sensible reason and integrity against the spirit of the constitution. If more than, say 60% disagree with any new law, then that law can be sent back for re-evaluation and amendment, or rejected outright. They could in a worst case scenario even call for a reformation of the legislative assembly itself if they believed that the membership had somehow become corrupted. The governing council would then have the final say over any new law. A governing council should not need more than 20 members - it needs to be of a size that is able to openly discuss the issues. The council could decide without fear of elections, or fear of political parties, or fear of the impact of special interest groups, or fear for their careers. The concept is for a sensible governance framework, without a requirement for politics or for public popularity contests.

The relative merits of Governed Democracy come down to a basic decision. It is simpler to remove the flawed processes entirely from the democratic system, or to try and fix or remediate the myriad of complicated problems? Our existing problems are inextricably linked to having a disinterested, busy and sometimes uninformed public electing strangers, and then being governed by those conflicted, misaligned and often unqualified and incompetent politicians.

We have presented a new democratic process, without politics, parties or the elections of strangers. All replacement processes are based on existing and working systems. Democracy itself is strengthened through a true independence and separation of powers of the three arms of government. No individual or group can wield unchecked power over the process. There can be little undue influence, corruption or misaligned incentives. For every risk, there is a mitigating governance process. Our collective decision making process is able to produce truly representative, informed and well considered decisions, for the greater good of all citizens. A democracy that is truly of the people, by the people and for the people.

Governed Democracy, a brief summary

Critically, this below process satisfies each and every requirement of our fourth democracy to produce the best possible democratic results. In doing so it also removes virtually all of the root causes of problems from within our current democratic process, while mitigating the risk of the few remaining problems which are inherent within democracy itself.

A section is also included on the functions and responsibilities that can be delivered by the general public, within the framework of the fourth democracy. Public participation in the process of democracy is considered an important advantage.

Democratic functions in Governed Democracy

Legislative - To manage the laws of the nation. This includes the following:
- Collectively decide whether to proceed with changes to the law based on a formal "for and against" case presented (by Independent Policy Assessment Department). A 60% yes vote approves changes.
- Collectively decide whether to proceed with constitutional changes based on a formal "for and against" case presented (by Independent Policy Assessment Department) An 80% yes vote approves changes.
- Approve individuals appointed to both the Executive arm of government and to the Judiciary, based on information presented on those individuals (by Independent Appointment Panels)

Executive - To enforce the laws of the nation, including the management of the administration of the laws of the nation and the public services.
- Independent Appointment Panels appoint individuals to run the executive arm of government
- Independent Appointment Panels appoint justices to the supreme/high courts

- Appoint all members of the legislative assembly from general society through a process similar to the existing jury duty selection process (4000 are randomly selected, for up to three months periods)
- Independent Governance Panels govern the Executive arm of government (appointed by Independent Appointment Panels)
- Independent Policy Assessment Department vets and prioritizes ideas for changes to laws or to the constitution. This can be also deferred to the legislative assembly if necessary.
- Existing public service groups formally construct each new law
- Independent Policy Assessment Department presents a case for and against new changes to law including a separate internal group vetting for factuality, reason and balance
- Implement any laws approved
- Run the executive arm of government

Judicial - to adjudicate and interpret the laws of the nation.
- Adjudicate on constitutionality of new laws
- Adjudicate on citizens and corporations under the law
- Adjudicate Legislative Change Proposal documents for the legislature

Public opportunities for contribution
Can submit new ideas, proposals and legislative and constitutional changes
Can serve in the legislative assembly
Can serve in Independent Appointment Panels, Independent Governance Panels, Independent Policy Assessment Department (including in fact checking areas), executive government and the judiciary

Note that all of the above new public service groups (e.g. IPAD), could include up to 50% membership of seconded members of the public to ensure diversity of opinion as well as balance, and to enable greater public participation in the democratic process.

Governed Democracy, a walk through

We will now take a look at some of the potential for how the new system may operate in practice.

Judiciary
Most of the processes of the judiciary for many democratic states do not change materially.

Executive
The President/Prime Minister and key cabinet members are now appointed for fixed terms through the Independent Appointment Panels, as well as by approval from the legislative assembly. Key selection criteria include an ability to make effective, evidence based decisions. Executive government appointments are considered an honour, capping off a successful career. The appointment panels have a register of qualified, intelligent and capable potential leaders – the best and brightest minds if you will, that they manage in an ongoing sense, to keep up to date. There is no wholesale replacement of the entire leadership team after elections, instead changes to leadership are phased in. In this way, new leaders can utilize the experience of the existing leadership team. Managing an area of government is now not materially different to managing a large corporation or public service department. There is no excessive media scrutiny, no cheap shots from opponents, no politics in general. Leaders of the executive government can now propose new expert committees and panels to make recommendations for changes and improvements, knowing that the recommendations will be actioned towards legislation and a vote in the legislative assembly. Politics will not get in the way of expert opinions. Rather, proposals will be assessed and evaluation of the benefits of any change will be prepared, and a vote on any changes will occur. Executive government members will no longer need to make promises to gain office, they will no longer need to object to existing leadership in order to gain political support. There can be a sensible, even extended

handover, between one leader and the next. There will be no politically based distrust between one leader and her predecessor. Leaders will no longer fear for the loss of their job or future based on their decisions. They decide actions based on verified information. There are no political conflicts between the executive and legislative branches, they can work together to solve problems. Conflicts of interest are managed by the independent governance panels. Executive government members meet with their governance panel once every 3 months, to communicate their major undertakings. The governance panel then vet for integrity in the executive leader's decision making. In rare cases, the governance panels may act to protect the integrity of the process.

New laws and policies

Anyone from society can propose a change to the law, or a new law. Many advocacy groups would continue to operate as they currently do, except that in the fourth democracy the advocacy group influence only extends up to the presentation of supporting information for a particular law. New proposals for policies are then prioritized for consideration based on a combination of their support level (number of signatories) as well as an initial independent assessment of the criticality of the proposal. All proposals will eventually be considered. All evaluations, reasoning and results of considerations are made publicly available.

For those policies that move forward, an initial proposal is presented to the public with calls for public input. This public input is then collated into a public case for and against the proposal. This case is then again presented to the public for comments and possible feedback or objections. Once this hurdle has been passed, the approved case is presented to the legislature for consideration, evaluations and for a vote. Again, there are no deals, no quid pro quo, no politics at all. Each policy is considered on its own merits alone. Policies can be for the long-term with no personal risk of consequence for any involved in the process. Policies based on new evidence (scientific or otherwise), no longer have to wait until most members of society have been painstakingly and slowly convinced over a long period of time. Instead, if the case for change is strong, then the process allows for people whose time is dedicated to the evaluation and who have seen all of the evidence for and against, to make an informed decision. Societal views can catch up afterwards, as they read the supporting evidence for the change after the decision. There will be no hidden decisions, no deals, no truly political compromises and no control from special interest groups or minor parties. Consequently, fully transparent policies can be proposed and ratified, with all from society able to contribute to the process and fully published reasoning behind the decisions. Public trust in the process should grow.

Appointment of the Legislative Assembly

Initially, for the first legislative assembly the whole group of 4000 people can be appointed through random allocation for a three month period. The group appointed is, by definition, diverse and decentralized - from a range of ethnicities, age groups and geographies. Employers are required by law to allow their employees to participate without consequence. All members of the legislative assembly are paid at above their current base salaries for the duration of service. The assembly members gather in their nearest capital cities, to serve directly on the legislative assembly. Each person is given two weeks of training in the process, as well as in the key requirements for making effective decisions. There are no elections held, no manipulation of the process and voting is by secret ballot. It is illegal for members of the public to seek out the names of current legislators or to approach them directly while in service. Legislators are protected under the law similarly to jurors. Legislators can contribute and can decide without consequence. Legislative assembly members can choose to discuss their experience of the process after they leave, or they can choose not to. Without the stigma of politicians, without conflicted interests and a history of corruption, appointees are considered to be doing their civic duty without excessive rewards. They are paid for their service, but it is still a service to society. There can be no incentive or reward for voting in any particular way.

Note also that fairly quickly a legislative proposal could be put forward to allow the nation to strategize for the future. A department of strategy could be created, which can consider options for the long-term benefit of the nation. These options can be submitted to the department by anyone from society. There is also an opportunity for individuals to be seconded into the department from society for periods of time to ensure that a broad range of ideas and approaches are considered. Without politics, a long term national strategy is then possible.

Voting on laws

After any training time, legislative members are presented with the case for and against for each legislative proposal. They are given time to make their decision. Anyone directly impacted by any new law more so than others can be exempted from voting. Voting is not allowed until all material is read and digested. The vote occurs without any direct influence by any special interest groups. Legislators vote individually, there is no peer influence amongst members. Voting takes place without deals, or negotiations, or politics. Voting also takes place over a period of time, each legislator may take a different time in deciding. The results are not published until all legislators have voted. Each person on the assembly gets one vote. After the creation of a case for a new law special interest groups have virtually no ability to influence any legislative assembly members, and this would be illegal in any case, as it is currently for juries. Even if influence of some members of the legislative assembly were somehow possible, unlike for politicians, those members would soon roll off the legislative assembly and the influence would disappear. If influence was somehow found, with the large number of people on the assembly extensive influence would be extremely difficult and would likely be discovered. There is an upper house irrespective, which can overrule if undue influence is suspected. If a majority of 60% approves then the law is passed.

Allowing society to propose new laws still allows for the existence of political organizations that gather and promote new ideas for change. They work within the existing framework to propose laws and contribute to the evidence base and reasoning for the laws. But after this is done it is up to the legislative assembly to independently decide upon the laws and proposals. The same advocacy organizations will be able to petition the executive arm of government for change to how the government is run.

It is an interesting quote from Thomas Jefferson – "Government is the strongest in which every man feels a part". It could hardly be said that many people in today's democracies would realistically feel a part of government.

The typical feeling would be more akin to a helplessness to influence policy and a distance from decision making – as countless surveys have indicated. In Governed Democracy, thousands of normal men and women from all parts of society would regularly become a real and influential part of government. Those people could then return to society to speak of the benefits of the process and what good they have done as a contributing part of it. Within 10 short years more than 40,000 people could have realistically contributed to the democratic process, having direct involvement in decisions for the future of society. More contribution would be possible through the regular secondment of people into departments like the Independent Policy Assessment Department, for periods of time. Within 50 years, more than 200,000 people could have directly and meaningfully contributed to the democratic process. This is aside from any advocacy groups which may spring forth, which would be motivated by the new-found ability to influence the legislative process.

After a period of time, society and the democratic process itself may become more stable. The requirement for new laws and policies may diminish, as the government processes mature. The number of new legislative changes may reduce significantly. The requirement for citizens to serve for 1-3 months at a time may reduce. It may even then be that legislative groups could be formed to decide only on one specific issue at a time.

Our examples revisited

Let's now reconsider all of the major examples given throughout this book, our "Ons". These are listed below, along with a very brief description, to help the reader identify each one. We consider generally how these examples throughout our text would be different under a Governed Democracy. Note that there are many overlaps in the below, many changes would help to resolve more than one of our previous problems. But these groupings are indicative only and not every contributing resolution has been listed for all problems. We want to demonstrate that all of our examples have been resolved and mitigated, with their root cause removed, in at least one way.

On avoidable infections (hand washing), On pharmaceuticals (Bad Pharma), On multinational tax avoidance (decades of unrestricted tax cheating)
Given that Governed Democracy enables any individual in society to contribute to the policy debate, individual scientists are significantly more likely to be able to gain attention and initiatives from both the legislative assembly and from the executive arm of government. It is no longer a requirement to convince a large portion of society before action is taken. A scientists or activist only needs to convince a small group of specialist staff of the value of any proposal. Compelling information and well considered arguments can stir government action before the general public has caught up with the need for policy change.

On Fidel Castro (Presidents' conflicts of interest)
Under Governed Democracy, a President faced with these critical decisions - about the threat posed by communism under Castro, would not have to worry about elections, or about approval ratings, or about any conflicts of interest. She could just focus on the issues and risks at hand, without fear of personal consequences. As well, to mitigate risk, any decisions made would be implicitly ratified by the independent governance panels, who could ask for

clarification, or further information, or could overrule if necessary. The risks associated with decisions around conflict would be vastly reduced.

On global conflict(soviet submarine), On political assertions (drug related crime), On 37th place (Texas development incentive error), On CIA assessments (government overruling the CIA), On the Battle of Britain (aircraft damage), On AIDS in South Africa, On pharmaceuticals (Bad Pharma), On the Space Shuttle Disasters (it has worked in the past), On ulcers (antibiotic solution), On the Rogers Commission (management risk assessments), On air safety (pilot incentives), On ratings agencies (AAA ratings for junk), On investment banks (short-term staff incentives)
These examples were used to illustrate a number of points about the importance of a sensible decision making process. The points were about the criticality of getting decision making right, the importance of root cause identification, the risk of depending on individuals to make key decisions, problems where a lack of scientific evidence is used, problems with incentive alignment, problems with non-sequiturs and failures of logic and reason. The resolution of these issues is about improving our process for decision making and minimizing our reliance on individuals. Our democratic process now includes a better decision making framework. Many of the decision making flaws underlying these issues would be identified and removed as a part of our formal Legislative Change Proposal. Problems and issues could be identified more quickly, evidence would be vetted, complex issues could more easily be identified and presented for resolution. The new decision making process encourages informed and well considered adjudication. There would be no misaligned incentives stopping a government from fixing a regulatory framework. Special interest groups would not have the influence to inhibit good policy. And nonetheless, our governance process (having a Governance Panel) would potentially have been able to mitigate the risk of leaving critical decisions to individuals, if these had instead been executive government decisions.

On tax reform (goods and service tax policy reversal)
Taxation reform would be evaluated without reference to the next election or to any special interest groups. There would be no threat of a looming election

loss for decision makers, no personal risk at all. There can be no incidents of skilled politicians trumping sensible policy, or policy reversals - just to win an election with populist policies. There are no deals or quid pro quo. Without politics, elections and politicians, these problems largely disappear. Instead, the results of any expert commissions can be actioned accordingly without fear. Legislators then consider the pros and cons for any proposed change on its own merits - decisions are based purely on the efficacy of change.

On lessons lost (Great Recession)
Under Governed Democracy, the reasoning for and subsequent lessons of past decisions are stored for posterity and available for future reference. Every previous political decision can be researched and included as examples, by the Independent Policy Assessment Department, since all cases for change are investigated. When any new policy is proposed, any similar reasoning for previous policy changes can be included. Evidence and lessons are accumulated by the process, rather than lost in the fog of constantly antagonistic campaigns between ever changing governments and leaders. Outgoing leaders are also free to pass on the lessons that they have learnt in office, without fear of political consequence. Incoming leaders have no reason not to trust their predecessors, and every reason to learn from their experience.

On "nearly perfected" government (Prussian democratic decline)
As has been said, the degradation to despotism is an ongoing possibility in any democratic government. A black swan event of this nature is an ever present, albeit low risk possibility. The way in which this is mitigated in Governed Democracy is through the true greater independence of the arms of government – no longer can one person or political party control more than one arm of government. The executive and judicial arms of government are independently nominated, albeit then approved by the legislature. There will also be no alignment of similarly minded zealots after an election, the processes that nominates the members of government works continually, rather than in cycles. As well, having an independent Governing Council (second legislature), reduces the risk of legislation which changes the power

229

structure within Governed Democracy. On top of these controls, the Governance Panels reduce the power of the executive government leadership. No individual can remove controls on their own and there is no possibility of political manipulation inspiring the populace to support risky changes to the legislature. Enshrining the new controls for the separation of powers of the various arms of government in the constitution, significantly reduces the risk of these being removed. Overall, the new system adds a range of checks and balances, over and above our existing democratic process, which vastly reduce the risk of any changes to the power structure and separation of powers. In Governed Democracy, the power lies in the process, not the individual.

On the rule by 37% (Brexit from Europe)
Any critical decisions made by the legislature are approved by a 60% majority. Statistically, the size of the legislative assembly means that the decisions are designed to have a very high probability of being representative of the majority of voters. There is also an automatic sunset clause for all legislative decisions, as well as a Governing Council to further reduce the risk of populist, poor decisions being made. As well, there is no political imperative (no politics at all), as there was for the British Prime Minister who was under pressure from his party and from his electorate. A Prime Minister no longer needs to concern himself with short-term popularity or elections. Any people deciding on a Brexit like decision are presented with the true costs and risks of any change, so are less likely to vote based on fear and uncertainty alone. The undue influence of any public political campaigns for change is reduced, since their facts and reason are independently vetted, and flaws highlighted.

On agnotology (industry manipulation of science), On opioids (avoidable drug addiction), On lead in society (lead damage from fuels), On the President's men (partisan policy zealots), On ratings agencies (AAA ratings for junk), On investment banks (short-term staff incentives), On 37th place (Texas development incentive error), On pharmaceuticals (Bad Pharma)
These examples have been grouped together since their risk has been mitigated through the same mechanisms in Governed Democracy. Ensuring

that we have a formal assessment of the pros and cons of any new government policy proposals, is more than likely to reduce our risk of jumping the gun on any new scientific discoveries or assessments. Allowing all from society to contribute, as well as reducing the influence of special interest groups, also severely reducing our risks. Special interest groups will have no influence beyond any other contributor to the case for policy change, they will have no politicians for direct appeals, and their contributions will be checked for factuality and reason. There can be no purchase of support by politicians and no threats of negative campaigns in subsequent elections. Basically, without politics, politicians and elections, special interest group power to control policy, largely disappears. At the same time, it will be significantly easier for any individual to gain the attention of the legislature and the executive government. Politics will not get in the way and large scale consensus is not required before sensible action can be taken.

On multi-party states (67 Italian government), On stable government (6 Prime Ministers in 8 years), On 89 votes (Liberal Democrat's 6100% vote increase), On political assertions (Nixon drug study), On sports governance (IOC and FIFA elections), On government gridlock (US government budget shutdown), On CIA assessments (government changes unpalatable reports), On units of measurement (Mars Climate Orbiter crash)
Without having politicians, political parties, or elections, these issues are simply impossible.

Applying *Deciding upon change*

The changes that accompany Governed Democracy are quite significant and these changes should be carefully considered. The *Deciding upon change* criteria which was proposed earlier can be used as a simple tool to evaluate the new democratic model. We need to compare the proposed model against the existing system to ensure that it is better overall. Basically, this is a potential change upon which we must decide.

1/ Is the proposed change enough of an improvement on the status quo, that it justifies the costs and risks of making the change itself?

We'll compare the two systems by considering the benefits of the new democracy vs the benefits of the old. In this case, for simplicity, the statement of benefits of each will also include the negative aspects of the alternative. In this way we can then more easily compare the benefits of one system vs the other.

For Governed Democracy, let's consider the benefits. With our new democratic process, a whole range of root causes of problems have been removed - we will not list them again here. Because these root causes have been removed the problems described earlier should disappear or be vastly reduced in likelihood. In particular, we should see the following benefits:

No self-interested politicians
No corrupt politicians
No unrepresentative political parties or factions vying for power. No single issue parties
No political conflicts of interest. No politicians worried for their careers
No politics in the appointment of the legislative assembly (no elections)
No politics at all in decision making
No ignorant politicians making ill informed decisions and mistakes

No risk of one political party controlling two arms of governments (or even three arms)

No politicians leading us into war for political gain

Apathetic voters have no influence but can if they get called up. No requirement for any in society to waste time on politics - unless they are called to serve – as a full time, paid job

No imperfect and ineffectual elections

No concerns about party or election funding

Violence can have vastly less influence, since voting is done behind closed doors, by unknown people, by secret ballot

There is no payback for political support at the expense of others

There is no block voting possible

Any media influence on people's perceptions and preferences can be nullified. In fact, there would be no politics at all for the media to cover, except after the democratic decisions are made

Virtually no possibility of electoral fraud

Virtually impossible for an external country to influence the political outcome of legislative changes

Vastly less incentive for short-term policy. There is now an opportunity for long-term policy planning

Policy is decided at the time, not through unreliable up-front promises

There are no more policy packages – one policy is decided at a time. Voting is for policy, not politicians too

No delays waiting for the support of a slow moving and disinterested populous. Instead, we only need to convince a single legislative body with informed and well considered arguments

No policy swing between political parties – no political parties at all

There is no incentive for individuals (politicians) to push simplistic and populist policies for their own good

No deals or policy compromises made to gain favour of political control

No ineffectual public or parliamentary debate, which focusses on point scoring and blame, instead of the issues. Any dishonest debate or manipulation is corrected, and vastly less effective

Special interest groups and money have no more influence than anyone else

Lessons are accumulated and retained for future decisions and legislation

Weaknesses in the separation of powers have been largely removed through a full independence of the three arms of government

Democracies do not waste enormous sums of money on inefficiently deciding the best policies through elections or political self-promotion

Next let's look at the root causes of problems that have not been fully removed. These potentially remain, although, with new governance the risks of these have been substantially reduced:
Legislators' decision making is complicated by other issues and consequences

> The vast majority of negative impact on legislators' decision making has been reduced since the conflicts and misaligned incentives of politicians have been removed. And yet, there is still a possibility that some legislators' complications remain. This is always the case for any human decision making process and we have reduced the risk as much as possible.

It is possible to gain benefits from political influence (of legislators)

> Again, although it is still theoretically possible for some legislators to gain benefit from their decisions, the vast majority of potential benefit has been removed. If there are any direct conflicts of interest for legislators then that legislator can be removed from the decision making process, which is easier to do when there are so many legislators involved. But there are some conflicts for which legislators cannot be removed because they affect too many legislators. But this is inevitable in any democratic process.

Leadership is a single point of failure and corruptible power, without governance

> We have added a governance framework to ensure that this risk is reduced when compared to our existing democratic process

The many can rule the few unfairly

> This is an inherent limitation of any majority based democratic system and can be especially difficult where there are a variety of ethnic and religious groups. Our change in this respect is to include a more effective Governance Council (as a second house of parliament), which does not have any of the problems of politics, which is not beholden to the masses for elections or for support. The Governance Council can be an effective check on majority rule. We also have reduced this risk considerably through a more effective

inclusion of the mandated vetting of arguments around policy, as
well as in our requirement for people to spend the time in
consideration of those policies before voting

Freedom of speech can be abused and have influence in representative
democracy

Public debate is invariably not sensible and rational

The media is not an effective, fair and balanced view of the world

These are all still true in any democracy. What has been done
however is to remove the influence of misinformation and
unreasonable arguments through the vetting of all evidence and
reason presented to legislators. Errors and flawed reasoning can be
corrected and highlighted with a balanced view presented in all
policy discussion papers. Presenting an independent source of truth
to legislators and ensuring that they have the time available for the
consideration of options, vastly reduces this risk.

Jobs for the boys

There is still a possibility that individual members of the executive
government can subsequently take roles in industries over which they have
favourably governed. However, there can be none of this for politicians
because they do not exist. And the executive government Governance Panels
are still able to ensure that this is less likely, and to intervene if necessary.
With executive government members being appointed for fixed terms and
only one term, this potential does reduce.

For Representative Democracy, let's consider the benefits.

For our existing representative democracy, the major benefit is, realistically,
the fact that it is a known quantity. The system does have its quirks, but it
has worked for a reasonable period of time. It is safe. It has delivered for
many nations. It may not be perfect, but it has been largely stable. Even
though there are many risks in our current democracy there is no risk
associated with any change.

The following is a list of potential negatives for Governed Democracy:

Populist policies can still be approved by a self-interested legislature.
Although we do see this risk can be realized in representative democracy as
well, there is a potential for it to cause greater issues in Governed
Democracy. To mitigate this risk, we have the capability of independent

235

government departments preparing a formalized case of evidence that clearly outlines the consequence of self-interested decisions and allows the legislature the time to make an informed decision. We also control the process by taking away the power of misinformation and misrepresentation from the process, enabling the spurious populist arguments to be dispelled. There is no incentive for politicians to promote and encourage populist policies to gain political advantage. An independent, non-political governance council can overrule any populist, poor decisions.

Too many changes proposed – the system may be inundated with change requests from the public. At the moment, politicians implicitly limit the speed of change since they reject most calls for change from the public. This has the effect of slowing many good changes, but it also stops too many unnecessary changes from happening and overwhelming the legislative process. There may need to be a governance process to mitigate this risk. The new prioritisation process for change would also implicitly reduce the rate of change. The number of changes is still limited by the requirement for an independent body to consider and create formalized documentation on each new policy proposal. This will limit the amount of change possible.

There is still no specific requirement for a long-term strategy. We do effectively lose some potential strategy that comes along with the formation of an aligned political party in representative democracy. Although we have removed the misaligned incentives which encourage short-term policies, we have not actually done anything to incentivize a long-term strategy. Our assumption here is that the individuals appointed to the executive government positions would develop a long-term strategy and work towards the greater good. In many ways the primary responsibility of a President is actually the long-term strategy for the nation. This is a requirement for the position. As well as this we have lost the disincentive to strategize for the future that overwhelms our current democratic process. It would be expected that a legislative change would occur to create a government long term strategy capability.

Cost comparison
Next, we need to compare the relative costs. Our assumptions here will be that firstly, these are only broad estimates of the comparative costs. The cost

comparison is not a material influence on our system of government. In reality, the more important part in improving our democratic process is to get the democratic processes right. If the new system produces a significantly better form of government - as long as the change is not cost prohibitive, then the benefit of improving the democratic system is well worth the cost. So, our analysis here is rather simplistic and high level just to check that the costs of any change are not potentially prohibitive. Since we are only concerned with an estimate of the cost change, our analysis will in some cases consider the people cost alone, since it is not considered that there will a material cost difference in other ways – and certainly not a prohibitive cost difference. Again, any cost differentials, when it comes to a preferred from of government, are considered relatively immaterial in comparison to the benefits of better government and governance.

So then, we shall consider only the high level changes the two different systems, and the number of people involved in each process. Effectively, in Governed Democracy, we replace two houses of parliament, which may contain approximately 1000 members (in the US 435 members of the House of Reps, 535 Senators), with two houses of parliament which may contain 4020 members (the new upper house is smaller). When you consider that currently each politician may have ten or more support staff, then the numbers, albeit different, are not significantly so. There will be a support staff requirement for Governed Democracy, but not near 10 per person.

At the same time, we significantly reduce costs by not having to run any elections and by not having to monitor politics and political donations (e.g. the FEC). We also increase cost in Governed Democracy through new departments like the Independent Policy Assessment Department (IPAD) and a number of Governance and Appointment panels. However, it is estimated that the overall cost to society in Governed Democracy would substantially reduce, since the substantial cost of running and funding elections and political parties is no longer necessary. There is also a vast reduction in cost for industry and society as a whole, as the requirement to lobby politicians and political parties largely disappears. The enormous cost of corruption also reduces.

The simple efficiency of running a democracy where only 4000 people need to critically consider and analyse change is an extraordinary benefit. We no longer need to engage 40 million or even 400 million voters to help decide policy (indirectly), through elections and politicians. We only need to employ the time of around 4000 people for decision making, and only for months at a time. We only need to expend the cost of convincing 4000 people of the need for change, rather than millions. This makes the whole process significantly more efficient. The benefit of course is not just in financial cost, but in time. Decisions can be made much more quickly than when we are dependent on taking the time to convince the whole populous. We can move more quickly on beneficial changes and improvements to our society. What has previously taken decades, to convince millions of largely disinterested, often confused and manipulated voters, could now happen vastly more quickly.

Overall, this simple high-level analysis would indicate that the overall costs would largely reduce between representative democracy and Governed Democracy. And irrespective, costs comparisons pale into insignificance once you consider the potential damage done to society through the poor decision making of existing democratic governments. Overall costs then should be a large net benefit for the new democratic process.

Risk comparison
The greatest risk is primarily around the unknown potential of the new system. We really can't be certain how it would practically operate. There are unknown unknowns. At the end of the day, we need to decide if these risks are greater than the potential, and more definable, rewards. However, this risk has been mitigated by choosing only known, working replacement processes in Governed Democracy.

At the same time, there are also many reductions in risk with the new processes. We have greater independence of the arms of governments, which protects democracy from itself and from a degradation to dictatorship. We also have more checks and balances on the system with a truly independent upper house as well as with our governance councils over the executive arm of government. Every single power within Governed Democracy has a fully independent body which can regulate and govern to ensure sensible decisions. In Governed democracy every arm of government has an independent control on its power.

2/ Is the proposal the best available option for dealing with the root cause or causes of the important issues or problems?

We've already been through a range of other proposals that have been made for dealing with some issues of our representative democracy, in the Chapter "Changes Proposed So Far". These proposals, even though many are good ideas, invariably do not resolve the root causes of the underlying issues. These options then do not materially change and improve our democratic process.

The verdict

So overall, the fourth democracy has removed the vast majority of the problems identified in our existing democratic system by removing the root causes of their failure. The minor problems that remain largely exist in both systems. A major advantage of the new system would be that of the true independence of the three arms of government. This gives significantly more stability and a much more balanced policy approach. The system could potentially save the enormous sums of money wasted currently on the ineffective processes of democracy, the electioneering and self-promotion. Allocated the same funds directly on evaluating and planning the best options for our future would deliver untold benefits, especially when coupled with the more effective collective decision making.

The major risks associated with this new system of democracy, as with any new system, are any problems that are unknown at this stage. Things that arise from the new structure that we are not yet aware of. And yet the system has a range of more comprehensive features to significantly reduce risk. In particular, there is a better governance framework for dealing with human imperfections and poor decision makers. A true advantage of the new system is the ability for the system to change more dynamically, unlike the existing process. This allows for the new democracy to more effectively improve its own process and to deal with any issues as they may arise.

Any overall decision is in many ways, somewhat subjective. However, given the number of problems removed, comparable high level costs between the two systems, and reasonable risks associated with the fourth democracy, the overall benefits certainly do overwhelmingly outweigh the cost and risk of change. A new democracy built with simple, effective and tried and tested processes. A democracy without politics, without compromises, without conflicts of interest and without the undue influence of special interest groups. A democracy whose decision makers have the time to make informed and well considered decisions. A democracy whose power is contained within its strengthened process and not in the hands of individual politicians. A democracy which enables the best possible ideas and solutions to be quickly identified and implemented effectively. A democracy which truly delivers a government of the people, by the people and for the people.

So, what now?

"The greater danger for most of us lies not in setting our aim too high and falling short; but in setting our aim too low, and achieving our mark" - Michelangelo

When I think of the future of our democracies in hundreds or even thousands of years' time, I cannot imagine representative democracy surviving in anything close to its current form. The existing system is so flawed that it cannot remain. As a society, we will at some stage wake up and fix our democratic process. Any advanced society would have created a more effective form of government. Change is inevitable, it is just a question of time.

But given how much hardship, devastation and waste is caused by our flawed system, why would we wait? The current problems and the potential for future catastrophic failures should compel as to act now.

So how could any democracy transition to a Governed Democracy? It would be best to take smaller steps first, to reduce risk and more importantly to deal with the major challenge - which is that of an extreme resistance to change in the general populous. This would undoubtedly need a phased transition.

These next steps are broad and high level. They can be worked out in much more detail later. But it is possible to transition safely and gradually to a vastly better form of government.

The first and least impact step would be to improve the debates for legislative change – within our existing democratic process. We can reduce the impact of lies and false premises on any legislative debate. This would ensure that the debates improve in quality, accuracy and accountability. That is, for each new law, independently create a publicly available case for and against, based on vetted contributions from all interested, including any costs and risks of change. Then have all of our legislators take the time in parliament to hear the vetted evidence and reasoning within those cases and make an informed and well considered collective decision (using IPAD as described previously). This could happen without changing anything else – the first step could actually initially leave our politicians and elections in place. We just mandate the independent creation of a case for and against, produced by the public service (with help from all who want to make contributions) and where necessary, vetted through a tribunal or courts.

The next step would be to transition to the independent appointment of the executive arm of government. We would change from a system where politicians appoint the executive arm of government, to a system where independent experts make those same appointments. To make this possible we need to create an Independent Appointments Panel, which would then determine formalised criteria for the vetting of candidates. This would be an expansion of the criteria proposed in this book, which is obviously just a high-level starting point. But delivering this option would vastly reduce our greatest risk of catastrophe, which is for our government to degrade to dictatorship.

For those democracies that do not already have an independently appointed judiciary, this could occur early as well. Again, we would create an appointments panel of experts to independently appoint the judiciary. Then we can transition to the new judiciary over time.

The next step could be the replacement of the politicians in the upper house through a similar independent appointments panel.

Finally, we could transition the lower house from elected politicians to a jury style legislative assembly. For a number of years afterwards then, each legislative assembly could be run in parallel to support the transition.

But our first real step, before any transition to a vastly improved democratic process, is based on the current limitations of the democratic process. For any change to occur in our current democracy – no matter how imperative or beneficial, it must first be widely popular. Ideas alone cannot create change right now. Those ideas must become popular enough to drive a political agenda. While this is still the case, we must work within the existing political process to bring about a better democracy.

Without widespread support politicians, political parties and special interest groups will never relinquish their stranglehold on power. Our politicians must know that without change their jobs are at immediate risk. So, the imperative for change needs to be widely communicated. A broad range of people need to hear about the importance of change and believe in the possibility of a better way.

The intention of this book is to help progress the right change. The changes proposed within are not unique, others have also called for some of these new democratic processes as well. But people must hear about the need for, and the benefit of, these solutions. If each of us can spread the word in whatever small way possible then we can all help to create a better future.

Why would we not start now?

Bibliography

This bibliography is not of the typical variety. It is more a list of reference material used. It is assumed that virtually all of the material contained in this book can be quite easily independently verified on any of a number of reliable websites. The internet does make fact checking easy. So, the emphasis here is to provide a list of sources of the book's information more as a convenience. Although every piece of information contained in this book has been verified in some way using a reliable source (usually two or more), and although there has been an effort to record all sources, this has not been a thoroughly scientific endeavour. No guarantee is made of the completeness of the below list – some websites may have disappeared, or the saving of every reference may have been imperfect. However, these should prove useful irrespective for those interested in the source of much of the information contained within this text. If something cannot be found, then the internet is a wonderful resource to fill in the unintended gaps.

Author/s	Reference Book/s
Fareed Zakaria, PhD Harvard	The Future of Freedom: Illiberal Democracy at Home and Abroad (Revised Edition)
Charles Tilly	Democracy
Dan Fagin	Toms River: A Story of Science and Salvation
Tim Weiner	Legacy of Ashes: The History of the CIA
Bruce Bueno de Mesquita, Alastair Smith	The Dictator's Handbook: Why Bad Behaviour is Almost Always Good Politics
Robert A. Dahl	A Preface to Democratic Theory, Expanded Edition
Arend Lijphart	Patterns of Democracy
Bernard Crick	Democracy: A Very Short Introduction

Richard P. Feynman	Surely You're joking Mr Feynman! What do you Care what other People Think?
Steven Johnson	The Ghost Map: The Story of London's Most Terrifying Epidemic-- and How It Changed Science, Cities, and the Modern World
James Surowiecki	The Wisdom of Crowds
Barry Ritholtz	Bailout Nation
Jane Mayer	Dark Money
Adam Grant	Originals
Andrew Cockburn	Kill Chain:The Rise of the High Tech Assassins
Francis Fukuyama	The End of History and the Last Man, Political Order and Political Decay
Philip Tetlock and Dan Gardner	Superforecasting:The Art and Science of Prediction by
Bethany McLean	All the Devils Are Here: The Hidden History of the Financial Crisis
Ben Goldacre	Bad Science Bad Pharma
Bryan Caplan	The Myth of the Rational Voter
Nate Silver	The signal and the noise Why so many predictions fail – but some don't

Author/s	Academic Paper
Michel Crozier, Samuel P. Huntington, Joji Watanuki	The Crisis of Democracy
Daniel Levy M.D, Thomas J. Thom	Death Rates from Coronary Disease – Progress and a Paradox, Editorial, New England Journal of Medicine
Julia Reedy	How the U.S. Low-Fat Diet Recommendations of 1977 Contributed to the Declining Health of

	Americans
David Rosner, PhD, MSPH, Gerald Markowitz, PhD	A 'Gift of God'?: The Public Health Controversy over Leaded Gasoline during the 1920s
Daniel Madden and Alyssa Keri	The Mathematics Behind Polling
Chairman, Craig Estes	Senate Committee on Natural Resources and Economic Development, Interim Report to the 85th Legislature, November 2006
Donald L. Horowitz, Professor of Law and Professor of Political Science at Duke University	The Challenge of Ethnic Conflict, Democracy in Divided Societies
Mancur Olson	The Logic of Collective Action
Anthony Petrosino, Carolyn Turpin Petrosino, John Buehler	"Scared Straight" and Other Juvenile Awareness Programs for Preventing Juvenile Delinquency, May 2002

Internet Information	Source
Google influence	http://www.theaustralian.com.au/business/wall-street-journal/paying-professors-how-google-buys-academic-influence/news-story/01a372c4f042369fa87e2c69425a6893
Drug company issues	https://www.theguardian.com/books/2012/oct/17/bad-pharma-ben-goldacre-review http://medicalrepublic.com.au/pharma-give-money-patient-groups/ https://www.statnews.com/2016/10/26/oxycontin-maker-thwarted-limits/ http://www.vox.com/science-and-health/2016/11/30/12945756/prescription-drug-prices-explained https://www.washingtonpost.com/news/to-your-health/wp/2017/03/07/surgeons-were-told-to-stop-

	prescribing-so-many-painkillers-the-results-were-remarkable/ https://www.nytimes.com/2014/10/24/business/davita-to-pay-350-million-to-settle-charges-of-illegal-kickbacks.html http://edition.cnn.com/2016/08/25/health/us-surgeon-general-letter-doctors-opioid-use/index.html https://www.theatlantic.com/health/archive/2017/06/nejm-letter-opioids/528840/ http://www.npr.org/sections/health-shots/2017/06/16/533060031/doctor-who-wrote-1980-letter-on-painkillers-regrets-that-it-fed-the-opioid-crisis
Greg Combet	https://meanjin.com.au/essays/political-life/
Daniel Kahneman decision making	https://hbr.org/2016/10/noise
President Dwight D Eisenhower's farewell address to the nation	http://mcadams.posc.mu.edu/ike.htm
MSG	https://www.pri.org/stories/2014-10-03/science-suggests-msg-really-isnt-bad-your-health-after-all
Social media issues in a democracy (Facebook)	https://www.bloomberg.com/view/articles/2017-06-08/democracy-never-faced-a-threat-like-facebook https://www.wired.com/2016/11/facebook-won-trump-election-not-just-fake-news/ *http://www.bbc.co.uk/news/technology-37983571* http://www.chronicle.com/article/A-Professor-Once-Targeted-by/238742
"Cholesterol is not a nutrient of concern"	https://health.gov/dietaryguidelines/2015-scientific-report/06-chapter-1/d1-2.asp
Dietary recommendat ions change	http://www.zoeharcombe.com/2015/11/diet-advice-for-diabetics/
Hand washing for	http://theconversation.com/hand-washing-stops-infections-so-why-do-health-care-workers-skip-it-

current healthcare	58763 http://www.npr.org/sections/health-shots/2015/01/12/375663920/the-doctor-who-championed-hand-washing-and-saved-women-s-lives http://www.pbs.org/newshour/updates/ignaz-semmelweis-doctor-prescribed-hand-washing/ http://www.npr.org/sections/health-shots/2015/01/12/375663920/the-doctor-who-championed-hand-washing-and-saved-women-s-lives
Hygiene issues and consequences in the US	https://www.ncbi.nlm.nih.gov/pubmed/21460463
Diet	https://academic.oup.com/jhmas/article/63/2/139/772615/How-the-Ideology-of-Low-Fat-Conquered-America
Pension problems in the US	http://www.cnbc.com/2016/10/07/us-state-public-pension-unfunded-liabilities-to-hit-175-trillion-moodys.html https://graphics.wsj.com/table/Connecticut_102015 http://www.reuters.com/investigates/special-report/usa-illinois-madigan/
Campaign finance in the UK	https://www.loc.gov/law/help/campaign-finance/uk.php#issues
AIDS in South Africa	http://www.nybooks.com/articles/2000/07/20/the-mystery-of-aids-in-south-africa/
Jean Mayer, of Tufts University (mass murder)	"8-week Blood Sugar Diet" by Dr Michael Moseley
Banking crisis	https://www.prospectmagazine.co.uk/magazine/the-secret-history-of-the-banking-crisis
Sugar	https://www.bloomberg.com/news/articles/2017-08-09/sugar-barons-amass-8-billion-fortune-by-mastering-u-s-politics http://www.nbcnews.com/health/health-news/sugar-industry-manipulated-heart-studies-review-finds-

	n646836
Lead in petrol	https://www.thenation.com/article/secret-history-lead/ http://www.lead.org.au/lanv8n1/l8v1-3.html https://www.ncbi.nlm.nih.gov/pmc/articles/PMC1779871/ https://en.wikipedia.org/wiki/Thomas_Midgley_Jr
FIFA corruption	https://www.bloomberg.com/quicktake/world-cup
Ratings Agencies	https://www.bloomberg.com/news/articles/2017-08-02/the-great-escape-how-the-big-three-credit-raters-ducked-reform
Texas tax incentive (37%)	https://www.texasobserver.org/chapter-313-texas-tax-incentive/ https://comptroller.texas.gov/economy/local/ch313/ https://comptroller.texas.gov/economy/local/ch313/ https://www.texasobserver.org/rationale-for-texas-largest-corporate-welfare-program-was-a-typographical-error/
Brexit	http://blogs.lse.ac.uk/brexit/2016/10/24/brexit-is-not-the-will-of-the-british-people-it-never-has-been/
Ulcers	http://www.jyi.org/issue/delayed-gratification-why-it-took-everybody-so-long-to-acknowledge-that-bacteria-cause-ulcers/ https://www.cdc.gov/ulcer/history.htm
General resources on democracy	https://www.theguardian.com/books/2013/nov/08/trouble-with-democracy-david-runciman "Choosing Electoral Systems: Proportional, Majoritarian and Mixed Systems" – Pippa Norris, Harvard University
Democratic violence	http://www.bbc.co.uk/news/world-africa-40807425 http://www.bbc.com/news/uk-england-36550304
Special interest influence (Kochs)	http://www.newyorker.com/magazine/2010/08/30/covert-operations http://www.nbcnews.com/politics/elections/rebuke-tennessee-governor-koch-group-shows-its-power-n301031

Peter Hartcher Quote	http://www.smh.com.au/comment/imagine-if-for-one-day-politicians-acted-like-problem-solvers-20170331-gvb54j.html
Poland democratic degradation	http://www.bbc.com/news/world-europe-40670790
Enron, Gramm and the loophole	http://www.nytimes.com/2008/11/17/business/17grammside.html
Mars Orbiter and the metric system	https://en.wikipedia.org/wiki/Mars_Climate_Orbiter https://en.wikipedia.org/wiki/History_of_the_metric_system
Australian Political leadership changes	http://www.abc.net.au/news/2015-02-10/australia-political-leadership-rollercoaster/6080126
Fund raising in politics	http://www.huffingtonpost.com.au/entry/call-time-congressional-fundraising_n_2427291 https://www.vox.com/2015/4/20/8455235/congress-lobbying-money-statistic http://fortune.com/2015/04/28/these-things-cost-more-than-all-lobbying-spending-in-2014/
Political Apathy	https://www.cambridge.org/core/journals/perspectives-on-politics/article/testing-theories-of-american-politics-elites-interest-groups-and-average-citizens/62327F513959D0A304D4893B382B992B
Diabetes	https://www.diabetes.org.uk/About_us/News/Twenty-devastating-amputations-every-day/ http://www.reuters.com/article/us-rates-diabetes-related-amputation/rates-of-diabetes-related-amputation-vary-across-u-s-idUSTRE78T3EZ20110930
Tobacco	www.who.int/tobacco/media/en/TobaccoExplained.pdf
Special interest influence on climate change	http://www.pbs.org/wgbh/frontline/article/robert-brulle-inside-the-climate-change-countermovement/ http://www.politifact.com/pennsylvania/statements/2017/mar/31/scott-wagner/pa-gopers-climate-change-theory-debunked-nope-not-/

Democratic corruption	http://www.bbc.com/news/world-middle-east-38548534 http://www.independent.co.uk/news/world/middle-east/benjamin-netanyahu-corruption-investigation-police-bribery-a7574391.html https://www.theguardian.com/world/2017/jul/12/brazil-president-lula-convicted-corruption http://www.bbc.com/news/world-asia-40750671
Party membership decline	http://blogs.lse.ac.uk/europpblog/2013/05/06/decline-in-party-membership-europe-ingrid-van-biezen/ http://democracyrenewal.edu.au/democratic-decline-renewal-britain-australia-nz http://www.smh.com.au/comment/are-we-seeing-the-death-of-the-twoparty-system-20140827-109bi8.html http://onlinelibrary.wiley.com/doi/10.1111/j.1475-6765.2011.01995.x/abstract
Gambling on poker machines in Australia	http://www.dailytelegraph.com.au/newslocal/hornsby-advocate/poker-machine-spins-on-a-roll-in-sydney-and-central-coast-for-record-billion-dollar-playing-action/news-story/92047198b9a6bc52f2b712f315fbe367 http://www.sbs.com.au/news/article/2008/04/27/playing-pokies http://www.abc.net.au/news/2016-09-27/pokieleaks-australians-urged-to-leak-gambling-industry-secrets/7878528
External Interference in elections	http://www.latimes.com/nation/la-na-us-intervention-foreign-elections-20161213-story.html
Tax avoidance	http://www.oecd.org/tax/oecd-presents-outputs-of-oecd-g20-beps-project-for-discussion-at-g20-finance-ministers-meeting.htm https://www.theguardian.com/global-development-professionals-network/2016/may/10/were-losing-240bn-a-year-to-tax-avoidance-who-really-ends-up-paying https://www.ft.com/content/3e0172a0-6e1b-11e6-9ac1-1055824ca907?mhq5j=e1 http://www.smh.com.au/business/the-economy/google-

	admits-the-ato-is-chasing-it-for-money-as-it-reveals-166m-tax-bill-20170428-gvunac.html http://www.smh.com.au/business/comment-and-analysis/ato-unlikely-to-recoup-the-29b-its-chasing-from-multinationals-20170406-gvewsz.html http://www.smh.com.au/business/the-economy/facebook-australia-pays-more-tax-following-government-crackdown-against-multinationals-20170427-gvudau http://www.smh.com.au/business/the-economy/chevron-loses-appeal-ordered-to-pay-more-than-300-million-in-tax-20170420-gvondk.html
Agnotology	http://www.bbc.com/future/story/20160105-the-man-who-studies-the-spread-of-ignorance
Plebiscite expense	www.bbc.com/news/world-australia-41156949
Mathematics and polling statistics	http://www.nss.gov.au/nss/
Scott Pruitt	https://www.nytimes.com/2017/08/11/us/politics/scott-pruitt-epa.html
Freedom House online election interference	https://freedomhouse.org/article/new-report-freedom-net-2017-manipulating-social-media-undermine-democracy
Political influence	http://www.smh.com.au/federal-politics/political-news/political-donations-are-an-unregulated-arms-race-senate-committee-told-20171102-gzda0o.html
Economic crises	http://beta.latimes.com/opinion/op-ed/la-oe-ioannidis-economics-is-a-science-20171114-story.html

Made in the USA
Las Vegas, NV
27 July 2021